FOOD
AS
MEDICINE
EVERYDAY

FOOD AS MEDICINE EVERYDAY

Reclaim Your Health With Whole Foods

Julie Briley, ND and Courtney Jackson, ND

nunm PRESS

Portland, Oregon

© 2025 and © 2016 by Julie Briley, ND and Courtney Jackson, ND

Revised and Expanded Second Edition 2025.

First Edition published 2016.

All rights Reserved.

Managing Editor: NUNM Press

Illustrations by Jesse Nellis

Photography by Jenny Bowlden, Vanessa Morrow and Kira Freed

Production: Fourth Lloyd Productions, LLC

Support for this project was provided by the Food As Medicine Institute
at The National University of Natural Medicine.

No part of this book may be reproduced without written permission from the publisher or copyright holder, except for a reviewer who may quote brief passages in a review; nor may any part of this book be reproduced, stored in a retrieval system, or transmitted in any form or by any means electronic, mechanical, photocopying, recording, or other, without written permission from the publisher or copyright holder.

National University of Natural Medicine

NUNM Press

49 S Porter Street

Portland, OR 97201

www.nunm.edu

Individuals with serious health problems need to be under the care of a physician.
Information in this book is intended to supplement, not replace, advice and treatments provided by one's doctor or trained health professional.

Printed in the USA.

ISBN: 979-8-218-70061-4

Library of Congress Control Number: 2025922210

To FAME series participants
—past, present, and future.

Table of Contents

Dedication *v*
Table of Contents *vii*
List of Tables *viii*
Foreword *ix*
Preface *xi*
Acknowledgements *xv*
Introduction *xvii*

Chapter 1   The Wisdom of Traditional Diets *23*
Chapter 2   Nourish Yourself with Fat *33*
Chapter 3   Nourish Yourself with Carbohydrates *43*
Chapter 4   Nourish Yourself with Protein *53*
Chapter 5   Food Label Reading *67*
Chapter 6   The FAME Plate *87*
Chapter 7   Strategies for Healthy Digestion *101*
Chapter 8   Balancing Blood Sugar *111*
Chapter 9   Exploring Sweeteners *123*
Chapter 10   Benefits of Breakfast *135*
Chapter 11   Habits for Health *141*
Chapter 12   Healthy Eating on the Go *151*
Chapter 13   Nutritious Lunches and Snacks *157*
Chapter 14   Shopping Guide and Everyday Superfoods *165*
Chapter 15   Kitchen Skills *177*

Recipes *187*
  All Seasons *189*
  Spring and Summer *229*
  Fall and Winter *245*

References *264*
Index *279*
About the Authors *295*
About NUNM Press *295*

List of Tables

Table 2.1 Food Sources of Fats 35

Table 3.1 Food Sources of Complex and Simple Carbohydrates 45

Table 3.2 Food Sources of Fiber 50

Table 4.1 Food Sources of Protein 57

Table 4.2 Vitamins: Functions and Food Sources 65

Table 4.3 Minerals: Functions and Food Sources 66

Table 6.1 Food Sources of Calcium 93

Table 6.2 Comparison of Macronutrients from Taco Bowls Examples 99

Table 8.1 Nutrition Values for Alcoholic Beverages and Mixes 119

Table 8.2 Important Nutrients and Their Food Sources for Blood Sugar Regulation 121

Table 15.1 Cooking Guidelines for Common Whole Grains 179

Table 15.2 Cooking Guidelines for Common Beans 181

Table 15.3 Cooking Guidelines for Dark Green Leafy Vegetables 183

Table 15.4 Saturated Fats and Their Smoke Points 184

Table 15.5 Unsaturated Fats and Their Smoke Points 185

Foreword

Billboards throughout Kansas City in the 1980s posted "learn CPR... save your huband's life", and classes based on the historic food pyramid were offered for women to learn "how to cook for your man with heart disease." Little did we know at that time that heart disease was also the number one health threat in women.

As the first women's heart center of its kind in the United States, we witnessed the impact of empowering women through education about their heart health that resulted in an impressive fall in heart attack and stroke, not only in women but also in men. Yet, the decline in death rates related to cardiovascular events slowed and then plateaued around 2011, and since then, death rates have been on the rise. Much of this is thought to be related to the obesity epidemic, largely related to our food choices, and complicated by confusion about and lack of credible resources dedicated to nutrition. The common culprit in the development of heart disease as well as other chronic illnesses, inclusive of cancer, diabetes and arthritis, is inflammation. We know that nutrition plays a significant role in reducing inflammation and preventing chronic disease.

As women are known for making 90% of the health care decisions for their families, our Saint Luke's Muriel I. Kauffman Women's Heart Center team feels strongly that it is our obligation to align our dedication to educating our community about nutrition with an expert in this arena. Our goal was to find a refreshing, nontraditional approach regarding education about affordable, nutrient-rich foods. A nationwide search led us to the National University of Natural Medicine (NUNM) and the Food as Medicine Institute (FAMI) in Portland, Oregon, where we experienced firsthand the excitement of the Food as Medicine Everyday (FAME) class participants as they prepared plant-based, unprocessed foods and engaged in educational lessons on nutrition.

We remain honored as a longstanding founding partner of the Food As Medicine Institute Alliance and proud to share the wisdom about nutrition through teaching FAME to our Midwest communities! We also recognize that physicians and health care providers lack a basic nutritional platform for which they can educate their patients. FAME has created such a contagious passion about nutrition that FAME electives are now offered to our medical students and cardiology fellows!

Congratulations, Drs. Jackson and Briley, on your second edition of *Food as Medicine Everyday*. Your wisdom about nutrition is elegantly outlined, and each chapter engages the reader with inspiration and empowerment! Thank you both for leading the way!

Tracy L. Stevens, MD, Medical Director
Marcia L. McCoy, RN, MSN, Director
Saint Luke's Muriel I. Kauffman Women's Heart Center

Preface

Food is intimately woven into the culture of naturopathic medical training and clinical practice. Since its inception in the United States in the early 1900s, the profession of naturopathic medicine has always incorporated the healing power of food into patients' treatment plans. The profession has evolved and adapted with modern medicine, but it has not forgotten the original connection to food as medicine.

Naturopathic doctors (NDs) are educated and trained at accredited naturopathic medical schools. Their medical training incorporates the best of both the art and science of traditional and conventional medical practices. Clinically, NDs can address acute and chronic health conditions, from hay fever to heart disease, from infancy through adulthood. As of 2025, twenty-three states as well as the District of Columbia, Puerto Rico, and the U.S. Virgin Islands regulate the naturopathic medical profession. In these states, naturopathic medicine is recognized as a distinct system of primary health care that, like conventional medicine, includes the diagnosis, treatment, and prevention of illness.[1]

Naturopathic medicine is distinguished from other medical professions by its Principles:

The Healing Power of Nature (*Vis Medicatrix Naturae*),

Identify and Treat the Causes (*Tolle Causam*),

First Do No Harm (*Primum Non Nocere*),

Doctor as Teacher (*Docere*),

Treat the Whole Person (*Tolle Totum*),

Prevention (*Preventare*).

This underlying belief in and understanding of the healing power of nature, including the potential for a whole foods diet to prevent, treat, and reverse many chronic diseases, is truly unique to this group of healthcare providers.

Naturopathic doctors follow a therapeutic order that does not rely solely on prescription medications or surgery. Instead, they may use one of many treatment options to address the whole person.

Examples include:

clinical nutrition and utilizing food as medicine

nutritional supplements

botanical medicine

homeopathy

lifestyle counseling

physical medicine, such as soft tissue and joint manipulation

hydrotherapy, the application of hot and cold water to the body to stimulate a healing response

intravenous (IV) therapy including vitamin and mineral infusions

minor surgery

prescription medications in some areas of the United States

While there are fewer naturopathic doctors compared to conventional medical doctors, there is a growing demand for naturopathic medicine, with several million Americans choosing to access naturopathic care annually.[2] Naturopathic doctors also provide something else that patients want from their doctors: time. NDs take time to listen, to understand their patients' concerns and goals, to educate and to create individualized and holistic treatment plans.

Within the conventional medical model, a widespread lack of formal nutrition education and clinical application of food as medicine is a known barrier to success in reducing the rates of chronic disease.[3] Compared to conventional medical doctors, NDs are exceptionally well prepared to fill this skill and knowledge gap. NDs complete extensive clinical nutrition training in addition to studies in naturopathic philosophy, which builds a foundation to use food as medicine therapeutically for mind, body, and spirit. They receive training regarding the history, biochemistry, and the benefits and challenges of prescribing specific therapeutic diets such as an elimination diet, anti-inflammatory diet, and Mediterranean diet. Combining this training with extended time face-to-face with patients, NDs can routinely make a difference in empowering their patients to make achievable and sustainable dietary changes.

We feel uniquely positioned to write this book about whole foods nutrition. With almost thirty years of combined clinical practice as naturopathic doctors, we have worked with our patients to develop individualized nutrition plans as part of their healthcare program, navigating obstacles and sharing reliable tools for success. Additionally, we bring our background as co-founders of a successful community-based, hands-on nutrition program at the National University of Natural Medicine, which has been offering whole foods nutrition education based on the Food as Medicine Everyday (FAME) principles for fifteen years. We are also experienced writers, who spend a lot of time translating complicated nutrition research into more easily digestible pieces. We know that poor dietary choices are one part of the problem of our current healthcare crisis. Food is medicine; therefore, food is part of the solution. It is time that we truly recognize this therapy and that we all learn how to use food as medicine everyday.

Julie Briley, ND
Courtney Jackson, ND

Acknowledgements

We were inspired to write the second edition of the FAME book due to the demand for an updated whole foods nutrition resource for the public and an updated guide for the FAME series. In addition, the FAME book serves as an academic resource for both undergraduate and postgraduate nutrition students as well as medical students. We remain appreciative to everyone who has been involved or supported the ECO Project and FAME series since 2010. We would like to acknowledge the National University of Natural Medicine (NUNM) for creating the Food As Medicine Institute in March 2014 as a dedicated center for evidence-based nutrition education for both community members and healthcare professionals.

More specifically, we would like to express our gratitude to Dr. Andy Erlandsen and Kira Freed who encouraged us to complete the new edition of the book. Dr. Andy Erlandsen, Dean of the School of Undergraduate and Graduate Studies and Director of the Food as Medicine Institute at NUNM, continues his commitment to the FAME series at NUNM. We value his support and expert review of the new edition. We sincerely appreciate Kira Freed, MEd, MScN, Nutrition Department Coordinator and FAME Educator at NUNM, for her contribution to the new recipes and new photographs featured in this edition, as well as her expert review. We extend our heartfelt thanks to Michael Chilton for his generous support of FAMI. The Michael and Simone Chilton Family Fund of the Oregon Community Foundation helped to make possible the publication of this second edition.

The FAMI Alliance, created between NUNM and Saint Luke's Muriel I. Kauffman Women's Heart Center, continues to inspire us. This alliance helped expand access to the FAME series in addition to creating a powerful resource for credible nutrition education for medical students and fellows. Marcia McCoy, RN, MSN and Dr. Tracy Stevens have been instrumental in promoting food as medicine in their hospital system and community.

We recognize the important work of previous FAMI Physicians, Dr. Pera Gorson, Dr. Cory Szybala, Dr. Shawnte Yates, and previous FAMI Nutrition Coordinators, Manda Draper, BSN, MScN and Julie Marks BSN, MScN. We celebrate the more than 100 nutritionists and doctors who are now trained to facilitate the FAME series in their communities. The FAME series at NUNM also continues to depend on the dedication and hard work of NUNM medical and graduate students to be able to offer programs through the Food As Medicine Institute.

To the leaders and community members who supported and helped organize the initial FAME series locations, we thank you! These include: Mt. Olivet Baptist Church, Schools Uniting Neighborhoods (SUN) Program at Gresham High School and Roosevelt High School, June Key Delta Community Center, White Shield Center, Open Meadows High School and Betties 360, United Methodist Church in Banks, Oregon, Coffee Creek Correctional Facility, and NUNM's own Charlee's Kitchen.

A special thanks to Karen and Mark Ward, owners of Jim's Thriftway, for their vision of change in the small town of Banks, Oregon, Charlene Zidell for her support of FAME at Coffee Creek Correctional Facility, and Lori Sobelson for her shared commitment to community outreach. Additionally, we remember the vision and the dedication of David Schleich, PhD, past president of NUNM, and Susan Hunter, MBA, who created the foundation for FAMI and the NUNM Press. Nancy Stodart and Richard Stodart brought their creative talents in designing this book. Jenny Bowlden, Vanessa Morrow, and Jesse Nellis enhanced each chapter through their beautiful photographs and illustrations.

To the late Bob and Charlee Moore, founders of Bob's Red Mill, we continue to be honored by your generous support and unwavering encouragement when we developed the FAME series. This book originally evolved because of our shared belief in the healing power of whole foods.

Final appreciation goes to our families for supporting all of our book meetings, recipe testing, and countless hours editing and writing. Thank you Jeffrey, Maya, and Bella. Thank you Doug, Alice, and Connor. Writing a book (and a second edition) is truly a family affair.

Introduction

Almost ten years have passed since the first publication of *Food as Medicine Everyday* (FAME) and fifteen years since the Food as Medicine Institute began offering community-based nutrition and cooking classes. What we find very inspiring is that the FAME Guiding Principles, then and now, continue to be supported by nutrition research and nutrition experts. These six principles have proven to be an enduring, trustworthy guide for anyone attempting to use food as medicine:

- Promote whole foods
- Encourage a diverse, primarily plant-based diet
- Include food from healthy animals
- Promote anti-inflammatory food choices
- Recognize that each individual has unique food needs
- Care about food and its sources

Unfortunately, in the past ten years, the health of Americans has not improved. Heart disease continues to be the number one cause of death, and 88% of Americans are considered metabolically unhealthy.[1] 38% of adults in the U.S. have prediabetes, and almost 12% of Americans have diabetes.[2] Nearly one-third of children born in the year 2000 or later will develop diabetes in their lifetime.[3] Almost half of American adults have high blood pressure.[4] More than 40% of Americans are now considered obese.[5] For an individual, it can be empowering to know that these and many other chronic health conditions are highly modifiable through diet and lifestyle choices.

Yet, engaging in sustainable behavior changes to support improved health outcomes, whether by an individual or a family or a community, is often a complex process. These behavior changes are strongly affected by social determinants of health (SDOH). The Center for Disease Control (CDC) defines SDOH as: the nonmedical factors that influence health outcomes. They are conditions in which people are born, grow, work, live, worship, and age. These conditions include a wide set of forces and systems that shape daily life such as economic policies and systems, development agendas, social norms, social policies, and political systems. SDOH, such as experiencing racism or poverty, can be more influential on health outcomes than a person's genetics or access to healthcare..[6,7] It can significantly impact a person's or family's ability to consistently access, afford, and prepare healthy food as well as their ability to receive nutrition education.

In the past several years, there has been increased effort at the the community, state, and federal level to address the impact of SDOH on healthy eating habits. For instance, there are more programs to expand the availability of fresh produce through prescriptions from healthcare providers, as well as a growing awareness to the need of conventional physicians to receive nutrition education as part of their training.[8] We hope to see these efforts continue to grow at all levels.

Accessing credible nutrition information is an important starting place for anyone interested in using food as medicine. It can be challenging to sift through the endless supply of dietary advice, often received on social media, and to know what to hold onto. The optimal diet we reference throughout this book is based on the Latin word *diaeta*, meaning way of living. This book is a reliable guide that will illuminate the benefits of eating whole foods as a *way of living*, rather than a short-term intervention. Instead of focusing on specific foods or beverages to always include or to always avoid, it's about the overall combination of habits of food intake, referred to as a *dietary pattern*. We will help unravel common myths about nutrition so that you can approach food with confidence, not confusion. Physicians, nutrition experts, dietitians, and foodies around the globe are all trying to create the perfect dietary plan for everyone. However, it doesn't exist. There is no single diet that everyone should follow or one that is metabolically correct for all people. Even so, it is important to point out the unifying themes among health care professionals that we can all agree upon: focusing on whole foods matters most, and reducing ultra-processed foods from our diets will lead to better health. This is the way to live for improved health. This is the diet.

The Standard American Diet, appropriately nicknamed the SAD diet, is calorie-rich, nutrient-poor, and contains a significant amount of ultra-processed foods. While there is no singular definition, it is generally recognized that ultra-processed foods are:

- composed of industrially-made food products versus naturally-occurring ingredients. They can include ingredients that were mechanically or chemically extracted or refined from whole foods, like starches, fats, and sweeteners, as well as manufactured chemicals, preservatives, and artificial flavors.
- cheaply made, allowing for greater profits for the industries that create these products.
- conveniently and strategically located for consumers to find.
- hyperpalatable, which means the food products are significantly pleasing to eat, often due to the purposeful manipulation of sugar, fat, salt, and carbohydrates in the ingredients.[9]

The intake of ultra-processed foods has increased in the past two decades, for both youth and adults.[10,11] More than 73% of the U.S. food supply is ultra-processed, which is 52% cheaper, on average, than the less processed alternatives.[12]

The NOVA classification system, which was developed by the Food and Agriculture Organization of the United Nations, is often referenced for a framework to define processed foods. It organizes foods into four groups based on the degree of processing: unprocessed or minimally processed, processed culinary ingredients, processed foods, and ultra-processed foods.

Unprocessed or minimally-processed foods. Foods may be exposed to grinding, drying, fermentation, pasteurization, cooling, and freezing. No oils, fats, sugar, or salt have been added.

Examples: fresh or frozen vegetables and fruits, bulk or packaged grains, eggs, beans, nuts, seeds, tea, fresh or frozen meat or fish, milk and yogurt.

Processed culinary ingredients. These foods are extracted from whole foods by natural processes like pressing, grinding, or refining. They are often added to home-cooked foods to enhance flavor.

Examples: cooking oils made from olive, avocado, and coconut, from nuts and seeds such as soybeans, corn, canola, and sunflower, butter and lard, honey and maple syrup, mined or sea salt.

Processed foods. These foods are manufactured by industries with the addition of salt, sugar, or oil to help preserve or to make foods more palatable. Most processed foods have two or three ingredients.

Examples: freshly made cheese, cured meats, canned fish, freshly made breads, salted or sugared nuts or seeds, fruits in syrup

Ultra-processed foods. Manufactured from industrial formulations, these foods are made up almost entirely from extracted products from whole foods like oils, fats, sugar, starches, or proteins. They often contain additional synthesized laboratory products to enhance flavor and shelf life.

Examples: packaged snacks, sodas, energy drinks, instant soups, margarine and hydrogenated oils, cake mixes, frozen pre-made meals, processed meats, sweetened cereal with chemical additives.[13]

Clearly, in many cases, making the healthier choice is unfortunately not the easier option. As naturopathic doctors, we regularly treat patients dealing with chronic disease due to a lifetime of unhealthy dietary choices and lifestyle habits. Inspired to expand our clinical work and to address community health, we co-founded the Food as Medicine Institute (FAMI) at the National University of Natural Medicine (NUNM). Since 2010, naturopathic physicians, nutritionists, and registered dietitians have facilitated a ten- to twelve-week series of community-based nutrition workshops, initially called the ECO Project which then evolved to the Food as Medicine Everyday (FAME) series. These workshops are characterized by interactive nutrition education as well as communal meal preparation and dining. In 2019, results were published from a pilot study of FAME participants with prediabetes or at risk of prediabetes. Participants were monitored before and after the 12-week FAME series, as well as at 6 and 12-months from the start of the program. The study results showed that after completing the FAME series, there was a shift toward healthier lab values associated with diabetes and heart disease risk, specifically a significant lowering in fasting glucose and C-reactive protein, a marker of inflammation. Additionally, participants showed, on average, improved cardiometabolic profiles at the 12-month follow up with reductions in C-reactive protein, fasting glucose, HbA1c, total and LDL cholesterol, and triglycerides.[14]

To date, thousands of participants from diverse cultures and different socioeconomic backgrounds have participated. Time and time again, participants with widely varied education backgrounds often arrive at the workshops with the same level of minimal nutrition knowledge. They share the same sense of confusion regarding the conflicting and rapidly changing nutrition fads that are widely marketed. Without a solid foundation regarding basic nutrition, it is no wonder that many of us are swayed to move away from the principles of healthy eating.

As practicing clinicians, we also understand the obstacles our patients face after they hear dietary advice in their doctor's office and then try to convert that knowledge into real action. People won't eat whole foods if there are obstacles of affordability and availability or if they do not know how to prepare meals that are healthy and delicious. FAME participants regularly report that they learn to navigate these obstacles. The FAME workshops provide multiple opportunities for participants to be in the kitchen with fellow community members, supporting one another. Together, they prepare and enjoy a meal as well as share their experiences about making dietary changes. In the end, they realize that they can make the same healthy recipes at home, and their meals will taste good.

> There are tons of websites out there focused on health and wellness that you can read, but until you start putting healthy habits into your lifestyle, success cannot be achieved. Dr. Jackson and Dr. Briley educated us on how to incorporate simple practices into our everyday actions through the ECO project. I was thrilled to learn how to make grains and greens that my husband thinks ROCK!
>
> Since coming to the ECO cooking classes, I look at recipes and how I'm living a bit differently. While I have always been a fit and healthy woman, they inspired me to try new recipes and make some of my already good habits even better! They taught me how to incorporate healthier choices into my busy lifestyle and that it is possible to be a working woman that can provide nourishing fresh meals for her family.
>
> —Jackie, ECO project, Mt. Olivet

For those who are unable to participate in a community-based FAME series, the FAME series is now also offered virtually. Additionally, this book can help you learn the FAME guiding principles as well as build a strong foundation in nutrition education to guide your daily diet. However, nutrition books and cookbooks are no substitute for time spent exploring, preparing, and enjoying whole foods. While this book will serve as an excellent nutrition resource, our hope is that it will inspire you to spend time in the kitchen and to enjoy a delicious meal. Starting today, you can improve your health and the health of your family by incorporating sit-down, family meals made with whole foods.

> My experience with FAME has been nothing short of transformative. Before this, I'll admit my cooking repertoire was fairly limited and my understanding of nutrition was somewhat superficial. I often found myself relying on processed foods and convenience meals without fully grasping how they might impact my diet and overall well-being.
>
> FAME opened my eyes to a whole new world of culinary possibilities and nutritional wisdom. The program's emphasis on whole, unprocessed foods, primarily plant-based, resonated deeply with me. I was fascinated to learn about the anti-inflammatory properties of various foods and how they can contribute to chronic disease prevention.
>
> One of the most valuable aspects of FAME has been the hands-on cooking component. Learning how to prepare delicious and nutritious meals using fresh, seasonal ingredients has been incredibly empowering. Witnessing the instructors' nutritional expertise and passion for food was truly inspiring. I was particularly excited to discover new ways to incorporate superfoods into my diet and have already started experimenting with ingredients at home.
>
> Not only did it expand my culinary skills, but it also deepened my understanding of how interconnected food, health, and well-being are. I have a renewed sense of

purpose and mindfulness around grocery shopping and meal preparation, carefully choosing ingredients that can sustain and benefit my health in the long run.

The greatest value of FAME lies in its ability to empower individuals to take control of their health through informed food choices, as it provides the knowledge, skills, and support necessary for lasting dietary change that can have a profound impact on one's overall well-being.

—Ernesto, Health educator for chronic disease prevention in Portland, Oregon

Chapter One

The Wisdom Of Traditional Diets

We recognize the many challenges that people face in order to eat healthy: lack of time, potential higher cost, lack of access to healthy foods, the overabundance of cheap, ultra-processed foods, and confusion about healthy eating. But, we also find ourselves in a unique situation in the evolution of humankind. The greatest threats to our health are no longer infectious diseases, which were the leading causes of death until the mid-1900s. Currently, it is our diet and lifestyle choices that are putting us at the greatest risk of disease.

The World Health Organization reports that non-communicable diseases (NCDs), or chronic diseases, such as heart disease, diabetes, cancer, and lung disease, are the major causes of death and disability worldwide. More than 80% of deaths in the United States, and 74% of deaths worldwide, are caused by these chronic diseases. Currently, public health officials, healthcare providers, governments, and multinational institutions are prioritizing how to approach this growing global challenge. The principal lifestyle factors that increase the risk of NCDs are physical inactivity, poor diet, tobacco use, and excess alcohol consumption.[1,2] In addition, the metabolic risk factors of these chronic diseases are high blood pressure, being overweight or obese, having high blood sugar levels, and high cholesterol. Unfortunately, in the United States, less than 13% of adults are considered metabolically healthy.[3]

Rather than letting this grim scenario be intimidating, we hope to use this information as a valuable perspective that can help encourage healthy, achievable, and sustainable behavior changes. We all have some control in mitigating the greatest threat to our health by making changes in daily lifestyle choices.

In this book we will focus primarily on how to move away from the Standard American Diet (SAD), which is highly processed and nutrient-poor, and toward a more whole foods, nutrient-dense diet. To understand how our current eating habits have brought us to less than ideal health, we must first look back in time.

A Brief History Of Food Production In America

The industrialization of food production in America in the late 1800s included innovations in farming machinery, the building of railroads for food transport, improvements in refrigeration, and the mechanization of food processing. Additionally, people were moving into the cities from the country, distancing them from a closer connection to their food. As a consequence, this transition over time led to a shift away from a diet that was locally sourced and minimally processed, which ultimately contributed to increased rates of chronic disease.

Grains

Humans began their dietary intake of wild grains more than 100,000 years ago![4] The inclusion of grains in the diet is considered an important part of human evolution because of the complex manipulation required to turn seeds of grain into edible and nutritious food. Wild grains were often dispersed over wide areas, gathered in small amounts by hand, and unavailable at certain times of the year. Due to these challenges, grains were eaten rarely and in small amounts.

Our relationship with grains in the diet changed significantly with the domestication of plants about 10,000 years ago. During this agricultural revolution, humans applied lessons learned over tens of thousands of years of grain harvesting and preparation to yield the greatest nutritional benefits from grains year-round. Grains were traditionally prepared by soaking, sprouting, and allowing a natural fermentation to occur for several days before being cooked and eaten. When we study

The average grocery store contains more than 30,000 products!

the anatomical parts of a whole grain, we learn that the bran, or the outer covering, contains naturally-occurring nutrient inhibitors, such as phytic acid. Phytic acid is the principal storage form of the mineral phosphorus that the plant will ultimately rely upon to grow. Phytic acid is not digestible by humans. Furthermore, phytic acid binds to important minerals like zinc, iron, calcium, and magnesium, making them less absorbable. Generations of humans discovered, through observation, that in order to maximize the nutritional intake of grains in their diet, they needed to cook, soak, ferment, or sprout the grains.[5]

During the Industrial Revolution, planting, harvesting, and processing of grains became faster because of newly invented machinery. In the second half of the 1800s, the number and size of farms increased dramatically, growing commodities such as corn, wheat, and cotton. Large scale agriculture in the United States and improved storage allowed for year-round availability of grains to the consumer. Initially, grains were processed only via stone milling tools and retained all their nutritional components: the germ, bran, and endosperm. With the creation of steel roller mills, the germ and the bran were removed, leaving only the endosperm. This starchy part of the grain was then turned into flour that would not go rancid or spoil as quickly. This processing allowed for a longer shelf life of food products like white bread or white pasta. Unfortunately, food products made with refined flours have lost valuable nutrition provided by the removed parts. This process of removing parts of the whole grain produces what we now refer to as refined grains or flour. Food manufacturers try to compensate for the lost nutrition naturally provided in a whole grain by enriching the product with synthetic vitamins or minerals.

We've come a long way from hand harvesting wild grains to the daily intake of large amounts of refined grains in the form of bread, pasta, pastries, tortillas, chips, and crackers, all readily and cheaply available to the modern consumer. While certain diets may encourage everyone to avoid all grains, we promote a return to some of the traditional ways of consuming whole grains, in balanced portions and with proper preparation.

The process of removing parts of the whole grain produces what we now refer to as refined grains or flour. Food manufacturers try to compensate for the lost nutrition naturally provided in a whole grain by enriching the product with synthetic vitamins or minerals.

Wild and Cultivated Greens

Like whole grains, wild and cultivated greens have been a part of many traditional diets and are a nutrient-dense food that is often missing in today's Standard American Diet. Dark green leafy vegetables are a great source of plant-based iron, calcium, and potassium. In addition, they are high in fiber and a rich source of beta-carotene (the precursor to vitamin A) and vitamin K, both of which are fat-soluble vitamins. Vitamin A is important for vision, immune support, reproduction, and growth. Vitamin K regulates blood clotting and helps maintain mineralization of the bones. Traditionally, greens were prepared with a healthy fat source which allowed for increased absorption of these fat-soluble vitamins. An example is cooking collard greens with a ham hock or the traditional use of olive oil with vegetable dishes in a Mediterranean diet. Greens are also high in antioxidants, which are important for keeping our bodies from accumulating damaging chemicals, known as free radicals, that contribute to aging and disease.

The Standard American Diet is lacking in vegetables, and in particular, dark leafy greens. We will introduce several familiar and tasty recipes with greens that will bring this nutritional powerhouse back into your family's diet.

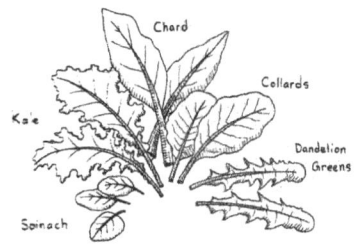

Dark green leafy vegetables are a great source of plant-based iron, calcium, and potassium. In addition, they are high in fiber and a rich source of beta-carotene (the precursor to vitamin A) and vitamin K, both of which are fat-soluble vitamins.

Meat, Dairy, and Eggs

There has also been a huge shift in the animal agriculture system that has increased the consumption of processed and ultra-processed meat in the American diet. For example, looking at the production of beef, pork, poultry, dairy, and eggs in the U.S., small farms have been widely replaced by large-scale, industrialized production, also referred to as factory farms. Huge feedlots, large industrial meatpacking plants, and government subsidies have fueled a massive expansion of cheaper, processed, and readily available meat and animal products.

Small-scale farming provided more time for animals to grow naturally and allowed access to land to roam, graze, and forage on their natural food sources, including grass, insects, and other vegetation. The economics of running small-scale farms generated higher prices and less availability. Consumers in the past were less likely to purchase large quantities of meat, naturally leading to a more plant-based diet.

Unlike small-scale farming, growth hormones and antibiotics are used extensively in the industrial model for faster animal growth. Today's meat industry, with its cramped living conditions and unnatural feeding practices, contributes to creating sick and stressed animals. Factory farming is also contributing to global public health concerns due to its emission of greenhouse gasses and its role in creating antibiotic-resistant bacteria due to the overuse and misuse of antibiotics.[6,7]

When we consider red meat specifically, industrial production creates less nutritious beef compared to small-scale farmers producing grass-fed beef. Conventional, or industrial meat, contains less vitamin E, beta-carotene, and antioxidants. Grass-fed beef is lower in fat compared to grain-fed beef and has a healthier balance of fats, including lower amounts of saturated fats and higher amounts of omega-3 fatty acids and conjugated linoleic acid (CLA).[8,9] This shift in the fatty acid profile and increased antioxidant content of grass-fed beef contributes to it being less inflammatory than conventional beef.

Animal foods such as meat, poultry, eggs, and dairy, can be a part of a healthy diet when you consider the source, processing, and amount consumed. But, there is a cause for concern when consuming large amounts of conventional and ultra-processed meats. Ultra-processed meat that makes its way into hot dogs, sausages, lunch meats, and chicken nuggets are high in other additives, such as sodium nitrites and nitrates, and preservatives that can have other negative health impacts.[10]

Fats

Fat has been considered a highly valuable part of traditional diets. Prior to the establishment of the current highly processed food system, populations around the world were sustained and nourished by nutrient-dense, minimally processed fats including:

- butter and ghee
- beef and lamb tallow
- lard (from pigs)
- chicken, goose, and duck fat
- unrefined coconut and palm oil

Animal foods such as meat, poultry, and dairy can be a part of a healthy diet when you consider the source, processing, and amount consumed. But, there is a cause for concern when consuming large amounts of conventional and ultra-processed meats.

cold pressed extra virgin olive oil

nuts and seeds

fish oils, including cod liver oil

Over the last century, the food industry has learned to extract and refine oils from plants like soy, safflower, sunflower, rapeseed (canola), and corn. An extensive, high-heat process is required that includes mechanical and chemical extraction of the oil, followed by bleaching and deodorizing the oil to obtain a neutral color and taste. The process is often referred to as RBD, for refined, bleached, and deodorized. This refinement process can also oxidize (damage) the fats, create harmful byproducts, and damage some of the health properties of the oils, including antioxidants like vitamin E and polyphenols.[11] These highly processed oils are common in the Standard American Diet due to their use in fried foods and ultra-processed foods. Additionally, people have moved away from cooking with butter, extra virgin olive oil, and animal fats and instead are using more processed fats such as margarine, imitation butter, or "vegetable oil", typically a combination of soy and corn oil.

If we don't include healthy fat in the diet, then we are missing out on a big nutritional opportunity! In Chapter Two, **Nourish Yourself with Fat**, we will discuss the benefits of healthy fats and how to choose and use minimally processed oils appropriately to maintain their nutritional value.

FAME Guiding Principles

Following the wisdom of a whole foods diet, our food philosophy will help you learn and make choices about the food you consume. Consider a spectrum of food. On one end is ready-made, ultra-processed food; on the other end are whole, unprocessed foods. Everyone makes choices somewhere on this food spectrum. Perhaps you are closer to one end, consuming highly processed foods and beverages daily. Or, you may already be committed to a whole foods diet, consuming fresh produce and healthy fats and avoiding processed foods. Most of us fall somewhere in between these nutritional bookends or even shift back and forth between them. Our goal is to motivate and support

choices closer to the whole foods end of this continuum. Rather than jumping from one extreme to the other, this journey is about gradual and sustainable behavior change based on education about food and learning the tools to be successful in your choices. What awaits you is pleasure in the process, and the enjoyment of delicious, whole foods using the information, tips, and recipes we provide. We hope that your relationship with food will change.

The wisdom found in traditional diets and our naturopathic medical training and clinical experience serves as the foundation for the FAME cooking series and this book. The following six guiding principles anchor us as we navigate a whole foods lifestyle in a highly processed food landscape:

Our goal is to motivate and support choices closer to the whole foods end of this continuum. Rather than jumping from one extreme to the other, this journey is about gradual and sustainable behavior change based on education about food and learning the tools to be successful in your choices.

- Promote whole foods.
- Encourage a diverse, primarily plant-based diet.
- Include food from healthy animals.
- Promote anti-inflammatory food choices.
- Recognize that individuals have unique food needs.
- Care about food and its sources.

Choose Whole Foods

Our post-industrialized society has systematically drifted away from eating whole foods from nature that provide a healthy balance of fat, protein, and carbohydrates. This move away from a nutrient-dense, fiber-rich, whole foods-based diet increases the risk of chronic diseases like heart disease and diabetes.

Eat a Diverse, Primarily Plant-Based Diet

Plants like nuts, seeds, whole grains, beans, legumes, fruits and vegetables are nutrient-dense, rich in fiber and antioxidants, and they help balance inflammation in the body. On the other hand, a low-fiber diet based on ultra-processed and nutrient-poor foods and excess animal products contributes to increased inflammation.

Include Foods from Healthy Animals

Foods from healthy animals are nutrient-dense, providing an excellent source of protein, in addition to nutrients such as iron, vitamin B12, and zinc. Animal meat, poultry, fish, dairy, and eggs can contribute to a well-balanced diet. However, diets high in excess animal products from the industrial food system are highly resource dependent in terms of land, water, and energy, which puts multiple stressors on the environment. We encourage a responsible and ethical animal agriculture system that takes into account the welfare of the farm workers, the animals, and the environment.

Promote Anti-inflammatory Food Choices

Diets composed of excess added sugar, poor quality fats, conventionally raised meats, and ultra-processed foods contribute to chronic inflammation. Chronic inflammation affects all systems in the body and contributes to the development of autoimmune, digestive, and neurological disorders, as well as diabetes and heart disease.

Recognize That Individuals Have Unique Food Needs

There is no one right "diet" for everyone. Life stage, health goals, healthcare conditions, lifestyle, and food allergies and sensitivities can all influence individual nutritional needs. An individual's cultural upbringing, food ethics, and access to food must also be taken into account regarding dietary recommendations. For example, age determines the need to prioritize certain nutrients over others. Infants require regular intake of fat-rich foods, ideally from breast milk, to support their growing brains. Elders require protein-rich foods to support metabolic changes that may decrease muscle mass. Additionally, specific illnesses ranging from ear infections to diabetes may be prevented or treated by food choices.

Identifying and treating patients with food sensitivities, which is the inability to properly digest certain foods, has been a foundational practice of naturopathic medicine. Food sensitivities or intolerances are common. It is estimated that more than 20% of people have a food intolerance, compared to about 2% of adults who have food allergies.[12] Food sensitivities can contribute to numerous symptoms, including headaches, mood changes, fatigue, acne, bloating, diarrhea, constipation, joint pain, and rashes.

> *Diets composed of excess added sugar, poor quality fats, conventionally raised meats, and ultra-processed foods contribute to chronic inflammation. Chronic inflammation affects all systems in the body and contributes to the development of autoimmune, digestive, and neurological disorders, as well as diabetes and heart disease.*

A food sensitivity is the result of an abnormal reaction of the immune system to a particular food. It can be difficult to identify because symptoms may not appear for hours to days after ingesting the food.

A person can be sensitive to any food or food group, but the most common sensitivities are to gluten, dairy, and eggs. Dairy sensitivities may be due to a lactose intolerance, which is a deficiency of the lactase enzyme, or it may be due to an inability to digest one of the milk proteins—casein or whey. A gluten sensitivity is different from a wheat allergy or Celiac disease, which is an autoimmune response triggered by gluten that damages the lining of the small intestine, affecting proper nutrient absorption. In addition, sensitivities to specific types of fermentable carbohydrates (also known as high FODMAP foods), or foods high in histamines (a chemical found naturally in certain foods), as well as reactions to various food chemicals and additives are also common.

A food sensitivity differs from a food allergy, which is an immediate response of the immune system that produces an IgE antibody. Food allergies can cause hives, wheezing, and swelling, and in the worst case, anaphylaxis, a life-threatening emergency. Food labels must clearly state if they contain one of the nine most common food allergens: milk, egg, fish, shellfish, tree nuts, peanuts, wheat, soy, or sesame.

Care About Food and Its Sources

Our choice of food can nourish us, or it can increase risk for disease. Food connects us to family, community, nature, and to other parts of the world. Food has played a central role in the social interaction of humans for thousands of years. We must begin to understand the connection between food production and dietary choices and how it relates to human and environmental health.

Macronutrients—The Big Players Of Nutrition

A diverse, whole foods-based diet provides a complete range of nutrition that is often absent in a diet high in ultra-processed foods. This includes healthy sources of fat, carbohydrates rich in fiber, and protein. Let us review some basics about nutrition which can help you better understand and communicate the value of whole foods. To begin, we will look at the importance of macronutrients.

Macronutrients are nutrients required in larger quantities in the diet for overall health: fats, carbohydrates, and proteins. All of these nutrients are needed to support energy, function, and structure. In the next three chapters, we focus on the importance of these macronutrients in the diet.

> "I came into the FAME series not understanding whole foods. I have learned so much about nutrition that I thought I knew, but didn't. I am more creative in the kitchen converting recipes to healthier choices. I have found my family has learned through my healthier choices and we are growing as a family in a healthy way. I have lost over 22 pounds in the 12 weeks."
>
> —Sherry, FAME series, Charlee's Kitchen

Chapter Two

Nourish Yourself With Fat

Eat Healthy Fat. It's Good For You!

THE SUBJECT OF DIETARY FAT CAN BE CONFUSING. MANY PEOPLE HAVE LIKELY HEARD CONFLICTING ADVICE ABOUT WHETHER TO eat a generally low-fat diet or perhaps even to try a very high-fat diet. We aim to demystify some of the confusion about fat in our diet because healthy fat is good for us, especially when it is part of a balanced diet.

Let's begin with a few basics to clarify some of the confusion about healthy fat:

- Fat is an important macronutrient to include in a daily diet. Healthy fat can include both saturated and unsaturated fats that can be found in both plant and animal sources of whole foods such as nuts, seeds, avocado, olives, dairy, fish and meat, as well as in cooking oils.

- A healthy dietary pattern includes primarily choosing minimally processed cooking oils made from unsaturated fats and including foods rich in omega-3 fatty acids.

- Smoking or overheating oils when cooking will cause oxidation to the fat, thereby increasing the risk of negative effects in the body. Polyunsaturated fats are at greater risk of becoming oxidized compared to saturated fats due to the differences in their chemical structure.

- Cholesterol is a type of fat naturally produced by your liver as well as a type of dietary fat. Food sources of cholesterol come from animal foods such as eggs, meat, seafood, and dairy. Misguided information has been promoted about the role of dietary cholesterol and disease. Food that contains cholesterol can be part of a healthy diet.
- Every person has individual nutritional needs, including which fats to include in their diet.

Understanding Dietary Fat

Fat is an energy-dense nutrient providing nine calories per gram compared to four calories per gram from protein and carbohydrates. The body digests fat more slowly than proteins or carbohydrates, providing a slow energy source, and fat helps to give you a satiated feeling from a meal. Fat is incorporated into cell membranes, affecting cellular function, and it influences levels of inflammation in the body as well as hormone production. This is why it is essential to choose healthy fats. Dietary fat also helps the body to absorb essential, fat-soluble vitamins, which are vitamins A, D, E, and K. Natural sources of fat in the diet come from both plants and animals and may include items in Table 2.1.

A quick review of some basic biochemistry is helpful to understand the difference between saturated and unsaturated fat. The chemical structure of fat has a glycerol base with three fatty acid chains attached. It is the fatty acids that can be saturated or unsaturated, which is a chemistry reference to how many double bonds occur within the fatty acid chain. Saturated fat contains no double bonds. Unsaturated fat contains one or more double bonds. The number of double bonds influences the physical characteristics of the fat. For instance, oils rich in unsaturated fat, like olive, flax, avocado, or sesame, tend to be liquid at room temperature. Compare these to foods rich in saturated fats, like butter, ghee, lard, palm, or coconut oil, which are solid at room temperature.

Table 2.1 Food Sources of Fats

Animal Sources Of Fats	Plant Sources Of Fats
Dairy: Butter, milk, cheese and yogurt (full-fat) Egg yolk Fish Red meat, Poultry, and Animal skin	Avocado and avocado oil Cocoa/chocolate Coconut and coconut oil Nuts and Seeds Olives and olive oil

Unsaturated Fats

The body relies on the metabolism of unsaturated fat to provide energy and to promote a healthy level of inflammation. Additionally, unsaturated fat surrounds and protects nerve cells, including those of the brain and eyes.

Unsaturated fat includes both monounsaturated and polyunsaturated fat. The mono (one) and poly (many) refer to the number of double bonds within the fatty acids. The number of double bonds in a fat influences the way it reacts to heat, light, and oxygen in the environment, a process called oxidation. The oxidation of the fat creates unhealthy free radicals and eventually causes the oil to become rancid. Compared to polyunsaturated fats, which have multiple double bonds, monounsaturated fats are more stable when exposed to oxygen or higher heat. Rich sources of monounsaturated fats include olive oil, a foundation of the Mediterranean diet, avocados and avocado oil, and nuts and seeds. Dietary patterns that include monounsaturated fats are known for their heart-healthy benefits.[1]

Polyunsaturated fats are also referred to as essential fatty acids because the body doesn't naturally make them. These include omega-3 and omega-6 fatty acids, and together these fatty acids influence inflammation in the body. Omega-3 fatty acids such as eicosapentaenoic acid (EPA) and docosahexaenoic acid (DHA) are found in most fish such as salmon, tuna, sardines, and cod. Some nuts and seeds like walnut, flax, chia, and hemp are high in alpha-linolenic acid (ALA), a plant-based omega-3 fatty acid, some of which is convert-

Sources of Monounsaturated Fats

Olives and olive oil
Avocados and avocado oil
Macadamia nuts
Peanuts
Sesame seeds
Chicken fat
Lard
Canola oil

Sources of Polyunsaturated Fats High in Omega-3 Fatty Acids

Fish (salmon, trout, halibut, cod, sardines, mackerel)
Shellfish
Pasture-raised meats
Flaxseed*
Chia seed*
Walnuts*
Hemp hearts*

---

*High in alpha-linolenic acid

ed to EPA and DHA. Dietary patterns that include regular consumption of omega-3 fatty acids, particularly from seafood, have shown cardio-protective benefits.[2] Omega-6 fatty acids are found in walnuts and sunflower seeds as well as in oils produced from soy, safflower, sunflower, rapeseed (canola), and corn. Because they are inexpensive to manufacture, these omega-6-rich oils are often used in ultra-processed and fast foods. Polyunsaturated fats are more susceptible to oxidative damage, and overheating these oils through repeated heating or through deep-frying is associated with increased risk of cardiovascular disease.[3]

The Balancing Act of Omega-6: Omega-3

Most people are consuming omega-6 and omega-3 fatty acids out of balance, which can promote inflammation. A healthy ratio of omega-6 to omega-3 in the diet is thought to range from 4:1 to 6:1, but the Standard American Diet contributes to an imbalanced ratio over 15:1. This contributes to health consequences associated with increased inflammation such as cardiovascular disease and diabetes.[4,5] To promote an anti-inflammatory diet, increase the amount of foods rich in omega-3 fatty acids in the diet. Reducing your intake of omega-6 rich oils in ultra-processed foods is another important way to improve this ratio.

Saturated Fats

In the body, saturated fats provide energy storage in adipose tissue (body fat), and they are incorporated into cell membranes, providing necessary stiffness and integrity. Dietary saturated fat can be found in both plant and animal sources such as full-fat dairy, fatty cuts of red meat, coconut oil, and palm oil. Because saturated fats are more chemically stable, they can be a good choice to cook with at higher temperatures. Eating saturated fat in balance with unsaturated fat can be part of a well-balanced, whole foods diet. However, the body can also convert excess carbohydrates in the diet into saturated fats, so they are not essential to include in the diet like polyunsaturated fats. A dietary pattern based on increased consumption of saturated fat

High in Omega-6 Fatty Acids
  Corn oil
  Soybean oil
  "Vegetable oil"
  Safflower oil
  Sunflower oil
  Grapeseed oil
  Canola oil
  Walnuts
  Conventionally raised meats

Animal Sources of Saturated Fat
  Dairy products (whole milk, full-fat yogurt, cheese, butter, ghee)
  Pork bacon, sausage, and processed meats
  Poultry skin (duck, chicken, turkey)
  Fatty cuts of red meat
  Egg yolks

Plant Sources of Saturated Fat
  Coconut meat and oil
  Chocolate
  Palm oil

from ultra-processed foods along with low intake of fiber and antioxidants from fruits and vegetables is linked to inflammation, high cholesterol, heart disease, and diabetes.[6,7]

Trans Fat: A Fat to Avoid

You've heard our message: Eat healthy, minimally processed fat. It's good for the body. However, there is one type of fat to avoid: industrial trans fat. Industrial trans fats increase inflammation in the body and are linked to heart disease and stroke.[8,9,10] Scientists discovered that bombarding unsaturated fats with hydrogen atoms creates trans fats, a far cry from a minimally processed fat. Another name for trans fat is **partially hydrogenated oils** or PHOs. Industrial trans fat was created to give food a longer shelf life: it goes rancid less quickly. This fat was often used in the fast food industry for frying and for stabilizing packaged food products. Due to an abundance of evidence linking industrial trans fat to an increased risk of heart disease, in 2015, the FDA took the significant step to remove this highly processed ingredient from the "GRAS" list ("Generally Recognized as Safe").

Natural trans fats do occur in small amounts in foods like dairy and meat from ruminant animals. At this time, natural trans fats in the diet have not been shown to contribute the same health risks as industrial trans fats.[11,12]

Bringing Fat Back To The Kitchen

Nutrient-rich, minimally-processed fats, like olive oil, butter, tallow, lard, ghee, and coconut, have been a part of traditional diets across the world. Not only can these fats add important nutrients, they also enhance the flavors of the meal! Knowing how to properly cook with fats is just as important as including healthy fats. Certain fats and oils withstand higher heat with less risk of oxidation, like saturated fats and certain unsaturated fats with higher smoke points. Recall the negative health implications of overheating polyunsaturated fats. The reality is that some degree of oxidation will occur with cooking oils. Eating antioxidant-rich foods is very important to counteract the negative health effects of oxidized fats in the diet. Antioxidant-rich foods include brightly colored fruits and vegetables, beans, beverages such as tea and coffee, and dark chocolate.

The following are general guidelines for cooking with and consuming minimally processed oils and fats. For higher heat needs, such as baking or sautéing, consider avocado oil, butter, ghee, or coconut oil. Choose extra virgin olive oil for recipes that require lower temperature cooking, as well as for salad or meal dressings. Unrefined, expeller-pressed sesame oil can be used for its distinctive flavor in stir-fries, sauces, and dressings, and generally has a medium-to-high smoke point. Grapeseed oil, which can be a sustainable by-product of wine production, is often marketed for its neutral flavor. However, the seeds have very high amounts of omega-6 fatty acids (about 70%) and often undergo extensive processing, increasing the risk of oxidation. With any oil you choose, be sure to review the oil's smoke point, and try to avoid overheating the oil. Refer to Table 15.4 and Table 15.5 in Chapter Fifteen, **Kitchen Skills**.

Rich in monounsaturated fat, canola oil is marketed as having a high omega-3 content and for its heart-healthy benefits.[13] This oil has an interesting history. Canola oil comes from the rapeseed plant, which is an inedible plant in its natural form because it contains a toxic compound, erucic acid. Originally, rapeseed oil was used for lamp fuel and as an industrial lubricant. In the early 1970s, the plant was bred to contain a lower amount of its toxic compound, leading to the name: Canola or Canadian Oil Low Acid. Similar to corn, soy, and safflower oils, rapeseed oil extraction requires a high amount of processing. This includes chemical extraction (using hexane, a petroleum-based product), high heat, and bleaching, exposing the sensitive omega-3 oils to stressors that may contribute to the oxidation of the fatty acids and the loss of valuable antioxidants.[14,15] If choosing canola oil, look for organic and expeller-pressed to help preserve the antioxidants.

In addition, the rapeseed plant is recognized as one of the most common genetically modified organisms, or GMOs. Learn more about why we encourage limiting or avoiding GMOs in food products in Chapter Five, **Reading Food Labels**. While increasing omega-3 fatty acids in the diet is a healthy goal, there are less processed fats to choose from than canola oil that will increase omega-3 fatty acids in

For higher heat needs, such as baking or sautéing, consider avocado oil, butter, ghee, or coconut oil. Choose extra virgin olive oil for recipes that require lower temperature cooking, as well as for salad or meal dressings.

the diet, including ground flaxseed, chia seed, hemp seed, walnuts, egg yolks from pasture-raised chickens, grass-fed beef, and most importantly, many types of seafood.

Demystifying Cholesterol

What exactly is cholesterol, and why do we care so much about it? Cholesterol is a type of fat, or lipid, made by the body and also consumed in the diet from meat, eggs, dairy, and animal fats. Cholesterol forms the building blocks of several hormones—including estrogen, progesterone, testosterone, DHEA—and vitamin D. It supports the structure of all the cells in the body, including brain cells. Cholesterol helps to repair damaged tissue in the body due to its role in creating healthy cell membranes. It is also used to make bile in the liver, which helps to break down dietary fat.

A high total cholesterol level is implicated in the development of heart disease because cholesterol can become trapped in the artery lining and create plaque which can impair blood flow. This is called atherosclerosis, a condition that increases the risk of heart attack and stroke. A blood test can evaluate a person's cholesterol level. Most people are familiar with LDL (low density lipoprotein) being known as the bad cholesterol and HDL (high density lipoprotein) being known as the good cholesterol. This is because LDL carries cholesterol to the arteries where it has the potential to cause plaque formation, and HDL carries cholesterol back from circulation to the liver for removal.[16] While a significantly elevated LDL cholesterol level is associated with an increased risk for heart disease, people can also have an elevated LDL cholesterol and not develop it. Additionally, there are different types and sizes of both HDL and LDL that have shown different impacts on the development of heart disease. Certain blood tests can look at these cholesterol subtypes to further shed light on a person's risk of heart disease.

The liver makes 75-80% of your total cholesterol levels, leaving only about 20-25% to be influenced by the diet. Medical conditions and metabolic triggers that influence cholesterol production in the liver include diabetes, low thyroid function (hypothyroidism), hormonal conditions like polycystic ovarian syndrome and menopause, physical inactivity, chronic stress, and poor sleep quality.[17] A person's family history, or genetics, can also influence their pattern of cholesterol production. As for dietary intake, saturated fat from both plant and animal sources is known to directly increase cholesterol levels, specifically LDL cholesterol. In addition, a dietary pattern that includes too little fiber and too much added sugar, refined carbohydrates, alcohol, and processed foods is also associated with elevated LDL.

The development of heart disease is a multifaceted process and includes other significant factors besides total cholesterol, LDL cholesterol, and dietary intake of fat. Factors known to increase the risk of heart disease include hypertension, tobacco use (smoking or chewing), physical inactivity, obesity, diabetes, poverty, chronic stress, depression, and excessive alcohol intake. Additional risk factors include a family history of heart disease, advancing age, and racial or ethnic groups that face health disparities, including African American, American Indian, Asian American, and Hispanic/Latinx people.

If you do have elevated cholesterol along with additional risk factors for heart disease, talk to your healthcare provider about creating an integrative plan to reduce your risk factors. Dietary and lifestyle recommendations may include: reducing the intake of highly processed foods and saturated fat, increasing fiber-rich foods, reducing added sugar, refined carbohydrates, and alcohol, increasing physical activity, optimizing sleep habits, addressing sources of chronic stress, smoking cessation, and managing elevated blood pressure.

What About Eggs?

Some people may choose to avoid whole eggs or egg yolk to try to help lower their cholesterol. Eating cholesterol in the diet (including from eggs) has been shown to raise both the protective, large HDL and the large LDL.[18] However, extensive nutrition research has shown little to no evidence that dietary cholesterol contributes to the development of cardiovascular disease.[19,20]

Since 2015, the Dietary Guidelines for Americans **removed** the recommendation to limit dietary cholesterol to 300mg per day and recommends to include eggs in moderation as part of a healthy diet.

The development of heart disease is a multifaceted process and includes other significant factors besides total cholesterol, LDL cholesterol, and dietary intake of fat.

Eggs are rich in protein, low in saturated fat, and contain important vitamins and minerals. For example, egg yolk provides fat-soluble vitamins A, D, E, and K, as well as B vitamins and choline. Choline is an essential nutrient to include in the diet to support metabolic and neurological health.[21] Egg whites provide protein and several B vitamins including B12.

There are some people who do show negative responses in their cardiometabolic health with a diet rich in cholesterol. In these cases, reducing dietary cholesterol may still be recommended. Otherwise, for most people, avoiding eggs is not as important as other dietary strategies to lower cholesterol. Consider choosing eggs made from pasture-raised chickens, because their diet influences the nutrient composition of their yolks.

And Finally—The Question Everyone Is Asking— Does Eating Fat Make You Fat?

Get ready for this . . . No. Eating healthy, whole foods sources of fat and minimally processed oils is good for you and a healthy metabolism. In 1977, public health recommendations for the U.S. population were made to reduce fat intake to less than 30%. Food producers responded to this recommendation by replacing fat, especially saturated fat, with highly processed and refined carbohydrates. We have since learned that contrary to those recommendations, replacing dietary fat with refined carbohydrates and added sugars is associated with an increased risk of heart disease and diabetes. Replacing some saturated fats and refined carbohydrates in the diet with unsaturated fats and whole grains has been shown to be beneficial.[22] Obesity medicine experts have recommended up to 30-34% of dietary calories from fat, primarily unsaturated fat, to support weight loss and a healthy metabolism for people who are overweight, obese, diabetic, or have prediabetes.[23] Read a label on a fat-free or low-fat product and see what has been added to compensate for the loss of flavor from the fat; often it is sugar, more refined carbohydrates, and/or salt. Remember, fat provides a consistent energy source for your day and helps you to feel satiated. We will teach you the balancing act of building a healthy plate that contains fat as well as carbs and protein.

The bottom line: you can learn to optimize the quality and quantity of fats you cook with and eat to support a healthy metabolism—and quite frankly, your food will taste better.

Chapter Three

Nourish Yourself With Carbohydrates

IF THERE IS A MACRONUTRIENT CATEGORY THAT AMERICANS ARE FAMILIAR WITH, IT'S CARBOHYDRATES! WE LOVE OUR CARBS. Consider the last time you consumed pasta, bread, cereal, chips, popcorn, rice, fruit juice, soda, or an energy drink. These foods and food products are packed with carbohydrates, some healthier than others. While many are highly processed, there are whole food sources of carbohydrates, including some of our favorites: carrots, sweet potatoes, black beans, brown rice, kale, spinach, and whole fruit. In general, plant-based foods will provide the large majority of the carbohydrates in the diet.

Carbohydrates provide numerous benefits, including:

- energy production for all the cells in the body, especially the brain,
- fuel storage in the form of glycogen,
- providing phytonutrients (including antioxidants), which are beneficial plant-based chemicals,
- helping balance cholesterol, and
- supporting a healthy digestive tract.

It is important to navigate carbohydrates well. Choosing poorly can lead to weight gain, insulin resistance and diabetes, cavities, heart disease, increased inflammation, and decreased immune function.

Learning the language of carbohydrates is important before venturing into label reading. Starch, fiber, and sugar all refer to carbohydrates.

Carbohydrates exist in two main categories: simple and complex. Simple carbohydrates can have two different structures and may be referred to as monosaccharides (a single sugar) or disaccharides (two sugars). Due to their simple structure, simple carbs are broken down quickly and provide a quick energy source. Complex carbohydrates are longer chains of simple carbohydrates, also called polysaccharides (many sugars). They take more time to break down and provide a slower energy source compared to simple carbs.

Simple Carbohydrates

Simple carbohydrates generally taste sweet and provide a quick energy source. Eaten in excess and without a balance of fats and protein, they can lead to blood sugar spikes and crashes. Excessive sugar intake is also associated with weight gain, poor dental health, and diabetes. The following are examples of the most common simple carbohydrates found in food:

Monosaccharides

Glucose: Main source of energy for the brain
Galactose: Part of lactose or milk sugar
Fructose: Sweetest of all sugars, found in fruit and honey

Disaccharides

Sucrose or refined "table" sugar (glucose + fructose)
Lactose or milk sugar (glucose + galactose)
Maltose (glucose + glucose)

Complex Carbohydrates

Complex carbs take longer to digest compared to simple carbs, and therefore provide a slower energy source. Fiber and starch are the two main types of complex carbohydrates, or polysaccharides, found in food.

Fiber is indigestible, and therefore cannot be broken down into simple sugars. Fiber provides many health benefits in the diet, which we will soon explore.

Starch is a complex carbohydrate that can be digested and broken down into simple sugars slowly, providing a good energy source for the body. Whole foods sources of starch often contain other valuable vitamins, minerals, and typically will also contain some fiber. Examples of whole foods that contain starch include whole grains, fruits, and root vegetables, such as potatoes, yams, and cassava.

Table 3.1 Food Sources of Complex and Simple Carbohydrates

Complex Carbohydrates	**Simple Carbohydrates**

Legumes and beans
Nuts and seeds
Vegetables
Whole grains
	Sugar
	Fruit juice
	Sweetened beverages:
	   soda, tea, energy drinks
	Honey, maple syrup, agave nectar
	Refined grains:
	   white pasta, white bread

Effects In The Body	**Effects In The Body**
Provide a slow energy source for your body and brain Fiber helps remove waste and cholesterol Increase the sense of fullness after eating Provide important fuel to sustain friendly bacteria in the gut	Provide a quick energy source for your body and brain Taste sweet Excess can lead to cavities, weight gain, and diabetes

Let Fiber Be Your Guide

Fiber provides many health benefits and can be a powerful guide in your journey towards including more plants in your diet. Many of fiber's health benefits are linked to its role as the primary energy source for the microorganisms known as the gut microbiome that live in the large intestines (or colon). The gut microbiome strongly influences the overall function of the human body. The greatest benefits from fiber come from including a variety of plant foods in the diet that contain diverse types of fibers and other healthy nutrients. Relying primarily on taking a fiber supplement or highly-processed foods that add in extra fiber won't provide the same benefits, although there are some situations where that can be beneficial.

Many of fiber's health benefits are linked to its role as the primary energy source for the microorganisms known as the gut microbiome that live in the large intestines (or colon). The health of the gut microbiome influences almost all of the systems in the body. The greatest benefits from fiber come from including a variety of plant foods in the diet that contain diverse types of fibers and other healthy nutrients.

Excellent food sources of fiber include whole fruits, vegetables, beans, peas, and other legumes, nuts and seeds, and whole grains. Notice that plant foods provide fiber while animal products, such as meat and dairy, do not. The fiber content of whole foods is often reduced when it is highly processed, for example when a whole fruit is processed into fruit juice, vegetables into vegetable juice, and whole grains into refined grains. Fiber is categorized as soluble or insoluble, though most plant foods contain both types.

Soluble fiber: This type of fiber dissolves in water in the digestive tract and creates a gel-like substance. It helps slow down digestion and contributes to a sense of fullness. Additionally, some soluble fiber can also be referred to as fermentable fiber, or a *prebiotic*, which provides a food source for the healthy bacteria in the large intestine. We will further discuss the role of prebiotics and the gut microbiome in Chapter Seven, **Strategies for Healthy Digestion.**

Sources of soluble fiber include: apples, pears, oats, vegetables, beans, peas, lentils, nuts, ground flaxseeds, and psyllium husk.

Insoluble fiber: This type of fiber doesn't dissolve in water and remains relatively unchanged in the digestive tract. It helps move food through the digestive tract and creates more bulk and softer stools.

Sources of insoluble fiber include: whole grains, nuts and seeds, dark green leafy vegetables, and fruit skins.

Resistant Starch: There is also a specific type of starch, called a resistant starch, which isn't digested into simple sugars like a typical starch. It acts more like a fermentable soluble fiber, or a prebiotic, and moves through the digestive tract undigested, where it reaches the large intestine and provides food for the gut microbiome.

Sources of resistant starches include: unripe bananas and plantains, beans and lentils, peas, and raw or soaked oats, such as overnight oats. Additionally, cooking and then cooling (refrigerating or freezing) starchy food, such as bread, rice and other grains, potatoes, and beans can increase the amount of resistant starch in the food.

In general, fiber intake in the United States is lacking, yet it can have a profound effect on your health. Focusing on increasing your dietary fiber is a simple strategy to improve your metabolic health and to help reduce the risk factors for several chronic diseases. A high-fiber diet has been shown to reduce the risk of developing heart disease, stroke, type 2 diabetes, breast cancer, and colon cancer.[1,2,3] The soluble fiber found in beans, oats, and ground flaxseed, for example, helps lower total and LDL (low density lipoprotein) cholesterol levels, therefore reducing risk factors associated with heart disease.[4] It also slows the absorption of dietary sugar in the digestive tract, which will help balance blood glucose levels and reduce the risk of diabetes.[5] In addition, higher fiber diets have been shown to help control blood pressure, promote weight loss, and decrease waist circumference.[6,7]

High-fiber foods will generally provide a sense of fullness and satiety with meals, decreasing the likelihood of overeating and unnecessary snacking. Generally speaking, high-fiber foods found in whole vegetables and whole fruits tend to be lower in calories per serving. An example of this is comparing one cup of apple juice (approximately 115 calories, 0 grams of fiber, 24 grams of sugar) to eating one whole apple with the skin on (approximately 65 calories, 3 grams of fiber, 13 grams of sugar).

Increase your fiber intake gradually, making sure to support the increased fiber with adequate hydration. Fiber and water work together to maintain healthy bowel elimination. You may temporarily experience increased gas with more fiber. Typically, as your intestines adjust to the new environment, the gas will diminish.

Whole Grains

Whole grains can be a good source of fiber in any meal. Examples of whole grains include: barley, brown rice, buckwheat, millet, oats, whole corn, whole wheat, wild rice, quinoa, teff, and amaranth. We previously discussed the change in processing of whole grains; let's now take a closer look at the change in nutrition, including fiber content, when whole grains are refined.

Whole grains provide complex nutrition from the combination of all parts of the grain, including the bran, germ, and endosperm.

The **bran** is the outer protective layer of the grain, also referred to as the husk or shell, which protects it from germinating until it is in the optimal environment. Not only is it a protective fibrous layer for the grain, it is an excellent source of dietary fiber. Bran also provides B-vitamins and trace minerals like iron. B-vitamins are an important part of many biochemical processes to create energy in the body and to support a healthy nervous system. Iron is required in red blood cells for proper oxygen transport.

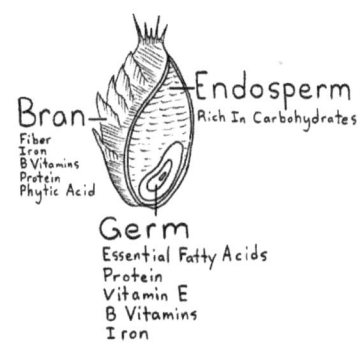

Whole grains provide complex nutrition from the combination of all of its parts, including the bran, germ, and endosperm.

The bran also contains a compound called phytic acid. Phytic acid prevents the plant from germinating in less than ideal environments. But in food, it can reduce the availability of minerals, such as calcium, magnesium, iron, and zinc. Certain cooking methods such as soaking, sprouting, and fermenting can decrease the amount of phytic acid and other nutrient inhibitors in whole grains.

The **germ** is the part of the grain that contains the genetic information for the plant to germinate or initiate growth. It provides essential fatty acids, a combination of omega-3 and omega-6, as well as vitamin E. The vitamin E, an antioxidant, works synergistically with the essential fatty acids to protect these valuable oils from oxidation. It is natural for whole foods to spoil over time. Thus, food manufacturers remove the germ from the whole grain to ensure a longer shelf life, which robs us of this valuable combination of nutrients.

The **endosperm** contains the necessary energy from carbs and protein for a seedling to initiate growth. It consists of starch, a digestible complex carbohydrate that the body breaks down into simple sugars. It also contains protein and some B-vitamins. Refined grains are the result of processing out the germ and the bran, leaving only the starch-rich endosperm.

So, how much fiber do you need? Our Paleolithic-era ancestors are thought to have consumed more than 100 grams of fiber a day! Today, the average American consumes only 16 grams a day. The USDA recommends 28 grams of fiber a day based on a 2000 calorie diet, or 25 grams for females and 38 grams for males. Yet, it is estimated that only 5% of the population is meeting that goal.[8] The lack of dietary fiber intake in the U.S. has become a public health concern, along with the low intake of other nutrients such as calcium, potassium, and vitamin D, due to their roles in disease prevention.[9]

Naturopathic doctors generally recommend aiming for at least 30 grams of fiber a day, and along with some medical organizations, may recommend up to 50 grams a day for some people. Aiming to increase the amount of fiber to a minimum of 30 grams daily will naturally propel you toward eating whole foods and a more plant-based diet.

Aiming to increase the amount of fiber to a minimum of 30 grams daily will naturally propel you toward a whole foods and more plant-based diet.

Here are some strategies to increase fiber in your diet:

- Beans and legumes can provide a fiber-rich alternative to animal protein in some meals and are great additions to soups and salads.
- Choose high-fiber, whole grains including quinoa, oats, and whole wheat over refined grains such as white rice, white bread, and refined pasta.
- Add vegetables to every meal. Salads or roasted vegetables make great side dishes.
- Snack on raw veggies, fruit, nuts, and seeds instead of chips and crackers. Carrots and hummus, apple slices and nut butters, and kale chips make healthy, fiber-rich snacks.
- Include fiber-rich, plant-based foods alongside the foods that contain no fiber, such as meat, dairy, poultry, and eggs.
- High-fiber foods such as chia seeds, raspberries, ground flaxseed, avocado, and dark leafy greens can be added to smoothies.
- Increase the resistant starches in your diet. Make overnight

oats instead of cooking them in the morning for breakfast. Freeze a loaf of bread and then defrost before using. Cook and cool whole grains, beans, and potatoes before reheating.

- Limit cookies and pastries, which are high in refined grains and sugar, and aim for sweets treats with more fiber. See recipes for **Chia Seed Pudding, Cocoa Loco Bars,** and **Coconut Berry Bliss.**
- Eat whole fruit and skip the fruit juice.

So, in the end, what's not to love about fiber? Refer to the chart to see how you measure up with your daily fiber intake.

Table 3.2 Food Sources of Fiber

Fresh & Dried Fruit	Serving Size	Fiber (g)
Apple with skin	1 medium	5.0
Apricot	3 medium	1.0
Apricots, dried	4 pieces	3.0
Avocado	1 medium	12.0
Banana	1 medium	4.0
Blackberries	1 cup	8.0
Blueberries	1 cup	4.0
Cantaloupe, cubes	1 cup	1.0
Figs, dried	2 medium	3.5
Grapefruit	½ medium	3.0
Orange	1 medium	3.5
Peach	1 medium	2.0
Pear	1 medium	5.0
Plum	1 medium	1.0
Raisins	¼ cup	2.0
Raspberries	1 cup	8.0
Strawberries	1 cup	4.5

Table 3.2 Food Sources of Fiber (cont'd)

Grains, Beans, Nuts & Seeds	Serving Size	Fiber (g)
Almonds	¼ cup	4.0
Amaranth, cooked	1 cup	5.0
Black beans, cooked	1 cup	14.0
Bread, whole wheat	1 slice	2.0
Brown rice, cooked	1 cup	4.0
Cashews	¼ cup	1.0
Chia seed, dry	2 tablespoons	10.0
Corn, sweet	1 cup	4.5
Edamame	1 cup	8.0
Flaxseed, ground	2 tablespoons	4.0
Garbanzo beans, cooked	1 cup	6.0
Kidney beans, cooked	1 cup	11.5
Lentils, red, cooked	1 cup	13.5
Lima beans, cooked	1 cup	8.5
Oats, rolled, cooked	1 cup	5.0
Quinoa, cooked	1 cup	8.5
Pasta, whole wheat	1 cup	6.0
Peanuts	¼ cup	2.0
Peas, cooked	1 cup	9.0
Pistachio nuts	¼ cup	3.0
Popcorn, air-popped	3 cups	3.5
Pumpkin seeds	¼ cup	4.0
Sunflower seeds	¼ cup	3.0
Walnuts	¼ cup	3.0

Table 3.2 Food Sources of Fiber (cont'd)

Vegetables	Serving Size	Fiber (g)
Beets, cooked	1 cup	3.0
Beet greens	1 cup	4.0
Bok choy, cooked	1 cup	3.0
Broccoli, cooked	1 cup	4.5
Brussels sprouts, cooked	1 cup	3.5
Cabbage, cooked	1 cup	4.0
Carrot, raw	1 medium	2.5
Carrot, cooked	1 cup	5.0
Cauliflower, cooked	1 cup	3.5
Celery	1 stalk	1.0
Collard greens, cooked	1 cup	2.5
Green beans	1 cup	4.0
Kale, cooked	1 cup	7.0
Onions, raw	1 cup	3.0
Peppers, sweet	1 cup	2.5
Potato, baked with skin	1 medium	5.0
Spinach, cooked	1 cup	4.5
Sweet potato, cooked	1 medium	5.0
Swiss chard, cooked	1 cup	3.5
Tomato (fruit)	1 medium	1.0
Winter squash, cooked	1 cup	6.0
Zucchini, cooked	1 cup	2.5

Chapter Four
Nourish Yourself With Protein

PROTEIN PROVIDES STRUCTURE IN THE BODY IN the form of connective tissue, bone, hair, and muscle. It creates the framework of antibodies in the immune system, hormones in the digestive system like insulin and gastrin, and neurotransmitters in the brain. Protein, through the formation of enzymes, controls every chemical reaction in the body.

Protein is composed of building blocks called amino acids, and humans depend on about 20 different amino acids to function. Nine of these are considered "essential" amino acids and must be acquired through the diet. Food that contains all nine essential amino acids are considered a complete protein. The essential amino acids include:

- histidine
- lysine
- methionine
- phenylalanine
- threonine
- tryptophan

isoleucine

leucine

valine

From a metabolic perspective, dietary protein serves as a slow energy source, especially when compared to refined carbohydrates, and it promotes satiety after a meal. Consumption of protein increases the metabolic rate greater than fat and carbohydrate intake, which is called a thermic effect.[1] A diet low in protein, or a diet based on poor quality protein, contributes to many symptoms such as fatigue, blood sugar dysregulation, mood instability, difficulty building muscle, hair loss, and hormone imbalances.

Animal foods provide complete protein and include beef, pork, lamb, buffalo, wild game (venison, elk), poultry, fish, eggs, and dairy foods such as milk, cheese, and yogurt. Plant-based protein sources include nuts like almonds, pistachios, and walnuts; seeds like hemp, chia, sunflower, and pumpkin; beans and legumes including soy beans (tempeh, tofu, and edamame) and peanuts; and whole grains. Certain plant-based proteins like soy, chia seed, buckwheat, quinoa, amaranth, and hemp provide a complete protein. Otherwise, eating a well-balanced and varied diet of plant-based foods fulfills the need for complete protein.[2]

Consuming adequate amino acids—and therefore protein—is very important in terms of the impact on a healthy body and a healthy mind. Here are some examples of how individual amino acids influence specific chemical and metabolic pathways in the body:

- **Tryptophan** converts into serotonin and melatonin, both of which support a healthy mood and restorative sleep.
- **Tyrosine** converts into stress hormones like adrenaline as well as thyroid hormone.
- **Phenylalanine** converts into pain-relieving endorphins.
- **Glutamine** provides a fuel source for the brain and enterocytes, cells that line the small intestine.
- **Arginine** converts into nitric oxide, a potent chemical that relaxes blood vessels.

Nonessential amino acids are made by the body from essential amino acids or through other metabolic processes in the body. They include:

alanine

arginine

asparagine

aspartic acid

cysteine

glutamic acid

glutamine

glycine

proline

serine

tyrosine

- **Cysteine** supports the creation of one of the body's most potent antioxidants, glutathione.
- **Leucine**, **isoleucine**, and **valine**, also known as branch chain amino acids, reduce muscle soreness after exercise.[3]
- **Glycine** may help to raise serotonin levels and assist with improved sleep.[4]

Determining an individual's protein requirement can be complicated because the amount needed changes with age, health conditions such as pregnancy, breastfeeding, or recovery from surgery, physical activity level, body size, and metabolic goals. For instance, the Recommended Dietary Allowance (RDA), which is the average amount of protein recommended to meet the nutrient need for most healthy adults, is 0.8 grams of protein per kilogram (kg) of body weight for adults. This translates to a:

150-pound person (equal to 68 kg) consuming approximately 55 grams of protein daily

200-pound person (equal to 91 kg) consuming approximately 73 grams of protein daily.

Another way to think about an individual's protein requirement is by calculating a percentage of daily caloric intake. The National Academy of Medicine recommends anywhere from 10% to 35% of total calories to come from protein for adults. For example, eating a 2,000 calorie diet, one could consume anywhere from 50 grams (10% of calories) to 175 grams (35% of calories) of protein per day.

There are certain communities of people that may benefit from increased protein intake. For people aged 50 and over, an increase in dietary protein is recommended: between 1.0–1.2 grams of protein per kilogram of body weight. Aging is associated with a decreased ability to digest and absorb protein as efficiently, as well as a decline in the anabolic response to protein, which is the ability to build muscle.[5] Athletes, or people engaging in regular, vigorous exercise, also have increased protein needs: up to 1.4–2.0 grams of protein per kilogram of body weight.[6] Depending on their metabolic and health goals, overweight and obese people can discuss with their healthcare provider how to determine their daily protein intake based on an adjusted

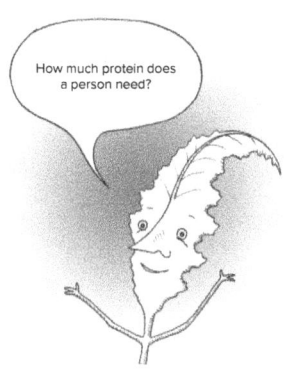

Determining an individual's protein requirement can be complicated because the amount needed changes with age, health conditions such as pregnancy, breastfeeding, or recovery from surgery, physical activity level, body size, and metabolic goals.

body weight, which is a modified weight calculation used to estimate appropriate nutritional needs. This may be 1.0–1.5 grams of protein per kilogram of adjusted body weight, for example.[7]

With such a wide range of potential protein intake, it can be beneficial to seek individualized advice. A naturopathic doctor can assess your individualized dietary needs relating to metabolic health, healthcare goals, and medical concerns and determine a healthy range of protein intake. For those with a history of kidney disease, it is essential to get guidance on protein intake because excess protein can place stress on the kidneys.

Check Table 4.1 to compare different food sources of protein. Be sure to compare animal sources with plant sources. Notice that animal foods (including meat, fish, and yogurt) as well as tempeh and edamame are excellent sources of protein per serving size, followed by legumes, beans, and seeds. Imagine ways to create a meal that would provide 25–30 grams of protein.

For people aged 50 and over, an increase in dietary protein is recommended, from 1.0–1.2 grams of protein per kilogram of body weight. Aging is associated with a decreased ability to digest and absorb protein as efficiently, as well as a decline in the anabolic response to protein, which is the ability to build muscle.

Table 4.1 Food Sources of Protein

Animal Foods	Serving	Protein (g)
Bacon (pork)	1 slice	3
Bacon (turkey)	1 slice	6
Beef	3.5 ounces	26
Bison	3.5 ounces	28
Bone broth	1 cup	9
Chicken	3.5 ounces	30
Dairy		
Cottage Cheese	½ cup	14
Greek Yogurt	¾ cup	22
Hard Cheese	1 ounce	7
Milk	1 cup	8
Yogurt	¾ cup	9
Eggs	1 large	7
Fish	3.5 ounces	24
Pork	3.5 ounces	27
Shrimp	3.5 ounces	20
Tuna	5 ounces, canned	30
Turkey	3.5 ounces	28
Venison	3.5 ounces	30
Plant Foods	**Serving**	**Protein (g)**
Beans and Legumes		
Beans (black, pinto, kidney)	½ cup, cooked	7-9
Green Peas	½ cup, cooked	4.5
Lentils	½ cup, cooked	12
Peanuts	¼ cup	8
Soy		
Edamame	1 cup, cooked	17

Table 4.1 Food Sources of Protein (cont'd)

Plant Foods	Serving	Protein (g)
Soy Milk (unsweetened)	1 cup	8
Tempeh	3.5 ounces	19
Tofu	3.5 ounces	8
Fruit		
Banana	1 medium	1
Blackberries	1 cup	2
Kiwi	1 cup	2
Orange	1 medium	2
Passion Fruit	1 cup	5
Grains		
Amaranth	½ cup, cooked	4.5
Brown Rice	½ cup, cooked	3
Buckwheat	½ cup, cooked	6
Corn Whole Kernel	½ cup, cooked	2
Oatmeal	1 cup, cooked	6
Quinoa	½ cup, cooked	4
100% Whole Wheat Bread	1 slice	3.5
Nuts and Seeds		
Almonds	¼ cup	8
Almond Butter	2 tablespoons	8
Cashews	¼ cup	5
Chia Seeds	2 tablespoons	5
Hemp Seed Hearts	3 tablespoons	10
Ground Flaxseed	2 tablespoons	4
Peanut Butter	2 tablespoons	8
Pecans	¼ cup	2.5

Table 4.1 Food Sources of Protein (cont'd)

Plant Foods	Serving	Protein (g)
Pumpkin Seeds	¼ cup	8
Sunflower Seeds	¼ cup	6
Vegetables	**Serving**	**Protein (g)**
Asparagus	6 spears	1
Broccoli	1 cup	5
Carrots	1 cup	1
Cauliflower	1 cup	3
Spinach	1 cup	3
Protein Powders	**Serving**	**Protein (g)**
Collagen Peptides	4 tablespoons (20g)	18-20
Hemp Protein Isolate	4 tablespoons (31g)	12-15
Pea Protein Isolate	4 tablespoons (28g)	24-27
Whey Protein Isolate	4 tablespoons (35-40g)	35-40

Is there any concern about increasing soy in the diet?

For many people, there exists some uncertainty about whether soy food is safe to eat in terms of breast health and thyroid health. High levels of the hormone estrogen have been linked to an increased risk of breast cancer, and soy contains phytoestrogens. Phytoestrogens can affect estrogen receptors in the body, but not in the same way as the hormone estrogen. There is consensus that eating soy in moderation, as part of a well-balanced diet, is safe for breast health and may actually be protective.[8,9]

Soy also contains goitrogens, which are chemicals that can interfere with thyroid function.[10] Current research shows that, as it relates to thyroid health, soy can be safely included in a well-balanced diet, even for people who have hypothyroidism.[11] A person may be more susceptible to any negative effects of goitrogens in their diet if they have an iodine deficiency. This can be prevented by regularly including iodine-rich foods in the diet from seafood (including seaweed), eggs, dairy, or by using iodized salt.[12] In addition, cooking, steaming, and fermenting soy can reduce its goitrogenic activity.[13] In vegetarian or vegan diets that include soy regularly, it is important to diversify protein sources and to include legumes, beans, nuts, seeds, dairy, and eggs.[14] We recommend choosing minimally processed, organic soy which includes tempeh, edamame, tofu, soy nuts, miso, tamari, and natto.

What About Meat?

Food from animals, such as red meat, poultry, fish, eggs, and dairy, can play an important nutritional role in a balanced diet for all ages, including supporting children's growth and development, supporting muscle growth for adults, and preventing muscle loss in the elderly. These animal foods are an excellent source of complete protein, providing all of the essential amino acids, and contain several important vitamins and minerals. Red meat, poultry, fish, eggs, and dairy contain variable amounts of fat-soluble vitamins and B-vitamins. They are the only source of naturally occurring vitamin B12. They are high in minerals, including selenium, phosphorus, zinc, and are the only source of heme-iron, a highly absorbable form of iron. Additionally, dairy and some canned fish with small, edible bones are excellent sources of calcium. These macro and micro nutrients can be more difficult to obtain through plant-based foods only.[15] In general, a dietary pattern that includes minimally processed animal foods along with diverse plant-based foods will help create a balanced diet. A diet that includes frequent consumption of ultra-processed animal foods, which can include certain sausages, bacon, hot dogs, deli meat, fast-food meat, and fried meats, is associated with an increased risk of heart disease, diabetes, and mortality.[16,17,18]

For some people, the choice to include animal products in their diet is a complex decision due to the current animal agriculture system, ethical and environmental concerns including the contribution to greenhouse gas emissions and antibiotic resistance, and individual health concerns. Additionally, eating meat, dairy, and eggs may be influenced by cultural and religious traditions, food access, and cost.

Poultry

Poultry is defined as foods from domesticated birds, such as the meat from chicken, turkey, ducks, and geese. The USDA also classifies the eggs from these animals as poultry.

The consumption of chicken has tripled since the 1960s and is currently the number one animal meat consumed in the U.S.[19] Chicken tends to be more affordable than red meat and fish, and poultry in general is leaner and lower in calories than red meat. A 3.5-ounce serving of chicken breast

Red meat, poultry, fish, eggs, and dairy contain variable amounts of fat-soluble vitamins and B-vitamins. They are the only source of naturally occurring vitamin B12. They are high in minerals, including selenium, phosphorus, zinc, and are the only source of heme-iron, a highly absorbable form of iron.

Pasture-raised chicken meat and eggs, which are from chickens that have had daily access to roam and forage in outdoor pastures, have been shown to have higher levels of omega-3 fatty acids and vitamins A, E, and D.

provides about 30 grams of protein. Chicken meat is lower in saturated fat than red meat and is a good source of unsaturated fats, especially heart-healthy monounsaturated fats. Pasture-raised chicken meat and eggs, which are from chickens that have had daily access to roam and forage in outdoor pastures, have been shown to have higher levels of omega-3 fatty acids and vitamins A, E, and D.[20]

Red Meat

Red meat is defined as the meat that comes from mammals, and it is generally more red colored when raw due to its higher myoglobin content. Myoglobin is a protein that contains iron and delivers oxygen to the muscles. Red meat includes the meat from cattle, pigs, sheep, goat, and game animals such as deer, elk, and bison. Beef and pork are the second and third most consumed meats in the U.S.

Depending on the source, red meat can provide 21-30 grams of protein in a 3.5-ounce serving. The protein content of both pork and beef can vary based on the cut of the meat, with leaner meats containing higher protein content. Lean meat will have less than 10 grams of fat (and less than 4.5 grams of saturated fat) in a 3.5-ounce serving. Extra lean meat will have less than 5 grams of fat (and less than 3 grams saturated fat). Ground beef and pork will often be labeled at 90/10 for lean or 95/5 for extra lean. Higher fat cuts of beef (ribeye, skirt steak, ribs, and brisket) and pork (pork belly, bacon, ribs) will contain less protein and more calories due to the higher fat content.

In addition to the cut of meat, the type and quantities of fat in red meat is influenced by the animal's diet. Beef and pork contain both saturated and unsaturated fats. The unsaturated fats include mono and polyunsaturated fats, and both omega-3 and omega-6 fatty acids. Pasture-raised animals are leaner with higher concentrations of omega-3 fatty acids and lower levels of saturated fats compared to grain-fed animals.[21]

Although some studies are conflicting, in general, a high intake of red meat (and not poultry or fish), and especially processed red meat, has been associated with an increased risk of heart disease and colon cancer.[22,23,24,25] To limit these risks, most health organizations recommend choosing lean cuts of red meat, consume appropriate portion sizes, and avoid ultra-processed red meat consumption.

Seafood

Seafood includes both fish and shellfish and is another excellent source of high-quality, lean animal protein. Fish is unique in that it is the best food source of essential omega-3 fatty acids EPA (eicosapentaenoic acid) and DHA (docosahexaenoic acid). Fish and omega-3 fatty acid consumption improves heart health, promotes fetal and infant growth and development, supports brain health and eye health, and is generally anti-inflammatory.[26] Oily, cold-water fish such as salmon, mackerel, tuna, herring, sardines, and anchovies are the highest in these anti-inflammatory fats. In addition, oily fish are one of the best food sources of vitamin D3. It is generally recommended by most health organizations to include at least two servings of fish in the diet each week.

Some fish can be high in mercury, a toxic heavy metal that can impact the nervous system, kidney, lungs, and other organs depending on the amount and length of exposure to this metal. The fish that are highest in mercury are typically larger, older, predatory fish that have had more time to accumulate the toxin, including sharks, swordfish, king mackerel, and tilefish. Pregnant and breastfeeding females, in particular, need to strictly limit their exposure to mercury due to the potential impact on the neurological development of the fetus and infant. The seafood typically lowest in mercury includes sardines, anchovies, salmon, trout, tilapia, cod, scallops, crab, and shrimp. The Environmental Protection Agency (EPA) maintains a "Best Choices" list for seafood low in mercury.

Another consideration when choosing fish is determining if it is wild-caught or farm-raised. Wild-caught means the fish was caught from its natural habitat, either a lake, river, or ocean, and that the fish fed on their natural food source of phytoplankton, insects, algae, krill, or smaller fish. Aquaculture is the commercial breeding of fish in large fish tanks, ponds, or open-ocean pens. Farmed fish are given a feed mixture based on the needs of the species that may include plant proteins, commonly from soy and corn, fishmeal, oils, vitamins, and minerals. Nutritionally, wild-caught and farmed fish contain similar amounts of protein. However, wild-caught

Fish is unique in that it is the best food source of essential omega-3 fatty acids EPA (eicosapentaenoic acid) and DHA (docosahexaenoic acid). Fish and omega-3 fatty acid consumption improves heart health, promotes fetal and infant growth and development, supports brain health and eye health, and is generally anti-inflammatory.

fish tend to be higher in omega-3 fatty acids, and farmed fish can generally be higher in fat and contain more omega-6 fatty acids.[27]

The choice of whether to choose wild-caught or farmed fish can be complicated due to cost, increased consumer demand for fish and seafood, and the differing environmental impacts of both overfishing wild fish and fish farming. The most sustainable option may depend on the specific species. There are several organizations that regularly review and analyze sustainably produced wild-caught and farmed fish, such as the Marine Stewardship Council, Monterey Bay Aquarium, and the Aquaculture Stewardship Council.

> **Cooking Techniques to Reduce Potential Carcinogens**
>
> Certain cooking techniques can create harmful compounds that, when found in high levels in the body, can contribute to inflammation and increase the risk of heart disease, diabetes, and cancer.[28,29,30] Heterocyclic amines (HCAs), polycyclic aromatic hydrocarbons (PAHs), nitrosamines, and advanced glycation end products (AGEs) are examples of compounds that can be created from chemical reactions that can occur between the protein, fats, or preservatives in meat when exposed to high temperatures, dry heat, or smoke. The cooking techniques that tend to produce more of these compounds are grilling, broiling, deep frying, pan frying, and smoking. The following are strategies to prepare meat that can greatly reduce the production of these potential carcinogens:
>
> - Marinate the meat, poultry, and fish prior to cooking. Choose or make a marinade that contains citrus juice, vinegar, garlic, onion, and antioxidant-rich herbs such as rosemary, oregano, thyme, basil, and turmeric.
>
> - Lower the heat on the grill, pan, or oven and avoid high heat if possible (over 400°F). Consider using indirect heat as a strategy when grilling. Flipping the meat often can also help prevent the surface from reaching higher temperatures. Avoid or limit overcooking, charring, or

blackening your meat. Avoid flame flare-ups when grilling.
- Cook meat with or in liquid. Use more moist heat and lower heat cooking methods, such as boiling, poaching, steaming, stewing, braising, pressure cooking, and slow cooking.
- Limit or avoid smoked meats and meat with nitrite or nitrate preservatives.
- Increase antioxidant rich foods! Antioxidants help protect cells from damage to their DNA. Pair antioxidant-rich foods alongside meat such as cruciferous vegetables (cabbage, kale, broccoli, cauliflower), berries, spinach, tomatoes, and bell peppers.

Good Things Come In Small Packages—The Role Of Micronutrients

Now that we have detailed the macronutrients (fat, carbohydrate, and protein) and emphasized the need to include all three in a healthy diet, we will focus on the smaller, but still important, micronutrients. Vitamins and minerals are micronutrients that occur in very small quantities in food and impact processes in the body related to immune function, growth, mood, bone health, and metabolism. Additionally, water can contain small amounts of minerals depending on its source and its level of treatment. Soil quality will also influence the mineral content of food. By eating a whole foods-based diet, you will naturally introduce rich sources of vitamins and minerals into your body. Highly processed foods often have these important nutrients removed or altered from their natural state. Check Table 4.2 and Table 4.3 to learn basic functions and whole food sources of these micronutrients.

Table 4.2 Vitamins: Functions and Food Sources

Vitamin	Functions	Food Sources
A (Vitamin A Palmitate, Beta-carotene)	Supports eyes and enhances immunity Antioxidant Fat-soluble*	Orange, yellow, and dark green vegetables (carrots, squash, spinach, kale), liver, pasture-raised beef, egg yolks, poultry
B Vitamins (Thiamin-B1, Riboflavin-B2, Niacin-B3, Pantothenic acid-B5, Pyridoxine-B6, Biotin, Cobalamin-B12, Folate-B9)	Supports numerous chemical reactions in the body that impact mood, energy, neurological development, and detoxification Water-soluble	Dark green leafy vegetables, meat, poultry, eggs, whole grains (bran), nutritional yeast
C (Ascorbic acid)	Supports immunity, collagen production, energy production, and blood vessels Water-soluble	Broccoli, cauliflower, citrus fruit, peppers, berries, melons
D (Cholecalciferol-D3, Ergocalciferol-D2)	Supports immunity, bone health, growth, and mood Fat-soluble*	Fish (specifically cod liver oil), milk from pasture-raised cattle and goats, mushrooms, and **sunshine—the best non-food source**
E (Tocopherols)	Antioxidant Fat-soluble*	Whole grains (germ), nuts and seeds, dark green leafy vegetables
K (Phylloquinones-K1, Menaquinones-K2)	Essential for blood clotting and bone health Fat-soluble*	K1-Dark green leafy vegetables K2-Produced by healthy gut bacteria

*Fat-soluble indicates that dietary fat in needed to absorb the vitamin.

Table 4.3 Minerals: Functions and Food Sources

Minerals	Functions	Food Sources
Sodium	Keeps fluid in balance in the body and supports energy Excess amounts may affect blood pressure in some people	Salt, processed and canned foods, seaweed
Potassium	Supports nerves, heart, muscles, and stress tolerance	Avocado, kiwis, bananas, cantaloupe, melons, spinach, dark green leafy veggies
Calcium	Builds strong bones and teeth	Dairy, dark green leafy vegetables (kale, spinach, broccoli), almonds, fish and animal bones, sesame seeds, beans, fortified orange juice, fortified plant-based milk
Iron	Binds and transports oxygen in the blood	Meat, poultry, fish, chocolate, dark green leafy vegetables, molasses, nuts, beans, fortified grains
Magnesium	Contributes to blood pressure regulation, smooth muscle relaxation, and healthy stress responses	Vegetables (especially dark green leaf veggies), nuts, seeds, beans, whole grains
Zinc	Supports immunity, hormone balance and healthy mood, and aids wound healing	Red meat, dark meat chicken, eggs, oysters, pumpkin seeds

Chapter Five
Reading Food Labels

I used to go shopping and buy groceries without looking at labels. Now, I look at all the labels on all items. I looked at a bottle of lemonade, and it had 26 grams of sugar per serving. I learned that a female's daily intake of "added" sugar should be no more than 24 grams. So, I had to walk quickly away from the lemonade.
—Beryl, ECO project, Mt. Olivet

I could really connect with the idea of moving towards whole foods. This idea helped in choosing foods at the grocery store (reading food labels and buying organic from the Clean 15 list) to eliminating foods containing additives, chemicals, and sugar. The changes affect my whole family. Thank you!
—Kathy, FAME Series, Charlee's Kitchen

IN ORDER TO MAKE THE HEALTHIEST CHOICES POSSIBLE WHEN SHOPPING, SKILL AND CONFIDENCE IN READING FOOD LABELS ARE important. When initially reading a label, many people will first look at the numbers and percentages in the Nutrition Facts section regarding the amount of fat, calories, sodium, or cholesterol. Other consumers may initially be attracted to the health claims on the front of the food label, such as low-fat, heart-healthy, or all natural. Food claims on the front of food packaging may have little to do with the actual nutrition in a food. Rarely does the conventional food industry have your health first and foremost in mind, and they will often use manipulative language on labels to sway your shopping habits.

Food label reading is an acquired skill that initially requires practice. Our goal is to provide guiding principles to follow as you begin this important habit. A bit of extra time at the grocery store dedicated to reading food labels will be time well spent. It will not be a perfect process, but it can be empowering as you choose the foods and ingredients you will be consuming and thereby impacting your health and the health of your family. Even small changes can have a huge impact on health.

Getting Started Reading Food Labels

You may find that the following food items either do not have a food label or only have one ingredient listed on the label: fruits, vegetables, fresh meat, poultry, fish, nuts, seeds, legumes, and whole grains. A single listed ingredient often indicates a whole food that has not been processed. However, when purchasing boxed, canned, and other packaged food, you will be confronted with more complex labels. Taking time to compare the labels of similar products can have a great impact on your health once you learn to recognize ingredients and misleading label claims. Oftentimes, there are convenient and more nutritious alternatives to ultra-processed foods that contain less additives, refined grains, and sugars.

Most shoppers are familiar with locating the two basic parts of a food label: *Nutrition Facts* and *Ingredients*. As we work to promote the benefits of a whole foods diet, we are going to reprioritize the process of food label reading and encourage you to begin at one particular location: the Ingredients. Let the Ingredients section of the label be your initial guide to a whole foods lifestyle.

Food claims on the front of food packaging may have little to do with the actual nutrition in a food. Rarely does the conventional food industry have your health first and foremost in mind, and they will often use manipulative language on labels to sway your shopping habits.

Steps For Reading A Food Label (Refer To Label 1)

Step 1: The Ingredients

This is the best place to start for understanding what is in the food and the level of processing that may have taken place. Assess the following, in order:

Length of the List: Without even reading the ingredients, take a look at the length of the list. The number of ingredients in a product can give you an idea of the degree of processing and the amount of additives. In general, when a product contains a large number of ingredients, it is likely that it is considered ultra-processed and contains added sugars, refined grains, and chemical additives such as preservatives and artificial colors and flavors.

Ingredients: Everything on the list should be a recognizable food item. If it is not, it is likely a highly processed food or a chemical additive. Next time you are shopping, ask yourself what you would expect to find in the food product if you were making the same thing at home. For example, if you are making chili at home, you might add beans, tomatoes, spices, onions, garlic, and other vegetables. Then, look at the ingredient list below of the Popular Canned Chili and compare what is common and what is surprising with a homemade version. Would you expect to find texturized vegetable protein, monosodium glutamate (MSG), modified cornstarch, or autolyzed yeast in your chili? Probably not!

Popular Canned Chili INGREDIENTS: Water, Beef, Cereal (oatmeal, corn flour), Chili Powder, Textured Vegetable Protein (soy flour, caramel color), Tomatoes (water, tomato paste), Sugar, Salt, Hydrolyzed Corn Protein, Hydrolyzed Wheat Protein, Modified Food Starch, Flavors, Autolyzed Yeast, Monosodium Glutamate, Spices.

Order of the ingredients: The ingredients are listed in order of the greatest amount to the least amount. Thus, the order will give you a good idea of what the main ingredients are in a food product.

Within the ingredients list, pay special attention to:

added sugar

Label 1

Nutrition Facts

About 5 servings per container
Serving size about 11 pieces (38g)

Amount per serving
Calories 160

	% Daily Value*
Total Fat 8g	10%
Saturated Fat 2.5g	13%
Trans Fat 0g	
Polyunsaturated Fat 1g	
Monounsaturated Fat 4g	
Cholesterol 0mg	0%
Sodium 140mg	6%
Total Carbohydrate 22g	8%
Dietary Fiber 3g	12%
Soluble Fiber 0g	
Insoluble Fiber 3g	
Total Sugars 8g	
Includes 8g Added Sugars	16%
Protein 4g	4%
Vitamin D 0mcg	0%
Calcium 10mg	0%
Iron 1.5mg	8%
Potassium 150mg	2%

* The % Daily Value (DV) tells you how much a nutrient in a serving of food contributes to a daily diet. 2,000 calories a day is used for general nutrition advice.

Ingredients: Whole grain oats, sunflower seeds, invert cane syrup, brown rice syrup, brown rice, peanuts, cane sugar, coconut, semisweet chocolate chunks (cane sugar, chocolate†, cocoa butter†, sunflower lecithin, salt), chocolate†, cashew butter, millet, peanut butter (peanuts), vegetable glycerin, cocoa†, acacia gum, sea salt, cherry puree concentrate, salt, white pepper, rosemary extract for freshness.

- Serving information →
- Amounts per serving →
- % of daily requirements →
- Ingredients →

fats and oils

refined grains

chemical additives

Added Sugar

Some foods may contain more than one type of added sugar, such as evaporated cane juice, brown rice syrup, corn syrup, and molasses, for example. Each sweetener may be added to the food in smaller quantities, which allows it to be individually listed further down on the ingredient list. However, if you were to combine all the added sugars, it may likely be the highest quantity ingredient in the product. Food companies can employ this tactic as a way to avoid having to list sugar as the number one ingredient. Also, foods that claim to have no sugar may have added artificial sweeteners instead. We will discuss these ultra-processed sweeteners in a later section, but these are chemicals that should be limited or avoided in a whole foods diet.

Label 2 represents a popular breakfast cereal and lists the food's second ingredient as sugar. In addition, further down on the label, three more added sugars are listed: molasses, fructose, and honey. The Nutrition Facts section shows 14 grams of added sugar per serving, which you will learn is equivalent to 3½ teaspoons of sugar in a 1 cup serving of cereal! Considering that some people might eat up to two servings of this cereal, that would equate to 28 grams, or 6 teaspoons of added sugar. This is close to or over the daily maximum amount of added sugar recommended for most adults, which we will review in Chapter Nine **Exploring Sweeteners**, and is not the best way to start the day.

Fats

Read the ingredient list to identify the source of any fats or oils and whether they are highly processed. In general, oils that are listed as extra virgin, virgin, unrefined, or cold expeller pressed would be considered minimally processed. Typically, these oils haven't been exposed to high heat, chemical extraction, and haven't been bleached or deodorized.

Label 2

Nutrition Facts

About 12 servings per container

Serving size 1 cup (42g)

Amount per serving

Calories 170

% Daily Value*

Total Fat 4.5g	6%
Saturated Fat 0g	0%
Trans Fat 0g	
Polyunsaturated Fat 1g	
Monounsaturated Fat 2.5g	
Cholesterol 0mg	0%
Sodium 360mg	16%
Total Carbohydrate 32g	12%
Dietary Fiber 2g	7%
Total Sugars 14g	
Includes 14g Added Sugars	28%
Protein 2g	
Vitamin D 0mcg	0%
Calcium 160mg	10%
Iron 5.4mg	30%
Potassium 110mg	2%
Niacin	15%
Vitamin B$_6$	15%
Phosphorus	4%
Zinc	15%

* The % Daily Value (DV) tells you how much a nutrient in a serving of food contributes to a daily diet. 2,000 calories a day is used for general nutrition advice.

Ingredients: Whole Grain Wheat, Sugar, Corn Meal, Canola Oil, Molasses, Fructose, Salt, Honey, Baking Soda, Calcium Carbonate, Soy Lecithin, Dextrose, Trisodium Phosphate, Rosemary Extract (Antioxidant). *Vitamins and Minerals*: Ferric Orthophosphate (Source of Iron), Niacinamide (Vitamin B3), Zinc Oxide, Pyridoxine Hydrochloride (Vitamin B6)

There are several refined oils that are commonly found in ultra-processed foods since they are cheap and abundant. These include soy, safflower, sunflower, rapeseed (canola), corn, and "vegetable oils." You will find that foods with ultra-processed oils are often accompanied by added sugars, refined grains, and chemical additives. For example, review the Ingredient List of Salad Dressing 1 compared to Salad Dressing 2.

Salad Dressing 1

Water, Soybean Oil, Vinegar, Corn Syrup, Modified Food Starch, Egg Yolks, Salt, Contains Less than 2% of Fructose, Xanthan Gum, Monosodium Glutamate, Phosphoric Acid, Garlic, Potassium Sorbate and Calcium Disodium EDTA (To Protect Flavor), Artificial Color, Polysorbate 60, Spice, Parsley, Onion, Natural Flavor (Contains Milk), Lactic Acid, Sucralose.

Salad Dressing 2

Organic Extra Virgin Olive Oil, Organic Apple Cider Vinegar, Water, Organic Honey, Organic Garlic, Organic Coconut Liquid Aminos (Organic Coconut Blossom Nectar, Water, Organic Apple Cider Vinegar and Sea Salt), Organic Dried Onion. Less Than 2% of: Organic Black Pepper, Xanthan Gum

Salad Dressing 1 is made with soybean oil, a refined oil. It also contains added sugar (corn syrup), artificial sweetener (sucralose), and several chemical additives including monosodium glutamate, potassium sorbate, EDTA, and artificial colors. Salad Dressing 2 contains a heart-healthy, minimally processed oil, extra virgin olive oil. It also contains more recognizable ingredients (apple cider vinegar, honey, garlic, dried onion), and contains only one chemical additive (xanthan gum).

Although trans fats, or partially hydrogenated oils, are no longer "GRAS", or Generally Recognized as Safe, and should be removed from ultra-processed foods, there can be up to 0.5 grams of trans fats per serving in a food product before it is required to be noted in the

You will find that foods with ultra-processed oils are often accompanied by added sugars, refined grains, and chemical additives.

Nutrition Facts portion of the label. A fully hydrogenated oil is not a trans fat, but it is found in ultra-processed foods and should be limited or avoided if possible. Review the ingredient list for any partially or fully hydrogenated oils.

Refined Grains

A food may be marketed as being a **whole grain** product even if it has mostly refined grains and only a small portion of whole grains. A common example is *wheat bread*. Often, the number one ingredient listed will be refined wheat flour. Avoid this marketing trap by looking for products that list 100% whole grains on the label. Remember to confirm any claims on the front of the label with the ingredient list. When reading a food label for grains and flours, the following are examples of whole grain ingredients: whole wheat, brown rice, whole corn or cornmeal, and whole oats. The following words signify that it is not a whole grain: refined, white, enriched, and degerminated.

Chemical Additives

Chemicals may be added to a food item to enhance its color, flavor, or shelf life. While the FDA has approved these additives to be Generally Recognized as Safe ("GRAS"), most food additives have not been tested to determine the long-term health consequences associated with regular intake in adults or children. Chemical additives can have wide-ranging negative health effects. Certain additives may be linked to increased incidence of allergies, asthma, attention deficit hyperactivity disorder (ADHD), obesity, heart disease, and cancer. There is increasing evidence that they may also impact gut health and the microbiome, hormones, behavior in children, and fetal development.[1,2,3,4]

Once GRAS chemicals enter the food system, widespread negative impacts can become more apparent and may prompt additional research to further study their effects. Sometimes, chemical additives that were once thought to be safe are eventually banned from the food industry due to their health consequences, such as the case with trans fat. In 2024, brominated vegetable oil (BVO) was removed from the GRAS list due to concerns of thyroid toxicity.[5] Even more recently, in January 2025, red dye #3 was banned due to evidence of it causing cancer in animal studies. Other countries and even several individual states within the U.S. have banned additional chemical additives including potassium bromate, propylparaben, artificial colors, titanium dioxide, BHA and BHT, azodicarbonamide, and carrageenan. Currently, those additives are all still considered "safe" by the FDA and are still in the U.S food system.

Due to the questions of long-term safety and potential negative reactions, it is best to review your food labels carefully and limit or avoid chemical additives as much as possible.

In general, chemical additives are not real food, and they add no nutritional benefit to the diet. They are much more common in ultra-processed foods. Due to the questions of long-term safety and potential negative reactions, it is best to review your food labels carefully and limit or avoid chemical additives as much as possible. The most common chemical additives are listed below. The only place to find this information is in the Ingredients List.

Flavor Enhancers:

    Artificial sweeteners: Aspartame (Nutrasweet® and Equal®), sucralose (Splenda®), saccharin (Sweet N Low®), and acesulfame potassium (Equal®)

    Monosodium glutamate (MSG)

    Natural and artificial flavors

Artificial Colors: Look for these listed as a color and a number.

    Yellow #5, yellow #6, and red #40 are the most common

    Red dye #3 (Currently the FDA requires the removal of red dye from food and beverages by January 2027.)

Preservatives:

    Sodium nitrite and nitrate

    Sulfites

    Butylated hydroxyanisole (BHA) and butylated hydroxytoluene (BHT)

    Ethylenediaminetetraacetic acid (EDTA)

    Sodium benzoate

Thickeners, Stabilizers, Emulsifiers, Conditioners:

    Brominated vegetable oil (The FDA required the removal from food and beverages by August 2025.)

Carrageenan

Guar gum

Xanthan gum

Azodicarbonamide

Potassium bromate

Step 2: Nutrition Facts

After reading the ingredient list and identifying what is in the food product, look more closely at the Nutrition Facts to learn more about the calories, fat, carbohydrate, protein, and vitamin and mineral content of the food. While the FDA does maintain standards for determining the measured amounts of the nutrients and calories in a food or beverage, what is listed on the Nutrition Facts may not be exact since there is variability in food sourcing and processing. However, these small variations will balance out over time within an overall healthy dietary pattern.

Keep the following in mind when reading the Nutrition Facts:

Serving Size and Servings Per Container

Although a food item may appear to be one serving, such as a small bag of chips, soda or juice, a can of soup, or one pastry, it can often contain more than one serving. Review the serving size and whether you are likely to eat or drink more than one serving. Multiply the number of grams of fat, carbohydrates, and protein as well as the calories by the total number of servings consumed to understand the total amounts.

Calories

Most adults should generally aim for about 1500–2000 calories a day. It is helpful to have an awareness about which foods and drinks tend to be highly caloric in order to reference how it contributes to your daily caloric intake.

Percent Daily Value (% DV)

This value helps you determine if a food or drink is high or low in a particular nutrient. Food or drink providing more than 20% of % DV

Most adults should generally aim for about 1500-2000 calories a day. It is helpful to have an awareness about which foods and drinks tend to be highly caloric in order to reference how it contributes to your daily caloric intake.

can be considered high in that nutrient, 10–19% is considered a good source of that nutrient, and less than 5% would be considered low in that nutrient.

Fat

The amount of fat per serving may not always be as important as the source and processing of the fat in the food, which is information you learn from the ingredient list. Recommended dietary fat intake can vary greatly based on the individual, ranging from about 50–90 grams for most adults. It is helpful to become familiar with which food sources are rich in fat, whether saturated, monounsaturated, or polyunsaturated. To give an example, a tablespoon of butter has 11 grams of fat, of which 7 grams are saturated. Compare this to a tablespoon of extra virgin olive oil, which has 14 grams of fat, 11 grams of which are monounsaturated. The USDA recommends limiting saturated fat intake to less than 10% of daily caloric intake.

Trans Fat. Although rare, remember that a food may contain small amounts of trans fats even if it lists 0 grams on the Nutrition Facts label. Read the ingredient list of the label to identify any partially hydrogenated oils.

Cholesterol

Meat, poultry, fish, dairy, and eggs contain cholesterol, while plant foods do not.

Sodium

Salt is composed of two minerals called sodium and chloride. Many packaged and processed foods, fast food, and restaurant food contain high amounts of salt and sodium to enhance the flavor, as well as for food preservation. For some people, excess sodium in the diet can increase the risk of high blood pressure, cardiovascular disease, and kidney disease. On the other hand, strictly limiting or avoiding sodium also has its own health risks and isn't recommended for the general population.[6,7] Sodium is an essential nutrient needed in the diet to maintain fluid balance in the body and for optimal nerve and muscle function.

Most major medical organizations recommend a maximum of 5.8 grams of salt per day, equal to 1 teaspoon, which contains about 2,300 mg of sodium. It is very easy to go over this limit by consuming ultra-processed foods and snacks and eating out frequently. When reviewing food labels, check the % Daily Value (DV) per serving for sodium content: 5% DV or less of sodium per serving (equal to less than 140 mg) is considered low sodium, and 20% DV or more of sodium (generally anything with >400mg per serving) is considered high sodium.

Sea salt generally contains the same amount of sodium compared to table salt. However, sea salt is less processed and may contain small amounts of minerals such as calcium, magnesium, and potassium.

Potato chips, French fries, pretzels, frozen meals, pizza, burritos, canned soups, beans, and vegetables are often high in sodium. Canned beans and veggies can be drained and rinsed to decrease the sodium content. In general, including more fresh fruits, vegetables, and whole foods in your diet, cooking at home, and decreasing fast food and processed food intake will help limit excess sodium intake.

Carbohydrates

Similar to fat, recommended dietary intake of carbohydrates can vary greatly among individuals based on need. Most adults generally should aim for between 150–225 grams. In general, a *low carb diet* would be considered consuming less than 100 grams of carbohydrates a day. It is helpful to become familiar with carbohydrate-rich food and the source of the carbohydrates. Recall that sugar, starch, and fiber are all sources of carbohydrates. Aim to include more fiber and less added sugar in the diet.

In the Nutrition Facts section, the Total Carbohydrates will be broken down into Dietary Fiber, Total Sugar, and Added Sugar. Some labels will further break down fiber into Soluble or Insoluble. The amount of fiber per serving can help you to determine if a food product consists of whole grains and complex carbohydrates or refined grains. In general, a refined carbohydrate product will have a low fiber content, 0 to 2 grams per serving, for example, while a whole grain product will generally have 3 grams or more of fiber per serving.

Label 3
White Bread.

Nutrition Facts
21 servings per container
Serving size 1 slice (30g)

Amount per serving
Calories 80

	% Daily Value*
Total Fat 1g	1%
Saturated Fat 0g	0%
Trans Fat 0g	
Cholesterol 0mg	0%
Sodium 140mg	6%
Total Carbohydrate 15g	5%
Dietary Fiber 0g	0%
Total Sugars 2g	
Includes 2g Added Sugars	4%
Protein 2g	

Vit. D 0mcg 0% • Calcium 120mg 10%
Iron 1mg 6% • Potas. 22mg 0%

* The % Daily Value (DV) tells you how much a nutrient in a serving of food contributes to a daily diet. 2,000 calories a day is used for general nutrition advice.

INGREDIENTS: ENRICHED UNBLEACHED WHEAT FLOUR (WHEAT FLOUR, MALTED BARLEY FLOUR, NIACIN, REDUCED IRON, THIAMINE MONONITRATE, RIBOFLAVIN AND FOLIC ACID), WATER, SUGAR, YEAST, CONTAINS 2% OR LESS OF EACH OF THE FOLLOWING: SALT, SOYBEAN OIL, YEAST NUTRIENT (AMMONIUM SULFATE), DOUGH CONDITIONERS (SODIUM STEAROYL LACTYLATE, ASCORBIC ACID, MONOCALCIUM PHOSPHATE), EXTRACT OF MALTED BARLEY, DEXTROSE, CALCIUM PROPIONATE (MOLD INHIBITOR), CALCIUM SULFATE (SOURCE OF CALCIUM), ENZYMES.

CONTAINS: WHEAT

Label 4
Whole Wheat Bread.

Nutrition Facts

17 servings per container
Serving size 1 Slice (45g/1.6oz)

Amount per serving
Calories 110

	% Daily Value*
Total Fat 1.5g	2%
Saturated Fat 0g	0%
Trans Fat 0g	
Polyunsaturated Fat 1g	
Monounsaturated Fat 0g	
Cholesterol 0mg	0%
Sodium 170mg	8%
Total Carbohydrate 22g	8%
Dietary Fiber 5g	17%
Total Sugars 5g	
Includes 5g Added Sugars	9%
Protein 5g	3%
Vitamin D 0mcg	0%
Calcium 0mg	0%
Iron 1mg	6%
Potassium 100mg	2%

* The % Daily Value (DV) tells you how much a nutrient in a serving of food contributes to a daily diet. 2,000 calories a day is used for general nutrition advice.

INGREDIENTS: Organic whole wheat (organic whole wheat flour, organic cracked whole wheat), water, organic cane sugar, organic 21 Whole Grains and Seeds mix (organic whole flax seeds, organic sunflower seeds, organic tri-color quinoa [organic black quinoa, organic red quinoa, organic white quinoa], organic ground whole flax seeds, organic triticale, organic pumpkin seeds, organic rolled barley, organic rolled oats, organic rolled rye, organic blue cornmeal, organic millet, organic rolled spelt, organic brown rice flour, organic amaranth flour, organic yellow cornmeal, organic KAMUT® khorasan wheat, organic sorghum flour, organic buckwheat flour, organic quinoa, organic poppy seeds), organic wheat gluten, organic oat fiber, contains 2% or less of each of the following: yeast, organic molasses, sea salt, organic cultured wheat flour, organic vinegar, organic acerola cherry powder, enzymes.

Whole grain products will often have higher amounts of protein.

Total Sugars will include Added Sugar and those that are naturally occurring in fruits, vegetables, and dairy, for example. The grams of Added Sugars refer to any sweetener that is added to the food. Review the total grams of sugar, and aim to limit added sugar intake.

Can you tell from looking at the Nutrition Facts section of Label 3 and Label 4, two common breads, which product is whole grain and which is refined? Label 3 Nutrition Facts shows 0 grams of fiber and 2 grams of protein per serving, and the Ingredients show *enriched unbleached wheat flour*, in addition to added sugar, soybean oil, and chemical additives. Label 4 Nutrition Facts shows 5 grams of fiber and 5 grams of protein per serving. The Ingredients show *whole wheat*, along with several other whole grains and seeds, such as flaxseeds and whole oats, and organic cane sugar.

Protein

Review the protein section to determine if the food provides a good amount of protein. Considering that most adults generally need anywhere from 75–150 grams of protein a day, a general guideline is to aim for 25 to 30 grams of protein per meal. You can determine if a serving will provide a decent addition to your protein intake or if you need to include another protein-rich food.

Vitamins and Minerals

Use the % DV to determine if the food or drink is a good (10–19%) or excellent (20% and over) source of a particular vitamin or mineral. Check the ingredient list to determine if the food or drink has been enriched with added vitamins or minerals or if they are naturally occurring.

Label 5
Popular Brand Of Cereal

Nutrition Facts

About 16 servings per container
Serving size 1 cup (36g)

Amount per serving
Calories 140

	% Daily Value*
Total Fat 1.5g	2%
Saturated Fat 0g	0%
Trans Fat 0g	
Cholesterol 0mg	0%
Sodium 190mg	8%
Total Carbohydrate 31g	11%
Dietary Fiber 0g	0%
Total Sugars 12g	
Incl. 12g Added Sugars	25%
Protein 1g	
Vitamin D 2mcg	10%
Calcium 0mg	0%
Iron 1mg	6%
Potassium 20mg	0%
Vitamin A	50%
Vitamin C	10%
Thiamin	35%
Riboflavin	40%
Niacin	40%
Vitamin B_6	25%
Folate 240mcg DFE (140mcg folic acid)	60%
Vitamin B_{12}	80%
Zinc	15%

* The % Daily Value (DV) tells you how much a nutrient in a serving of food contributes to a daily diet. 2,000 calories a day is used for general nutrition advice.

INGREDIENTS: Rice, Sugar, Canola and/or Soybean Oil, Salt, contains 1% or less of: Natural and artificial flavor, Red 40, Yellow 6, Yellow 5, Blue 1, Tumeric Oleorsin (color), BHT and BHA added to preserve freshness. VITAMINS & MINERALS: Sodium Ascorbate and Ascorbic Acid (Vitamin C), Niacinamide (Vitamin B3), Reduced Iron, Zince Oxide, Vitamin A Palmitate, Pyridoxine Hydrochloride (Vitamin B6), Thiamin Mononitrate (Vitamin B1), Riboflavin (Vitamin B2), Folic Acid, Vitamin D3, Vitamin B12.

Review the Nutrition Facts section of Label 5, a popular cereal marketed to children, to see several added vitamins and minerals. However, the cereal contains 12 grams of added sugar per serving, 0 grams of fiber, and only 1 gram of protein. Packaged foods producers will add vitamins and minerals to their foods in order to market their products as having higher nutritional value. Don't be fooled. Some of these products may still have high amounts of added sugar, refined fats, refined grains, and even chemical additives.

Label Reading In Action

When you think of peanut butter, imagine what ingredients you would expect to actually be in peanut butter. Most people would say ground peanuts. Yet, Label 6, Peanut Butter One has added sugar and contains highly processed hydrogenated oils. The Nutrition Facts information is actually quite comparable between the two different types of peanut butters, but the level of processing between the brands is quite different. Label 7, Peanut Butter Two contains only two, simple ingredients. You wouldn't be able to see that information just by looking at the numbers in the Nutrition Facts section.

To practice some of the steps that we have outlined, start reading labels that you already have at home. Some ideas of labels to look at include a box of cereal, a salad dressing, a loaf of bread, or a can of soup. Find three products with food labels and follow Steps 1 and 2 above. Ask yourself the following questions:

Would you consider this to be a whole food product or an ultra-processed food?

What are the sources of added sugars, and how much has been added?

Are there any highly processed oils? How do you know?

Is this food a good source of fiber or protein?

Does it contain any chemical additives?

Label 6
Peanut Butter One

Nutrition Facts

Serving Size 2 Tbsp (33g)

Amount Per Serving

Calories 190

	% Daily Value*
Total Fat 16g	21%
Saturated Fat 3.5g	17%
Trans Fat 0g	
Cholesterol 0mg	0%
Sodium 140mg	6%
Total Carbohydrate 8g	3%
Dietary Fiber 2g	9%
Total Sugars 3g	
Incl 2g of Added Sugars	4%
Protein 7g	7%
Vitamin D 0µg	0%
Calcium 17mg	2%
Iron 0.5mg	2%
Potassium 184mg	4%
Vitamin E 2mg	10%
Niacin 5mg	30%

*The % Daily Value tells you how much a nutrient in a serving of food contributes to a daily diet. 2000 calories a day is used for general nutrition advice.

Ingredients: Roasted Peanuts, Sugar, Contains 2% Or Less Of Molasses, Fully Hydrogenated Vegetable Oils (Rapeseed And Soybean), Mono And Diglycerides, Salt. Product Information: • *See nutrition information for fat and saturated fat content • 7g Protein Per Serving* • Gluten Free • Kosher Pareve. Allergens: Contains Peanut Ingredients. Product Disclaimers: N\A

Label 7
Peanut Butter Two

Nutrition Facts

Serving Size 2 Tbsp (32g)

Amount Per Serving

Calories 180

	% Daily Value*
Total Fat 16g	20%
Saturated Fat 2g	11%
Trans Fat 0g	
Cholesterol 0mg	0%
Sodium 50mg	2%
Total Carbohydrate 6g	2%
Dietary Fiber 3g	10%
Total Sugars 1g	
Incl 0g of Added Sugars	0%
Protein 8g	8%
Vitamin D 0µg	0%
Calcium 32mg	2%
Iron 1mg	4%
Potassium 247mg	6%
Vitamin E 2mg	15%
Niacin 6mg	40%

*The % Daily Value tells you how much a nutrient in a serving of food contributes to a daily diet. 2000 calories a day is used for general nutrition advice.

Ingredients: Organic Peanuts, Contains 1% Or Less Of Salt. Product Information: • *See nutrition information for fat content • 8g Protein Per Serving* • Gluten Free • Natural • Kosher Pareve. Allergens: Contains Peanut Ingredients. Product Disclaimers: N\A

Common Label Claims And Certifications

Now that you know how to read the most important part of a food label, the Ingredients list, and you know how to navigate the Nutrition Facts, let us focus on some of the claims and labeling that might be found on the front of a label, can, jar, or box.

Healthy

The FDA recently updated its requirements to be able to claim that a food is "Healthy" on its label. A healthy food or product must contain fruit, vegetables, whole grains, low or no-fat dairy, or protein-rich foods such as lean meat, poultry, seafood, eggs, beans, nuts and seeds. There are also certain limits for the amount of saturated fat, added sugar, and sodium allowed in the food, however that amount varies based on the type of product. For example, the maximum amount of added sugar allowed in a grain product such as cereal is 5 grams per serving and less for other foods. The maximum amount of sodium allowed in any food is 230 mg per serving. The maximum amount of saturated fat is 2 grams per serving in a food product, or 20% of total fat for oils, spreads, and dressings. Currently, there is no symbol for the "Healthy" claim.[8]

Organic

Foods labeled organic have been certified by the USDA or a third-party agency. For produce and plant-based foods, organic signifies that it has been grown without the use of synthetic pesticides or fertilizers and with seeds that are not genetically engineered (GE). In addition, organic packaged and processed foods must not contain any artificial colors, flavors, preservatives, or any GE ingredients.

Organic meat and poultry are from animals fed organic feed only and without any animal by-products. They cannot be given any growth hormones or antibiotics. In addition, the meat must not be irradiated, which means treated with radiation to prevent food borne illness and extend shelf life. The animals must also be raised on an organic pasture and given access to the outdoors year round.

Consider the following as you navigate whether or not to purchase organic foods.

Benefits of purchasing organic foods:

- decreased exposure to toxic chemicals, including pesticides and fertilizers,
- increased nutrient quality of food, including some vitamins, minerals, and antioxidants,[9,10]

Foods labeled organic have been certified by the USDA or a third-party agency. For produce and plant-based foods, organic signifies that it has been grown without the use of synthetic pesticides or fertilizers and with seeds that are not genetically engineered (GE).

- better for the environment, and
- decreased toxic exposures to farm workers.

Additional purchasing factors to consider:
- possible increased cost of organic foods,
- availability, and
- difficulty of local farmers to become certified organic due to cost of the certification. Buying local, non-organic food may still provide you with an option for pesticide-free produce. Talk to your local farmers about their food production practices.

In addition to the USDA's Pesticide Data Program, the Environmental Working Group is an independent organization that rates fresh produce annually according to their residual pesticide content and creates a consumer-friendly guide. If you are just starting to purchase organic produce, using the Dirty Dozen and Clean Fifteen list for shopping may help you navigate what foods to purchase organic. However, the primary goal for children and adults is to increase the consumption of fruits and vegetables, whether choosing organic or not.

The list is updated every year, but to give you an example of what you might find, the 2025 Dirty Dozen, which contain the highest amount of pesticide residue on fresh produce, includes: spinach, strawberries, greens (kale, collard, and mustard), grapes, peaches, cherries, nectarines, pears, apples, blackberries, blueberries, and potatoes.

The 2025 Clean Fifteen, which contains the lowest amount of pesticide residue on fresh produce, includes: pineapple, sweet corn, avocados, papaya, onions, sweet peas, asparagus, cabbage, watermelon, cauliflower, bananas, mangoes, carrots, mushrooms, and kiwi.

Additionally, rinsing your produce under running water, peeling the skin of fruits and vegetables, scrubbing root vegetables like potatoes, and discarding the outer leaves of leafy greens and cabbage can help minimize your exposure to pesticide residues. Soaking produce in a baking soda solution (2 cups water, 1 teaspoon baking soda) for 15 minutes and then rinsing under water may further breakdown and remove some of the surface pesticides found on produce.

Free-Range

Free-range is a label regulated by the USDA for poultry meat only—chicken, turkey, and duck– but not for eggs. Free-range means that the animals have had access to the outdoors for more than half of their lives. However, this definition can be loosely interpreted, and farms may not be regularly inspected. Some farms may allow the chickens to roam freely in a large pasture for most of the day, returning to the indoors only at night. Because the term does not address the population density or the quality of the outdoor environment, it could mean they have a small area of dirt or gravel, having to stand with minimal movement due to crowding.

Grass-Fed

Grass-fed refers to cattle or lamb that have only been eating grass or hay and are not being fed grain or animal by-products. Grass-fed animals have continuous access to large areas of pasture to roam and to graze on their natural grass diet. Compared to conventional beef, meat from cattle raised on a grass-based diet is leaner and more nutritious, with increased omega-3 fatty acids and total conjugated linoleic acid (CLA), a precursor to a form of anti-inflammatory omega-6 fatty acids. In addition, it also contains higher amounts of beta-carotene and vitamin E, as well as antioxidants such as glutathione and superoxide dismutase.[11,12]

However, even with this label, there can be confusion. Animals may be grass-fed for a portion of their lives and then be fed grains like corn and soy in order for them to gain weight quickly before being processed into meat. In order to determine if the cattle were grass-fed for their entire lives, you can look for labels such as 100% grass-fed and grass-finished.

The USDA only offers a grass-fed certification program for smaller farms and ranches. However, there are several independent organizations that offer grass-fed and finished certifications and labels. Without a certification and label from a reputable organization, there is no regulation of labeling of grass-fed or finished beef.

Cage-Free

You may find this label on chicken, turkey, or more commonly, eggs. It means the chickens were not raised in cages. It does not necessarily mean that the animals had access to the outdoors or even access to large areas indoors. This label is minimally regulated.

Pasture-Raised

Another term, pasture-raised, generally signifies that the animal had access to outdoor pastures, versus gravel or dirt, in order to freely roam and graze for food. You might find this label on eggs, butter, pork, chicken, turkey, and beef. This label is minimally regulated, but certain independent certifications, such as Certified Humane or A Greener World (AGW), can help identify meat and eggs produced from pasture-raised farming.

Natural

Food products with the term *natural* may be the most confusing and misleading food label claim. Generally speaking, a food labeled as natural, with the exception of meat and poultry, may not carry much weight. Broadly, it means that the food was minimally processed and free of synthetic additives, but this label is not regulated. Some cereals, condiments, breads, soups, or peanut butters are labeled as *All Natural*. Look deeper into the ingredient list to be sure it is not just a marketing strategy.

However, meat and poultry that are labeled natural are regulated by the USDA. In these cases, it means that the product should be free of artificial colors, flavors, sweeteners, and preservatives. Natural meat and poultry must be minimally processed and not altered from the original raw product. Natural meat on a label represents little to do with what the animal was fed or what environment the animal was raised in; it is only referring to the processing of the animal.

Genetically Modified Organisms (GMOs), Genetically Engineered (GE), or Bioengineered (BE) Foods

Genetically modified organisms (GMOs), also referred to as genetically engineered (GE foods) or bioengineered (BE foods), were first introduced into the food system in the 1990s, ultimately allowing technology to alter and add genetic material into our food supply. These foods have not evolved naturally. It has been estimated that over 70% of conventional, processed foods in the U.S. may contain ingredients that are genetically modified. The most common GE foods are corn, soy, rapeseed (canola), and sugar beets, which make their way into the food supply as corn syrup, corn oil, corn starch, soybean oil, canola oil, and granulated sugar.

As of June 2025, the USDA will require mandatory labeling of GE foods that will state that a food is "bioengineered" or "derived from bioengineering." Many countries around the world have taken a stronger stance against GE foods aside from just labeling and have completely banned or strictly limited the use of GE foods.

One cause for concern with GMO foods is the lack of long-term studies examining their effects on human and environmental health. Additionally, there is unpredictable contamination of organic crops with GMOs.

The Non-GMO Project is one of a few independent organizations that verifies that a product is at least 99.1% GMO-free, with the aim of 100%. Look for a label and seal that says Non-GMO Project Verified or for a certified organic product. If you see the general label that says "GMO-Free," know that it may not have been verified by a third party.

The most common GE foods are corn, soy, rapeseed (canola), and sugarbeets, which make their way into the food supply as corn syrup, corn oil, corn starch, soybean oil, canola oil, and granulated sugar.

Whole Grains Stamp

The Whole Grains Council verifies if a food product is a good source of whole grains or if it is a 100% whole grain product. A food product with the basic stamp contains some whole grains, at least 8 grams, but it will also still contain refined grains. The 50% stamp indicates at least half the grains included are whole grains. The 100% whole grain stamp identifies products that are made completely with whole grains, including the bran, endosperm, and germ.

The Whole Grains Council verifies if a food product is a good source of whole grains or if it is a 100% whole grain product.

Not all food companies are using the whole grain stamp, but as we previously outlined above, you can also determine if a product is a whole grain product by reading the ingredient list.

BPA-Free (Bisphenol-A)

Although labeling isn't required or regulated, some food products in cans and plastic containers may note on their label that they are BPA-free. BPA (Bisphenol-A) is a chemical that is commonly used in the inner lining of canned goods such as soups, tomatoes, beans, vegetables, and fruits. It is also used in many plastic goods such as bottled water, juice, soda, baby bottles, plastic toys, and the lining of sales receipts. BPA leaches out of these products and can ultimately be absorbed into the body. BPA is considered an endocrine disruptor due to its similar chemical structure to estrogen produced in the human body. Thus, it mimics estrogen and can bind and activate the same receptors. Exposure to BPA may contribute to thyroid, nervous system, and reproductive system dysfunction, as well as affect hormonally-influenced cancers, such as breast and prostate.[13,14]

Many countries and individual states in the U.S. have banned or restricted the use of BPA. Currently, there are no restrictions on BPA use from the FDA. Despite lack of government action, companies have been moving away from using BPA in their products due to consumer demand. Unfortunately, some of the chemicals that manufacturers are using instead of BPA may turn out to be just as harmful. The bottom line is to generally limit or avoid foods and drinks packaged in plastic when possible. Tomato sauce, crushed tomatoes, salad dressings, and condiments such as mustard, sauces, oils, and vinegar can be found in glass jars.

Congratulations! You are ready to hit the aisles with your new label reading skills! Remember: reading the Ingredients is one of the most important things to do when becoming a conscientious shopper. We also recommend expanding your food shopping experiences by visiting local health food stores and farmers' markets. Don't be afraid to ask where the food came from and how it was grown or raised. Many local farms welcome visitors, and you can see firsthand how produce

BPA is considered an endocrine disruptor due to its similar chemical structure to estrogen produced in the human body. Thus, it mimics estrogen and can bind and activate the same receptors. Exposure to BPA may contribute to thyroid, nervous, and reproductive system dysfunction, as well as affect hormonally-influenced cancers, such as breast and prostate.

is grown and animals are raised. Because of the lack of clarity in food label claims, including cage-free and free-range for example, having a direct conversation with the person who raised the animals can clear up any confusion.

Keep in mind that some small farmers may not be able to afford organic or grass-fed certifications for their food labels. Smaller farming operations are often growing food organically and in a more natural environment than some of the large-scale farms that do the bare minimum to achieve and afford certification.

We hope you become inspired to learn more about what is in your food and where it comes from. The next time you are out grocery shopping, make the best decisions you can with your new knowledge and skills regarding label reading. You are well on your way to reclaiming your health with whole foods.

Chapter Six

The FAME Plate

Since I was 13, I have tried dozens of diets (Atkins®, Weight Watchers®, and Nutri-System® to name a few). I find it very comforting to know that I really can't go wrong with whole foods and a well balanced plate with greens, whole grains, protein, and fats. I will never go to the grocery store again without examining a label, buying a leafy green, and thinking of FAME!

—Allison, FAME Series, Charlee's Kitchen

THE AMOUNT OF FOOD COMMONLY SERVED AT A RESTAURANT HAS DRAMATICALLY INCREASED OVER THE LAST 20 TO 30 YEARS. Think about the enormous pasta portions served in many restaurants. Consider the sheer volume of a 32-ounce Big Gulp® soda or a 20-ounce Venti® latte. The notion that bigger is better has paralleled our worsening health. Bottomless sodas, super-size French fries, and free baskets of bread have become the norm when eating out. At grocery stores, many types of nutrient-poor, ultra-processed foods such as flavored chips, sweetened cereals, and frozen, premade meals are sold in greater quantities at lower prices due to bulk packaging and cheap ingredients. While this may be convenient and economical to the consumer, it often promotes increased consumption of low-quality foods at a cost to health.

Large portion sizes of commercially available food and beverages have been connected with metabolic syndrome, insulin resistance, and obesity.[1,2] Simply being served large portion sizes leads to increased caloric intake, and many people are not even aware they are consuming more calories than they want or need. Research shows that limiting (or using appropriate) portion sizes will decrease food intake.[3] Just as important to consider as portion size is the type of food on the plate. A meal composed of ultra-processed food will also likely lead to increased caloric intake. One compelling study showed when people consumed ultra-processed foods, they tended to eat up to 500 more calories a day.[4] By creating the healthy habit of including more minimally processed foods in a meal and by understanding and using appropriate portion sizes, we are less likely to overeat.

Serving Size Versus Portion Size

The serving sizes that are on the Nutrition Facts label are standardized measurements of food that are set by the FDA. A portion size is the amount of food that is actually consumed in one sitting.

In the past thirty years, the portions consumed in America have increased between two to five fold.[5] People are often unaware that packaged foods, bottled drinks, and restaurant meals often contain more than one serving. For example, the Dietary Guidelines suggest that a standard bagel serving size is three ounces, yet the average bagel sold is six or more ounces. Most people will eat a whole bagel as a portion, thus eating two or more servings. This doesn't mean you cannot enjoy a whole bagel. Just be aware that there are multiple servings in the portion size.

The reality is, as access to hyperpalatable and cheaper, ultra-processed foods has grown, Americans are eating more than they ever have. Additionally, restaurants and grocery stores are marketing the idea that *more* and *bigger* is better.

Nutritional Guidelines And Healthy Plates

The federal government (USDA) promotes MyPlate, a nutritional guideline using a plate as a visual aid to create healthy meals. There

20 years ago		Today
3 in	Bagel	6 in
8 oz	Soda	20 oz
8 oz	Coffee	16 oz
5 cups	Popcorn	20 cups
500 Calories	Pizza	850 Calories

are many examples of healthy plates created by various professional and governmental nutrition organizations and educational institutions.

The plate we present to you focuses on whole foods and allows for variation from person to person. A person may need less carbohydrates or more protein, for example, depending on what is best for their individual needs. A person's cultural background and their ethical choices in regard to animal products will also affect what is included on a healthy plate.

We will start with what food to include on your plate and then look at how much.

The FAME Plate

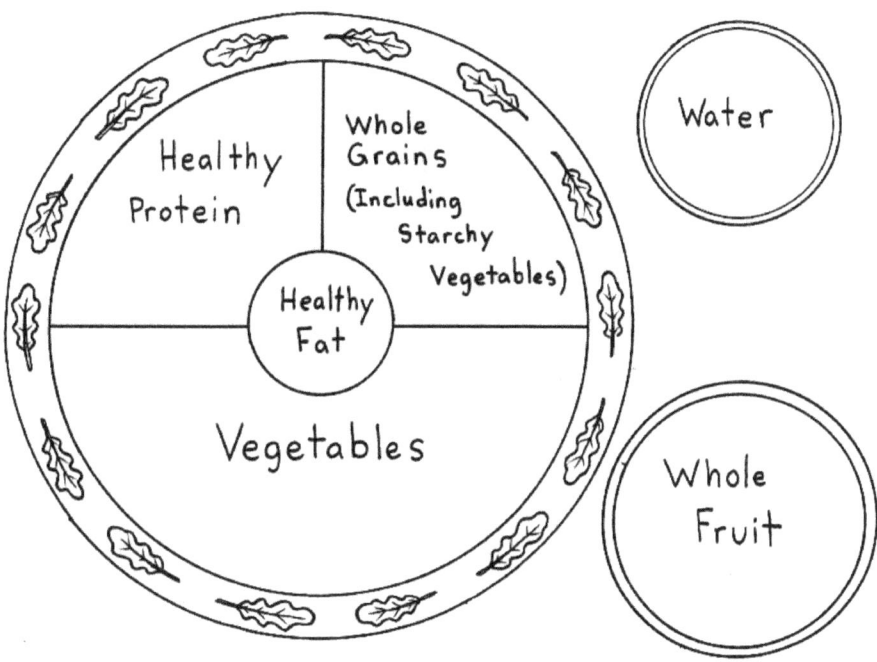

The following steps will help you learn how a dinner, lunch, or even a breakfast plate would look with food in healthy portions:

1. Use a normal-sized plate: approximately 10.5 to 11 inches in diameter. Measure the plate. Plates are sometimes up to 14 inches in diameter, which may also make it more difficult to eat appropriate portions.
2. Fill half the plate with non-starchy vegetables.

    Examples: all dark green leafy vegetables (spinach, chard, kale, collards), lettuce, broccoli, bok choy, cauliflower, onion, garlic, leeks, Brussels sprouts, carrots, celery, asparagus, bell peppers, cucumber, summer squash, tomato (fruit), mushroom (fungus).

3. Fill one-quarter of the plate with whole grains and/or starchy vegetables.

   Examples: all whole grains including brown rice, corn, quinoa, oats, and whole grain pasta or whole grain bread. Starchy vegetables such as potatoes, yams, sweet potato, beets, or winter squash.

4. Fill one-quarter of the plate with animal protein, or a combination of plant-based protein.

   Examples: meat, poultry, wild game, fish, eggs, dairy, beans and lentils, nuts and nut butters, seeds, tempeh, tofu, edamame.

5. The middle circle targets the inclusion of healthy fats and oils.
   Examples: avocado or avocado oil, olives or extra virgin olive oil, butter or ghee, full-fat dairy, nuts and nut butters, egg yolk, coconut or coconut oil, lard and tallow.

6. Whole Fruit: includes berries, pears, apples, citrus, melons, grapes.

7. Beverage: drink water.

Tips For Creating The FAME Plate

- Fruit does not need to be eaten at every meal, but it is definitely part of a healthy diet and can be used in any meal or as a snack. The general trend is that Americans (especially children) disproportionately choose fruits over vegetables.[6] To bring back balance, notice how much more space vegetables have on the typical FAME Plate. Fill half your plate with vegetables, and you'll be on the right track!

- Most foods contain a combination of macronutrients (fats, carbs, and protein) and may fit into more than one category. Quinoa is a complete protein, but it is also a good source of complex carbohydrates. Beans are similar, containing both fiber and protein. Nuts are high in healthy fats and also contain some

The FAME Plate is only a guideline. It doesn't need to be a perfect science or created at every meal. If one gets overly focused on the details, the big picture of moving toward a whole foods diet may be lost. Remember, each person has an individual relationship with food based on many factors including family and cultural traditions, food allergies or sensitivities, and health goals. Therefore, food groups and portions may be individualized.

protein. While the FAME Plate has separate sections, whole foods fall into more than one nutrient category. Place a food into the category it fits best for each meal.

- The FAME Plate is only a guideline. It doesn't need to be a perfect science or created at every meal. If one gets overly focused on the details, the big picture of moving toward a whole foods diet may be lost.

You can simplify the FAME Plate method by asking yourself these three questions when creating a meal: Where is the protein in this meal? Where is the healthy fat? And where are the fiber-rich foods? Remember, each person has an individual relationship with food based on many factors including family and cultural traditions, food allergies or sensitivities, and health goals. Therefore, food groups and portions may be individualized.

What About Dairy?

Unlike some plate models, dairy, which most commonly includes milk, yogurt, and cheese, does not get its own section on the FAME Plate. Due to its nutrient density, dairy is certainly an important part of a healthy diet for many people. It can provide a high quality source of protein and fat, contributing to those sections of the FAME plate, as well as several micronutrients including calcium, phosphorus, potassium, vitamin D, and B vitamins (including B12). It does not need to be included in every meal, as it is often suggested. Dairy can be a problematic food choice for those with a dairy allergy or sensitivity or for those with lactose intolerance. Compared to White Americans, lactose intolerance is highly prevalent in certain ethnicities, including African-Americans, American Indians, Hispanics or Latinos, and Asian-Americans.[7] Additionally, other people may choose to avoid or limit dairy due to ethical, environmental, or other personal reasons.

Milk consumption has been steadily decreasing in the U.S. over several decades.[8] The USDA's My Plate currently recommends three cups of dairy per day for adults and children over nine-years old. The USDA provides several alternatives to drinking three cups of milk to meet this dairy recommendation, such as low-fat yogurt, cheese, or fortified soy milk. Unsweetened soy milk, but not other plant-based alternatives like almond, rice, or coconut milk, is recognized as the best alternative to cow's milk due to its similar nutrient profile, specifically its protein content and fortified micronutrients. It is really important to pay attention to the nutritional differences with other non-dairy alternatives. Most non-dairy milk, cheese, and yogurt will be lower in protein and fat as well as calcium and vitamin B12, if they are not fortified.

The large majority of milk in the U.S. comes from dairy cows raised within the industrialized food system. If they do not meet the standard to make organic milk, then these cows very likely have been exposed to growth hormones, reproductive hormones, and antibiotics. Conventionally-raised cows are also not completely pasture-raised, thus decreasing the micronutrient status of the milk, including decreased beta-carotene, vitamin E, omega-3 fatty acids, and CLA (conjugated linoleic acid).[9]

Dairy foods and beverages can definitely be part of a healthy, whole foods diet for those who tolerate and choose to include dairy. Specifically, fermented dairy, such as yogurt, kefir, or aged cheese, may be beneficial for reducing risk of cardiovascular disease.[10] When available, choose dairy products from organic, pasture-raised cows, sheep, or goats.

Building Healthy Bones

The body needs adequate dietary calcium to build strong bones, especially in childhood and adolescence. In the United States, dairy-based foods and beverages are the primary sources of calcium as well as Vitamin D. However, in later adulthood, calcium is often overemphasized compared to other influential factors on bone health. The majority of evidence looking at the association of dairy intake and fracture risk in adults has shown a protective effect, though results have been inconsistent.[11,12,13,14] The type of dairy consumed and how it was processed seems to make a difference in these

Other factors to promote bone health in adulthood that are just as or more important than dietary calcium are regular weight-bearing exercise, vitamin D status, and eating a variety of foods that provide adequate protein, vitamin K, and other minerals besides calcium.

studies, and the habit of eating fermented dairy may exert a protective effect.

Promoting bone health and preventing osteoporosis are more complicated than just looking at calcium intake. A variety of risk factors must be assessed such as one's childhood nutrition habits, a family history of osteoporosis, gender, hormone status (for example, low estrogen during menopause), smoking status, a personal history of low body weight, fracture history, and medication use. Other factors to promote bone health in adulthood that are just as or more important than dietary calcium are regular weight-bearing exercise, vitamin D status, and eating a variety of foods that provide adequate protein, vitamin K, and other minerals besides calcium. There is a synergy and balance of other vitamins and minerals found in dark leafy green vegetables, including vitamin K, beta-carotene, magnesium, iron, and more, all of which are needed for bone health. Be sure to include leafy greens that contain highly absorbable calcium like kale, broccoli, and bok choy.[15] While spinach contains considerable calcium, it is not easily absorbable because of high levels of oxalic acid. Additionally, calcium supplements or foods and beverages fortified with calcium may be needed in the diet if plant-based alternatives are chosen over dairy.

Table 6.1 provides a useful guide of calcium levels in common foods. Notice there is more calcium in one cup of cooked collard greens (358 mg) or in 3-ounces of sardines that contain soft edible bones (325 mg) than in one cup of whole milk (300 mg).

Table 6.1 Food Sources of Calcium

Food Item	Calcium (mg)
Almonds (1/4 cup)	95
Barley (1 cup)	57
Black turtle beans (1 cup, cooked)	103

Table 6.1 Food Sources of Calcium (cont'd)

Food Item	Calcium (mg)
Bok choy (1/2 cup, cooked)	79
Broccoli (1 cup, cooked)	94
Brussels sprouts (8 sprouts)	56
Butternut squash (1 cup, cooked)	84
Cheese, hard (1 oz)	200-250
Collard greens (1 cup, cooked)	358
Figs (10 medium, dried)	269
Great northern beans (1 cup, cooked)	121
Green beans (1 cup, cooked)	58
Kale (1 cup, cooked)	94
Lentils (1 cup, cooked)	37
Lima beans (1 cup, cooked)	32
Mustard greens (1 cup, cooked)	150
Navel orange (1 medium)	56
Navy beans (1 cup, cooked)	128
Peas (1 cup, cooked)	44
Pink salmon (3 oz, cooked, with bone)	181
Pinto beans (1 cup, cooked)	82
Rhubarb (1/2 cup, cooked)	174
Sardines (3 oz, Atlantic, in oil, drained)	325
Sesame seeds (1 tablespoon)	90
Spinach (1/2 cup, cooked)	115
Tempeh (1 cup)	184
White beans (1 cup, cooked)	161
Whole milk (1 cup)	300
Yogurt (1 cup, low fat)	425

Daily Servings

Exactly how much food should be on the plate? If your plate looks like the FAME Plate at each meal, you are probably doing well maximizing your nutritional intake. Again, this is just a visual guide. Most meals won't have each food perfectly in its section and many foods overlap categories. The food on some plates may fit into the distinct categories and locations on the plate, for example: fish (protein, fat), sautéed vegetables, quinoa (whole grain, protein), and olive oil (healthy fat). For other meals, the plate might mix all sections together. Consider a big salad with salad greens, carrots, cucumbers (vegetables), with hard-boiled eggs and nuts (fat, protein), and avocado and olive oil for dressing (healthy fats). In addition to what foods are on the FAME Plate, it is important to take into account how much food is on the plate at each meal. This amount will ultimately depend on each individual's metabolic needs. As a starting point for most people, using visual aids and common household items can help in remembering appropriate portions, aside from actually measuring them out. Look at the Portion Size Guide for references.

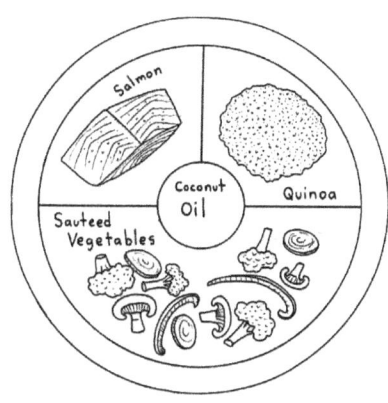

Here are some examples of portion sizes using the guide, including general amounts (in grams) of the primary macronutrient (protein, fat, or carbohydrate) in a portion size, visual aids to help determine a portion size, as well as suggestions for how to build a healthy plate:

Vegetables

On the FAME Plate, non-starchy vegetables are prioritized. Choose at least two servings at each meal, or six or more servings a day:

- 1/2 cup cooked non-starchy vegetables (5 to 10 grams of carbohydrates)
- 1 cup raw vegetables (5 grams of carbohydrates)
- 1 cup of salad greens (1 to 2 grams of carbohydrates)

Whole Grains And Starchy Vegetables

In the whole grain and starchy vegetable section, include one of the following choices:

1 cup starchy vegetables such as potato, yam, squash, beets (15 to 27 grams of carbohydrates)

1/2 cup of cooked whole grains (20 to 25 grams of carbohydrates)

1 cup cooked oats (27 grams of carbohydrates)

2 slices of whole grain bread (30 grams of carbohydrates)

Protein

Protein intake depends on body size and individual metabolic needs. Include one of the following at each meal:

3 to 4 ounces of meat, poultry, wild game, fish (20 to 30 grams of protein)

If choosing vegetarian or plant-based proteins, choose a combination of 2 to 3 of the following for each meal or 1 to 1.5 servings of a protein-dense food like tempeh or edamame.

1/4 cup of nuts or seeds (5 to 8 grams of protein)

2 tablespoons of nut butters (8 grams of protein)

1/2 cup cooked beans and legumes (7 to 9 grams of protein)

1/2 cup cooked quinoa, buckwheat, amaranth (4 to 7 grams of protein)

1 egg (7 grams of protein)

1 cup of whole milk or yogurt (8 grams of protein)

1 to 1½ ounces of cheese (8 grams of protein)

2 tablespoons chia seed (5 grams of protein)

3 tablespoons hemp hearts (10 grams of protein)

3.5 ounces of tofu (8 grams of protein)

3.5 ounces of tempeh (15 grams of protein)

1 cup shelled edamame beans (19 grams of protein)

Fats and Oils

Include 1 to 2 different sources of healthy fat per meal (grams of fat per serving included):

1 tablespoon butter or oil—coconut, olive oil, avocado (14 grams of fat)

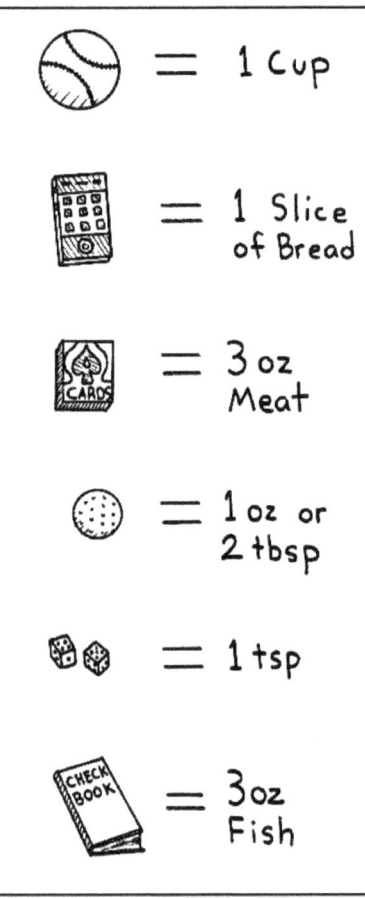

Portion Size Guide

2 tablespoons of nut butter (16 grams of fat)

1/2 medium avocado (11 to 15 grams of fat)

1/4 cup of nuts or seeds (14 grams of fat)

1/4 cup olives (15 grams of fat)

3 tablespoons shredded coconut (9 grams of fat)

1/4 cup full-fat coconut milk (12 grams of fat)

1 cup whole milk or yogurt (9 grams of fat)

1½ ounces of cheese (13 to 15 grams of fat)

Fruits

Include 1 of the following in every meal or with snacks throughout the day:

1 medium-sized whole fruit (15 to 30 grams of carbohydrates)

1/2 cup of fresh cut or frozen fruit (5 to 15 grams of carbohydrates)

Tips For Creating Appropriate Portions

When Buying Bulk

- Re-package oversized foods into appropriate-sized containers.

When Eating Out

- Split your entrée with a friend or family member.
- Ask to have half the entrée boxed to go, and eat it for a meal the next day.
- Skip the "free" bread or chips served before the meal.
- Avoid appetizers. They tend to be high-calorie and nutrient-poor food. Order a salad as an appetizer instead.
- Substitute French fries, chips, or white rice side dishes for vegetables or beans. Most restaurants offer a salad or sautéed vegetables.
- Keep it simple if traveling or eating out regularly for work. Order salad or vegetables with a source of protein.

- Ask if there is a small or kid-size portion for occasional fried foods or consider splitting desserts.

When Eating At Home

- Serve meals onto plates according to the FAME Plate method, and keep the serving dishes away from the dining table.
- When choosing to eat seconds, choose more vegetables, protein, or whole fruit first.
- Avoid eating snacks out of the bag while multitasking with work, school, or watching TV. Put the appropriate portion size of the snack in a bowl.
- If feeling hungry and lunch or dinner is a couple of hours away, first try drinking a glass of water and wait 10 minutes. Dehydration can often mimic hunger. If still hungry, eat a healthy snack (like a small handful of nuts or veggies with hummus, for example) to avoid overeating at mealtime.
- When choosing healthy whole foods that are balanced in protein, fats, and carbohydrates, as well as eating in a way that encourages healthy digestion, the body will tell you when it is full and satisfied. Listen closely.

Putting The FAME Plate Model Into Practice

The FAME Plate promotes an approach to building a well-rounded meal based on including more whole foods from plants as well as foods made from healthy animals. The FAME Plate model also recognizes that individuals have unique food needs depending on their life stage, health goals, or food sensitivities, for example. Below is one example of how a person can modify a common recipe for a taco bowl in order to help them meet their individual macronutrient goals (protein, fat, and carbohydrates, including fiber) as well as their caloric needs. Adapting some of the individual ingredients can change the nutrient density and the metabolic effects of the meal. In general, by filling half the plate with non-starchy vegetables, and including whole grains, you are decreasing the space available for less nutrient-dense, refined carbohydrates. By emphasizing healthy fat with every meal, you are providing your taste buds as well as your brain with a sense of satiety. By including a healthy portion size of protein on your plate, you further ensure a feeling of satiety and sustained energy between mealtimes.

Table 6.2 Comparison of Macronutrients from Taco Bowls Examples

	Calories	Protein (% calories)	Fat (% calories)	Carbohydrates (% calories)
Example 1	680	20 grams (12%)	20 grams (26%)	100 grams (59%) including 9 grams of fiber
Example 2	540	27 grams (20%)	18 grams (30%)	70 grams (51%) including 19 grams of fiber
Example 3	485	40 grams (33%)	19 grams (35%)	38 grams (31%) including 14 grams of fiber

Table 6.2 shows the comparison of the calories and macronutrients of the following three taco bowl examples. Consider a basic taco bowl **(Example 1)** that contains the following portions:

Ingredients:

1 cup cooked white rice (equaling two times the serving size)

½ cup cooked pinto beans

¼ cup shredded cheddar cheese

2 tablespoons guacamole

2 tablespoon sour cream

½ medium tomato, diced

2 tablespoons chopped green onions

¼ cup pico de gallo

A simple substitution of 1 cup brown rice for the 1 cup of white rice increases the fiber and protein content of the meal by 2 grams. Additionally, brown rice provides a wider range of micronutrients compared to the white rice.

This next example **(Example 2)** follows the FAME Plate portions for a vegetarian taco bowl, with added emphasis on enhancing the protein and fiber content of the meal:

Ingredients:

½ cup cooked quinoa

¾ cup cooked pinto beans

¼ cup shredded cheddar cheese

2 tablespoons guacamole

2 tablespoons low-fat, plain Greek yogurt

½ medium tomato, diced

2 tablespoons chopped green onions

1½ cup chopped greens (romaine lettuce, kale, mixed greens)

¼ cup pico de gallo

There is a reduction in total calories and a shift in the macronutrients, with a lower percentage of calories coming from carbohydrates as well as increased fiber and protein.

This final example **(Example 3)** follows the FAME Plate portions to create a taco bowl that includes animal protein and is adjusted to be a higher protein and lower carbohydrate meal.

Ingredients:

3.5 ounces cooked chicken

¾ cup cooked pinto beans

¼ cup shredded cheddar cheese

2 tablespoons guacamole

2 tablespoon low-fat, plain Greek yogurt

½ medium tomato, diced

2 tablespoons chopped green onions

1½ cup chopped greens (romaine lettuce, kale, mixed greens)

¼ cup pico de gallo

Chapter Seven
Strategies For Healthy Digestion

I have relaxed around food in general and preparing whole foods—it takes time and it's worth it to eat food I know is good for me and my family. This is a big deal for me. Before this class, I was always worried about weight management. My time with this project has freed me from this negative preoccupation.

—Patricia, FAME Series, Charlee's Kitchen

Where does digestion start? In the mouth? In the stomach? Actually, the digestive process starts in the brain! Consider the following visualization exercise:

Sit with your eyes closed. Take a few deep breaths. Now, imagine that there is a lemon sitting on a table. Take a knife and slice the lemon. Take half of the lemon and squeeze it into a glass. Pick up the glass and take a sip of the fresh squeezed lemon juice. How do you feel? Did you notice any changes in your body?

Most people will begin to salivate or feel their mouth pucker with just the thought of the lemon juice. Salivation indicates that the mouth has secreted enzymes that begin the digestive process. Just by imagining food, your body has started physiological processes to break down food!

Most people have heard the phrase, "You are what you eat." But, it is more accurate to say, "You are what you eat, digest, absorb, and eliminate." Digestion is a complex process that turns the food we eat into usable energy and nutrients for the body. Digestion is also very heavily influenced by the state of mind or environment we are in while eating. Consider the last time you ate a meal in one of the following situations: driving a car, talking on the phone, working on a computer, scrolling through social media, while reading, during a stressful discussion, while watching TV, or when in a hurry.

All of the above activities have the potential to affect your digestion in a negative way. To understand this more, let's look at the way our nervous system *directly* influences digestion.

The Nervous System

Generally speaking, the nervous system responds to our environment and to our thoughts in two distinct ways: the sympathetic and the parasympathetic systems.

The Sympathetic State

The **sympathetic state** is also known as ***fight or flight***. The classic example is the concept of being chased by a bear. When escaping from a bear, the sympathetic state helps the body to run faster and fight harder. Currently, people don't usually find themselves running from a bear very often. But, we can equate these physiologic changes to any stressful situation in which we might find ourselves.

The diagram on the next page shows some of the effects on the body when in a sympathetic state. Notice what happens to the digestive process when in this state. Many of the digestive processes are slowed or impaired, including saliva flow, digestive enzyme secretion, and the intestinal contractions that move the food along. While the sympathetic nervous system is a natural and necessary part of our human reaction, modern society and busy lifestyles tend to create a state of stress—both actual and perceived—including when we are eating meals. Rushing to work and school, balancing hectic schedules, dealing with financial stress, and the constant bombardment of negative news and media: all of these factors can contribute to an overactive sympathetic nervous system.

Sit with closed eyes. Take a few deep breaths. Now, imagine that there is a lemon sitting on a table. Take a knife and slice the lemon. Take half of the lemon and squeeze it into a glass. Pick up the glass and take a sip of the fresh squeezed lemon juice. How do you feel? Did you notice any changes in your body?

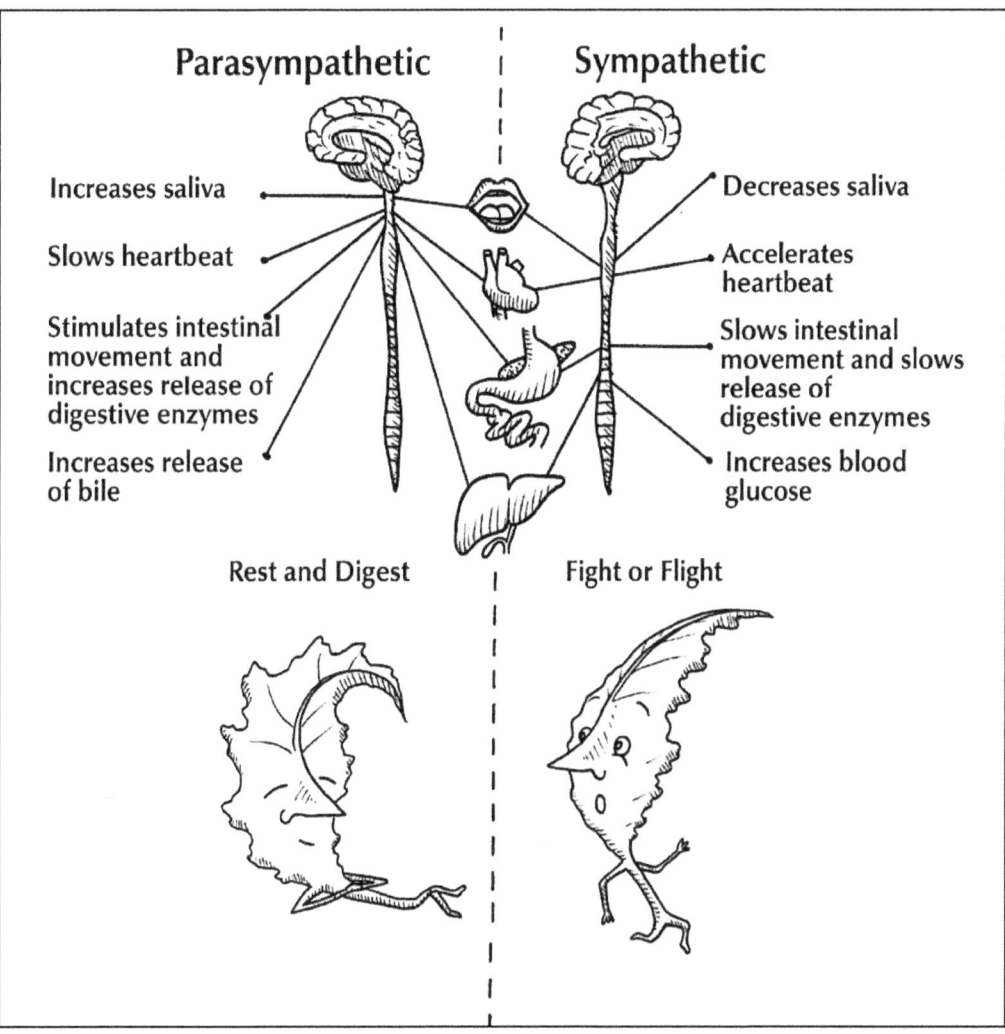

The Parasympathetic State

The **parasympathetic state** is known as ***rest and digest.*** In a calm, low-stress environment with limited stimulation, the body will be in a parasympathetic state. Notice what happens with digestion when in a parasympathetic state: saliva and digestive enzymes are secreted, and the intestinal muscles move the food along for optimal digestion, absorption, and elimination. Digestion will improve, which typically reduces minor digestive complaints, such as gas and bloating, that often accompany rushed eating. In a restful state, we are also more likely to notice when we feel full, decreasing the chance of overeating. While most people lead busy lives and often find themselves eating in stressful situations, there are ways to create an environment for eating that will help stimulate the rest and digest response.

Strategies For Healthy Digestion

- Avoid multitasking; just eat. Turn off or put away all electronic devices, including TVs, phones, tablets, and computers during meals.
- Take the time to put the food on a plate and find a comfortable space to eat. Sit down while eating. If eating at work, find an area to eat other than at a desk.
- Take ten deep, slow diaphragmatic breaths, or belly breaths, before beginning to eat. This is a powerful and simple way to support the parasympathetic nervous system. It is also a good time to acknowledge and give thanks for where the food came from and who prepared it. Practicing gratitude is linked to reduced stress.[1]
- Practice mindful eating. Savor the smell, texture, and taste of your food. Observe how you feel before, during, and after the meal.
- Chew your food well. Put down the fork between bites, and aim to chew each bite until the food is almost liquid before swallowing.
- Eat slowly and stop eating before feeling completely full. If you are eating fast or are distracted while eating, there is the potential to overeat.
- Stay hydrated. Water is essential to support proper digestion, nutrient absorption, and elimination. Aim to drink water throughout the day and with meals. For some people, drinking large amounts of water with meals may worsen symptoms of reflux.
- Include various herbs and spices in your meals. Not only will they enhance the flavor and aroma of the food, but many of them have been used traditionally to support digestion, including turmeric, fennel, ginger, garlic, cinnamon, mint, lemon, cayenne pepper, and black pepper.[2]
- Include raw apple cider vinegar (ACV) in your meals. It's a great addition to dressings for salads and veggies or in marinades for

Notice what happens with digestion when in a parasympathetic state: saliva and digestive enzymes are secreted, and the intestinal muscles move the food along for optimal digestion, absorption, and elimination.

red meat, poultry, and fish. Raw ACV is fermented and may contain probiotics, supporting healthy gut bacteria, and it can help balance blood sugar after meals.[3,4] Alternatively, drink 1 to 2 teaspoons of ACV in a small glass of water 15 minutes before meals. Some people notice an improvement in heartburn symptoms when consuming ACV, although research for those benefits are limited.

- Aim to incorporate more bitter foods into your diet, such as dark leafy greens (arugula, dandelion greens, mustard greens, kale), cruciferous veggies (broccoli, cabbage), radicchio, artichoke, and citrus fruits like lemon, lime, and grapefruit. Even unsweetened coffee, tea, and cocoa powder are bitter. There is a long history of using bitter extracts of herbs, referred to as "bitters," as a digestive tonic. In general, bitter foods help stimulate many digestive functions, including the production of enzymes, stomach acid, and bile.[5,6]

Avoid multitasking; just eat. Turn off or put away all electronic devices, including TVs, phones, tablets, and computers during meals.

Practice mindful eating. Savor the smell, texture, and taste of your food. Observe how you feel before, during, and after the meal.

These digestive strategies are often effective at dealing with minor digestive complaints such as gas, bloating, and heartburn that are the result of eating in a stressed or sympathetic state. However, there are many other factors that also affect digestion, absorption, and elimination. Some examples include the health of the microbiome, food sensitivities and allergies, medications, chronic inflammation from a Standard American Diet and lifestyle, and certain medical conditions like inflammatory bowel disease and celiac disease. We will further explore the gut microbiome because of its essential role in health and disease.

The Gut Microbiome

The digestive tract is home to a complex and dynamic ecosystem of microorganisms referred to as the **gut microbiome**. It is primarily made up of bacteria, but also contains species of viruses, yeast, and other fungi. Gut flora, specifically the healthy bacteria, is a key component of the immune system. Trillions of bacteria reside in the digestive tract, helping to maintain the intestinal barrier, which is a layer of protection that prevents harmful microorganisms from invading the digestive tract. In addition, the gut microbiota support the digestion and absorption of nutrients, elimination of toxins, regulation of bowel movements, and the balance of hormones and inflammation.

In the last few decades, microbiome research has been growing rapidly due to advancing technology. Many diseases have now been linked to *dysbiosis,* or an imbalance in the microbiome, including inflammatory bowel disease (IBD), heart disease, diabetes, obesity, liver disease, some cancers, asthma, allergies, many skin conditions (acne, rosacea, psoriasis, eczema), neurological disorders such as Parkinson's and Alzheimer's disease, autism spectrum disorder, depression and anxiety, and some auto-immune diseases.[7] Hippocrates is known for stating that "all diseases begin in the gut." It is clear that the microbiome plays a complex and vital role in health and disease.

While the science on the microbiome continues to evolve, it is generally accepted that the development of the microbiome starts at birth and will change throughout the lifespan. Here are some of the many factors that may influence the microbiome, some that may be in your control and others that are not:[8,9,10,11,12]

- Genetics
- Birth and early childhood (mode of birth and infant feeding methods)
- Age
- Environmental and lifestyle factors: exercise, sleep and the circadian rhythm, geographic location, exposure to industrial toxins and pollutants, smoking, chronic and heavy alcohol use, and acute and chronic stress
- Antibiotic use. Antibiotics kill pathogenic (harmful) bacteria, but they also kill healthy bacteria and increase the susceptibility for overgrowth of other harmful bacteria and yeast.
- Medications can impact the microbiome, including: proton pump inhibitors, statins, metformin, laxatives, NSAIDs (non-steroidal anti inflammatories), opioids, SSRIs (selective serotonin reuptake inhibitors), and other mood disorder medications.
- Diet. This is one of the biggest factors in the development and maintenance of the microbiome.

Diet and the Microbiome

It is important that healthy bacteria are replenished and supported regularly through the diet to support a healthy microbiome. In general, a dietary pattern focused on whole foods that includes a balance of protein, healthy fats, and is high in fiber will support a diverse and balanced microbiome. On the other hand, the Standard American Diet contributes to imbalances in the gut microbiome because it is high in refined sugar, unhealthy fats, ultra-processed foods, and chemical additives yet low in fiber and fermented foods.[13]

Prebiotics are specific dietary fibers that provide healthy food sources for the microorganisms in the gut. *Probiotics* are live, healthy bacteria and yeast that are found in fermented foods that help replenish the gut flora. When healthy bacteria have healthy food sources, they will produce postbiotics. *Postbiotics* are compounds that provide the many benefits associated with a healthy microbiome, including the production of short-chain fatty acids such as butyrate, vitamins including vitamin K and some B vitamins, and other anti-inflammatory compounds.

Dietary strategies to support a healthy microbiome include:

Eat foods high in prebiotics

There are specific types of soluble fiber that are also prebiotics, such as inulin, fructans, beta-glucan, pectin, and some oligosaccharides. Foods that are especially high in these prebiotic, soluble fibers include Jerusalem artichokes, jicama, chicory root, garlic, leek, onions, oats, dandelion greens, apples, chia seeds, flaxseeds, beans, nuts, and berries.

Recall that resistant starches are also a good source of prebiotics. This includes unripe bananas and plantains, beans and lentils, peas, raw or soaked oats, and other foods with starch that have been cooked and cooled, such as whole grains, potatoes, and beans.

Include food sources of polyphenols

Polyphenols are phytonutrients, or chemicals found in plant foods, that are known for their antioxidant and anti-inflammatory properties. In addition, they have shown to have prebiotic-like effects in the gut.[14] Polyphenols are found in brightly colored fruits and vegetables. If you follow the advice to *eat the rainbow,* it will help increase your intake of polyphenols and many other nutrients.

Polyphenols are found in fruits, especially berries, cherries, grapes, pomegranate, and apples, and in vegetables like artichoke, onions, and spinach. In addition, nuts and seeds such as flaxseed, almonds, hazelnuts, pecans, and coffee, tea, and cocoa powder are high in polyphenols.

A diverse diet is key!

Research shows that eating *30 or more* different plant foods each week results in a more diverse microbiome.[15] Including a variety of whole grains, beans, fruits, vegetables, herbs, nuts, and seeds throughout the week can help you achieve this goal. Count the number of plant foods you eat during a typical week, and set a goal to try adding a few new plant foods to your diet each week.

Include probiotics in the diet

Probiotics are found in fermented foods that contain *live active cultures.* Although this label does not confirm the number or quality of organisms, it can be helpful to identify if a food contains probiotics. In addition, in the Ingredients, you might find the name of one or more genus (group) of bacteria, most commonly *Lactobacillus, Bifidobacteria,* or *Streptococcus,* which also signifies there are probiotics. Since the amount of probiotics can vary naturally in a fermented food, the best option is to eat a variety of fermented foods, and to aim to include them in your diet every day.

Not all fermented foods contain probiotics. The following fermented foods are the *most likely* to contain live active cultures:

dairy (cow, goat, sheep): yogurt, kefir, some cheeses, cultured sour cream, raw (unpasteurized) milk
non-dairy: some yogurt, kefir, or cheeses
kombucha
kimchi
raw and unfiltered apple cider vinegar
lacto-fermented pickles, sauerkraut, or other vegetables

soy foods: soy yogurt, unpasteurized tempeh, miso, tamari, natto, and fermented tofu with live active cultures

There are a few other considerations when choosing certain fermented foods, especially dairy products, pickles, and kombucha.

Conventional yogurt is made from milk that is pasteurized, which is a high-heat process that kills bacteria, both friendly and harmful. To make yogurt, live cultures are then added to ferment the pasteurized milk. However, oftentimes, a second heat process is used to treat the yogurt, killing most of the live cultures, again. Some yogurts have live cultures added in a second time, making it a good source of probiotics, and some do not. Kefir, on the other hand, is a fermented milk drink that almost always contains a good source of probiotics. Cheeses that are aged, but not heated, may contain probiotics such as cottage cheese, swiss, provolone, or feta. Other dairy products that are cultured, like sour cream or buttermilk, may contain some probiotics. However, aside from yogurt and kefir, live cultures in dairy are not as common, so review the label carefully.

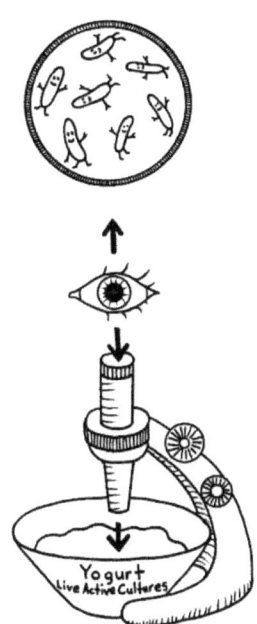

Most commercial brands of pickles and sauerkraut are made with vinegar and not fermented. If the ingredient lists vinegar and there is no label indicating live active cultures, then it will likely not be a source of probiotics. Fermented pickles, sauerkraut, kimchi and other fermented vegetables will be found in the refrigerator section of a grocery store, not on a shelf, which is another indicator that they may contain probiotics.

Kombucha, a fermented tea drink, is a good source of probiotics, but may contain a significant amount of added sugar. Often sugar is added to kombucha after fermentation to make it taste sweeter. Check the label, and choose low or no added sugar options.

It is important to note that traditional sourdough bread is a naturally fermented or leavened bread. It can be easier to digest, and may contain lower amounts of gluten. However, it does not contain live active cultures after baking, so it is not considered a probiotic food. However, if made from whole grains, it can provide prebiotics.

In addition to eating fermented foods, there are high quality probiotic supplements which provide specific strains and amounts of healthy bacteria. They may be recommended to support diets that are lacking daily fermented food and to help replenish the microbiome. In addition, they support digestion, the immune system, and can be indicated to prevent or improve many conditions.

As gut microbiome research continues, we will continue to learn more about the intricate connections between the gut and health and disease. Due to its vital role in so many systems in the body, supporting your microbiome and optimizing digestion is an important strategy for overall health.

Chapter Eight
Balancing Blood Sugar

Consider the following example of a daily routine: Sara works full-time and generally enjoys her office job in marketing even though it requires long hours and can be stressful to meet multiple deadlines. Sara begins her day by peeling herself out of bed, not feeling rested from the night before. She has to hurry out the door to get to work on time, but she does find time to make her daily stop at her favorite coffee shop for a vanilla latte and a scone. Sara looks forward to this daily ritual, not only for the energy boost she gets from the caffeine but also for the social interaction. Around 10:30 a.m., after a few hours of work, Sara feels tired, irritable, and very hungry. She usually has a granola bar to hold her over until lunch. After sitting behind a desk all morning, Sara usually walks to her building's cafeteria for lunch to grab a piece of pizza, side salad, and a diet soda. She finds her energy picks up at the lunch break. After returning to work, Sara anticipates her daily 3 p.m. energy crash and grabs an energy drink from the office kitchen to pull her through until 5 p.m. Sara looks forward to having a glass of wine with friends at the end of a packed workday. She heads home and throws a pasta dinner in the microwave while sitting down to enjoy some TV before bedtime.

Sara would say she is a relatively happy, positive person, but she would love to have more energy during the day, to sleep more deeply at night, and to lose some weight. She admits to low motivation regarding increasing daily physical activity, since she devotes most of her energy to work and to spending time with friends. Sara's story is a typical example of someone eating the Standard American Diet, which is low in nutrients and high in calories, and in her case, includes frequent consumption of caffeine and alcohol, too. Sara will likely be able to continue this routine for a few years before she becomes increasingly frustrated with her low energy, has some nagging health symptoms, and seeks medical advice. Sara can benefit from some practical support to balance her blood sugar on a daily basis.

The body works very hard to maintain blood sugar (glucose) levels within a healthy range. If the level goes too low, it is called *hypoglycemia*. This often happens when we skip meals during the day or, ironically, as a consequence of feasting on too many sweets or refined carbohydrates. Common symptoms of hypoglycemia include fatigue, irritability, foggy thinking, dizziness, and in extreme cases, fainting and loss of consciousness. On the other hand, the body can experience *hyperglycemia*, or elevated blood sugar levels, for months or years without showing any noticeable symptoms. This is another kind of danger: silently elevated blood sugar can put one at risk for insulin resistance, metabolic syndrome, prediabetes and type 2 diabetes, and heart disease. Additionally, it is difficult to maintain a healthy weight when the body is put through extended periods of either low or high blood sugar.

Blood sugar levels are influenced by food and beverage choices as well as by the interaction of several hormones. Understanding basic hormone functions in the body is an important foundation for balancing blood sugar.

Hormones 101

Insulin

The pancreas secretes insulin when blood sugar rises following a meal. Refined and simple carbohydrates cause significant glucose spikes after a meal that are especially effective at stimulating the release of insulin. When the body is balanced, insulin unlocks the door of the cells for glucose to enter from the bloodstream. When the body is imbalanced by poor dietary choices, a sedentary lifestyle, chronic stress, or medical

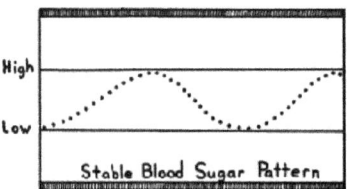

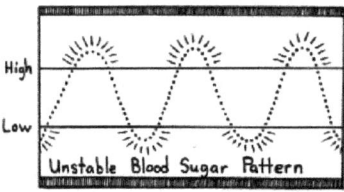

The body works very hard to maintain blood sugar (glucose) level within a healthy range. If the level goes too low, it is called hypoglycemia. *This often happens when we skip meals during the day or, ironically, as a consequence of feasting on sweets. Common symptoms of hypoglycemia include fatigue, irritability, foggy thinking, dizziness, and in extreme cases, fainting and loss of consciousness.*

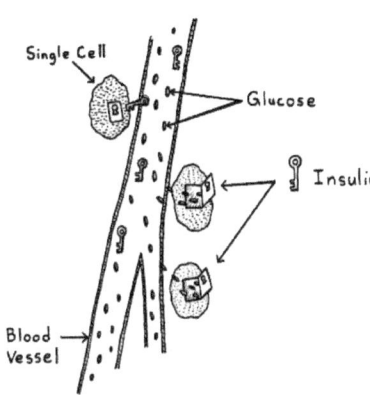

When the body is imbalanced by poor dietary choices, stress, or medical conditions such as diabetes or metabolic syndrome, the cells of the body become resistant to insulin activity. This means that insulin is at the cell to unlock its door, but it does not open. This is called insulin resistance.

conditions such as type 2 diabetes or metabolic syndrome, the cells of the body become resistant to insulin activity. This means that insulin is knocking at the cell door to unlock, but it does not open. The body will respond initially by having the pancreas secrete even more insulin, to knock louder. This is called **insulin resistance**. This condition raises the risk for prediabetes (and ultimately diabetes). Insulin resistance promotes weight gain around the abdomen, which can contribute to increased inflammation in the body and disrupts weight loss efforts.

Glucagon

The body has a buddy hormone to counterbalance insulin. In times of fasting or low blood sugar, the pancreas releases glucagon, which works to release glycogen, which is stored glucose from the liver, making it available in the bloodstream for cellular energy. The insulin-glucagon relationship represents the body's ability to maintain blood sugar balance quite well even under an episode of fasting or high-caloric feasting. If these episodes of excess or deficient caloric intake occur chronically over years, this self-regulating system begins to show signs of dysfunction.

Cortisol

Also known as the stress hormone, cortisol is secreted by the adrenal glands, which are located above each of the kidneys. Cortisol, when released during times of stress (whether physical, mental, or emotional), will cause a rise in blood sugar, which ultimately leads to an insulin response. Cortisol also decreases the effects of insulin at the cell doors, increasing the risk of insulin resistance. The effect of chronic stress on insulin resistance contributes to blood sugar dysregulation and frequently to weight gain around the midsection.

Metabolic Syndrome or Insulin Resistance Syndrome

Metabolic syndrome is considered to be a cluster of common chronic health conditions including insulin resistance, impaired glucose tolerance, abdominal obesity, reduced HDL-cholesterol, elevated triglycerides, and hypertension. Metabolic syndrome and insulin resistance often precede the development of heart disease or diabetes.

Those who are overweight or obese are at increased risk, especially those that carry extra weight specifically around their waist. While it is characterized by a dysregulation of insulin, several other hormones such as cortisol and the sex hormones (estrogen, progesterone, testosterone) can influence the development of this condition. Certain medical conditions like sleep apnea, PCOS (polycystic ovarian syndrome), and fatty liver disease, as well as the life stage of menopause increase the risk of this syndrome. The strongest dietary and lifestyle risk factors for the development of metabolic syndrome are regularly consuming an excess of refined carbohydrates and added sugar, low fiber intake, lack of physical activity, chronic stress, smoking, excess alcohol, and poor sleep quality.

Diabetes Mellitus

Diabetes mellitus is characterized by fasting hyperglycemia (elevated blood glucose) and glycosuria (spilling of excess glucose in the urine). Diabetes is a chronic disease that requires strict management and often multiple treatments, including dietary and lifestyle changes, nutritional supplements, and medication. This is not to say that the symptoms and health consequences of diabetes cannot be successfully managed, but it requires a lifetime commitment.

What To Know About Type 2 Diabetes

More than one in ten adults in the U.S. have type 2 diabetes. According to the CDC, one in three children born after the year 2000 will develop type 2 diabetes in their lifetime. Adult onset or type 2 diabetes results from abnormal pancreas function caused by insulin resistance. Type 1 diabetes differs from type 2 diabetes in that type 1 is due to an autoimmune disease that destroys the ability of the pancreas to produce insulin. People with this condition require insulin therapy.

Over time, the excess blood sugar deposits in the smallest blood vessels (the capillaries), resulting in increased risk for atherosclerosis (heart disease), nephropathy (kidney disease), retinopathy (eye disease), and neuropathy (nerve disease). Excess blood sugar also causes an increased risk of infections due to depressed immunity and poor wound healing.

Symptoms a person with type 2 diabetes may experience include polydipsia (increased thirst), polyuria (increased frequency of urination), fatigue, and eventually unexplained weight loss. Some people have diabetes and are not experiencing any symptoms at all. While the body is quick to react to significantly low blood sugar levels, years can pass before one realizes the consequences of unmanaged hyperglycemia.

Diabetes management requires regular blood glucose monitoring to measure the impact of different foods and activities on blood sugar levels. Exercise is key, as are diet, sleep, stress management, and often medications. Diagnosis can be determined by a visit to a primary care provider, who will look for:

- Elevation of fasting blood sugar above 126 mg/dl on two separate blood tests or elevation of non-fasting blood sugar above 200 mg/dl.
- Hemoglobin A1c (HbA1c) of 6.5% or higher. HbA1c is a blood test that measures average blood sugar levels over the previous three months.
- Pre-diabetes is recognized as having a fasting blood sugar over 100 mg/dl or a HbA1c between 5.7% and 6.4%.

Genetics, social and socio-economic factors, and environmental exposures do influence the prevalence of diabetes. However, by shifting lifestyle habits with a focus on exercise, diet, and weight loss if indicated, there may be up to a 60% reduction in the risk of developing diabetes.[1]

Essential Strategies To Balance Blood Sugar

The hormones discussed earlier, insulin, glucagon, and cortisol, are impacted by both behavior and lifestyle choices as well as by the foods you eat. Consider the following strategies to support balanced hormones and blood sugar.

1. Protein, Fat, and Fiber

Include slow energy sources like protein, fat, and fiber at every meal to help support healthy blood sugar levels. Together, these nutrients help to slow the absorption of simple carbohydrates in a meal, promote satiety, and support metabolism.

2. Be cautious about skipping any meals

For many adults, skipping a meal can negatively impact their blood sugar and also disrupt a sense of satiety and consistent energy throughout the day. For example, skipping breakfast and drinking only coffee or working through lunch can contribute to blood sugar dysregulation, leading to symptoms like cravings for sweets or an afternoon energy crash. Skipping a meal can also make it more difficult to consume an optimal daily intake of protein, fiber, and micronutrients that all support balanced blood sugar.

3. Break the Fast

The habit of eating breakfast can further support a healthy metabolism and sustained energy throughout the day, and may even improve resilience to stress.[2,3,4] This is especially true for children and adolescents.[5,6] Skipping breakfast can also impact the cortisol response, especially for females.[7] Refer to Chapter Ten, **Benefits of Breakfast**, for more information about the importance of this meal.

Allowing for an extended nighttime fast of at least 12 hours, meaning no caloric intake from food or beverages, is a healthy habit to develop. Beyond 12 hours of fasting, the body switches from primarily using glucose for energy to fatty acids. This metabolic switch has shown several health benefits that reduce cardiometabolic risk factors and support healthy weight management as well as gut health.[8]

4. Be Aware of Late-Night Eating

While there is no specific definition for late-night eating, it generally refers to the habit of eating dinner or calorie-rich snacks close to bedtime. Late-night eating may impair feelings of satiety and increase daytime cravings, contribute to unhealthy weight management, and increase the risk for developing diabetes.[9,10,11,12] While a person's work schedule or other time restraints can contribute to the habit of late-night eating, as can psychological factors or cultural influences, aim to eat your last meal or snack several hours before bedtime.

Late night eating may impair feelings of satiety and increase daytime cravings, contribute to unhealthy weight management, and increase the risk for developing diabetes.

5. Limit Simple Carbohydrates

Avoid or limit common refined carbohydrates that may contribute to blood sugar imbalances:

- refined grains like white pasta, white bread, white rice;
- highly processed snacks and desserts: cookies, candy, chips, pastries;
- soda, fruit juice, sweetened coffee drinks, and energy drinks;
- added sugar, honey, maple syrup, and any other added sweeteners consumed in excess (explored further in Chapter Nine, **Exploring Sweeteners**);
- alcoholic beverages.

Alcohol Drinking Patterns

Moderate Use	Heavy Use	Binge Drinking
Females: 1 or less drinks a day, 7 or less drinks in a week	Females: 8 or more drinks a week	Females: 4 or more drinks on one occasion
Males: 2 or less drinks a day, 14 or less drinks in a week	Males: 15 or more drinks a week	Males: 5 or more drinks on one occasion

A standard drink is defined as 12 ounces of beer (5% alcohol by volume), 5 ounces of wine (12% alcohol by volume), 1.5 ounces of 80-proof spirits, or 1 ounce of 100-proof spirits.[13]

The research around whether there are any health benefits attributed to alcohol intake for adults over 21-years old has been heavily scrutinized in the past several years. Alcohol is also known as ethanol, and it is a known toxin. It is produced during the fermentation process of grains and fruits. Previously, there was an understanding that *moderate* alcohol intake, as opposed to none or heavy, likely offered some degree of cardioprotective benefits, such as reduced risk of heart disease and diabetes. Current research findings are challenging those interpretations of the data regarding the benefits of moderate alcohol intake.[14]

It is clear that heavy alcohol intake is not associated with any health benefits, and reducing intake from heavy to moderate or less can lead to significant cardiovascular benefits.[15] If there are any benefits to low to moderate alcohol intake, they must be weighed against the well-known health consequences related to alcohol. Alcohol is classified as a carcinogen, meaning it is capable of causing or increasing the risk of certain cancers, including oral cancers, liver cancer, breast cancer in females, and colon cancer. Drinking just one serving of alcohol a day increases a female's risk of developing breast cancer.[16] There is no known safe amount of alcohol for pregnant women or teenagers. Other significant personal and societal consequences associated with alcohol use include alcohol use disorders and alcoholism, as well as as high blood pressure, obesity, fatty liver disease, depression, anxiety, suicide, and deadly accidents.[17] Alcohol disrupts deep, restorative sleep, which can lead to several negative health consequences.

Alcohol provides calories but no additional nutrient value and may contribute to weight gain if its impact on total daily caloric intake is not taken into consideration. The serving size, type of alcohol, and type of mixer consumed are important considerations in the context of added calories. Many mixers are high in added sugars, including tonic water, juices, sodas, and pre-mixed cocktails. See Table 8.1 to compare the serving size, alcohol content, and calories of common alcoholic beverages.

To complicate matters, there is also data to consider showing that adults who follow a traditional Mediterranean alcohol drinking *pattern*, which consists of *moderate consumption* of red wine during meals, spread out through the course of a week, and *does not* include binge drinking, have a reduction in all-cause mortality.[18] While red wine contains several phytonutrients, including resveratrol and other polyphenols, which are cardioprotective, these phytonutrients can also be consumed from non-alcoholic sources. It is generally agreed that the overall pattern of this Mediterranean dietary tradition, including the pro-social attributes, the inclusion of whole foods rich in antioxidants, and drinking the wine with a meal in moderation, are likely to be contributions to any possible health benefit.

Because of alcohol's well-known health risks and the fact that alcohol is not an essential part of a well balanced diet, limit or avoid alcohol as much as possible. If you do enjoy drinking alcohol, consider following the Mediterranean alcohol drinking pattern and choose an occasional glass of red wine with a meal with friends.

While red wine contains several phytonutrients, including resveratrol and other polyphenols, which are cardioprotective, these phytonutrients can also be consumed from non-alcoholic sources.

Table 8.1 Nutrition Values for Alcoholic Beverages and Mixes

Beverage	Serving Size (oz)	Alcohol Content (g)	Carbohydrates (g)	Calories
Regular beer	12	14	13	150
Distilled spirits, 80-proof (gin, rum, vodka, whiskey, scotch)	1.5	14	Trace	100
White wine	5	14	4	120
Red wine	5	14	4	120
Champagne	4	12	4	100
Hard Cider	12	12–16	25	200
Hard Seltzer	12	14	2	100

Alcohol content varies based on ABV, or Alcohol by Volume, which is expressed as a percentage. Caloric content may also vary.

6. Stress management

Practice stress management techniques daily, such as deep breathing, meditation, yoga, walking outside, gentle exercise, saying words of gratitude, talking with a trusted friend, or playing with a pet. These activities are time-tested lifestyle choices that help people adapt to a stressful world.

7. Move every day

Building and maintaining muscle strength is essential for maintaining insulin sensitivity and glucose regulation, not only during exercise, but all day long! Movement does not always have to mean a trip to the gym. Movement includes activities of daily living like cleaning the house, walking the dog, or playing with children. Daily movement is non-negotiable for those most at risk for pre-diabetes or those who have started to develop metabolic syndrome. Walking after meals can be especially effective for lowering post-meal glucose levels, even shorter walks of 5-10 minutes.[19] Avoid sitting for long periods of time. Interrupt every sixty minutes of sitting with a few minutes of stretching or walking. Include weight training or resistance training routines a couple times a week, such as lifting free weights or machine weights or including body weight resistance exercises like squats, lunges, and push ups, in order to maximize the impact of lean muscle on regulating blood glucose.

8. Sleep

Maintaining a healthy sleep and wake cycle is essential to health and to maintaining balanced blood sugar and hormones. Chronically disrupted sleep increases the risk for prediabetes. Aim to be in bed before midnight and to sleep for at least seven hours nightly. Sleep in a cool and very dark room. Avoid excessive caffeine during the day, and avoid eating meals and drinking alcohol close to bedtime.

9. Stay hydrated

It is possible to think you are hungry when you are actually thirsty. A good guideline is to drink half your body weight (in pounds) in ounces of water daily. If you have been diagnosed with heart or kidney disease, check with your doctor before significantly increasing water intake.

10. Tips and Tricks

Finally, the following nutrition tips may be included as part of comprehensive approach to balancing blood sugar, reducing risk of prediabetes, and improving post-meal glucose control:

- Add 1-2 tablespoons of apple cider vinegar along with 1 tablespoon of extra virgin olive oil to a meal.[20]
- Eat ¼ cup of nuts a day.[21]
- Include ½ teaspoon of cinnamon in meals and beverages.[22,23]
- Food order matters. Eat your protein and veggies first! [24,25]

Making lifestyle changes takes time and commitment, as well as constant inspiration and motivation. Surround yourself with positive people who will support you along the way.

Table 8.2 Important Nutrients and Their Food Sources for Blood Sugar Regulation

Nutrient	Function	Food Sources
Vitamin C	Influences collagen production, wound healing, immune function, and serves as a potent antioxidant.	Broccoli, bell peppers, citrus fruit, Brussel sprouts, strawberries
Vitamin D	Supports a healthy immune response and bone health, reduces insulin resistance, provides benefit to cardiovascular health.	Fish and cod liver oil, fortified dairy, mushrooms, and sunshine—the best non-food source
Zinc	Aids in wound healing, supports a healthy immune response and insulin function.	Oysters and other seafood, red meat, poultry, legumes, nuts, pumpkin seeds
Chromium	Improves insulin sensitivity.	Broccoli, tomatoes, romaine lettuce, green beans, whole grains (bran), brewer's yeast
Omega-3 Fatty Acids	Anti-inflammatory, incorporated into cell membranes, supports insulin function.	Fish and cod liver oil, pasture-raised meat, poultry and eggs, wild game, ground flaxseed, chia seeds, walnuts, hemp seeds
Antioxidants	Reduces oxidative damage and improves vascular health.	Blueberries, all brightly colored fruits and vegetables, tea, coffee, dark chocolate

Chapter Nine
Exploring Sweeteners

It is not surprising that Americans are over-consuming added sugar. Humans have a built-in desire for sweet food, and there is an abundance of cheap, added sugars in today's food supply. It is well established that the excess consumption of sugar is contributing to obesity, heart disease, diabetes, dental cavities, decreased immune function, and other metabolic disorders.

Added sugar in food or drinks contributes to the intake of discretionary calories, which are calories that are not essential to provide energy or nutrients for the body. The body doesn't need added sugar in the diet, so aiming to limit or avoid added sugar on a daily basis and saving it for rare occasions is ideal. In the Nutrition Facts section of a food label, Total Sugar will include both naturally occurring and added sugar. Added sugars will be listed separately on the label and does not include the natural sugars found in whole foods and unprocessed whole fruit, vegetables, and dairy.

In addition to identifying the amount of added sugar, it is important to identify the source of the added sugars. For that information, you should read the ingredient list. It is not as easy as simply looking for the word 'sugar.' Here are some additional ingredients found on labels that indicate that there are added sugars:

> **INGREDIENTS:** AGAVE, BROWN SUGAR, CANE CRYSTALS, CANE JUICE, CANE SUGAR, CORN SWEETENER, CORN SYRUP, CRYSTALLINE FRUCTOSE, DEXTROSE, EVAPORATED CANE JUICE, FRUCTOSE, FRUIT JUICE CONCENTRATES, GLUCOSE, HIGH- FRUCTOSE CORN SYRUP, HONEY, INVERT SUGAR, LACTOSE, MALTOSE, MALT SYRUP, MOLASSES, RAW SUGAR, SUCROSE, SUGAR, SYRUP, COCONUT SUGAR, DATE SUGAR, PALM SUGAR

The American Heart Association recommends that females consume less than six teaspoons of added sugar a day and that males consume less than nine teaspoons of added sugar a day.

The most common products with added sugar include beverages such as soda, juice, energy drinks, and sweetened coffee drinks, in addition to sweets such as cookies, pastries, candy, and ice cream. However, added sugar is also found in many processed foods including cereal, granola bars, breads, peanut butter, yogurt, salad dressing, condiments, and sauces. It is helpful to have a reference point for an upper limit of added sugar intake. The American Heart Association (AHA) recommends that females consume less than 6 teaspoons of added sugar a day and that males consume less than 9 teaspoons of added sugar a day.

While teaspoons are a great visual when measuring sugar at home, food labels present sugar in grams and calories. Remember this approximate measurement: 1 teaspoon of sugar = 4 grams = 15 calories. Another helpful visual reference is that a packet of sugar contains 1 teaspoon of sugar, or 4 grams, or 15 calories.

The AHA recommendations can be converted into the following approximate amounts:

6 teaspoons = 25 grams of sugar = 100 calories

9 teaspoons = 36 grams =150 calories

As for children and teenagers in the U.S., the amount of added sugar consumed daily is staggering. The National Health and Nutrition Examination Survey (NHANES) found that on average, children aged 2–5 years consume 12 teaspoons of sugar a day, children aged 6–11 years consume 17 teaspoons, and adolescents aged 12–19 years consume 18 teaspoons (more than 1/3 cup!) a day.[1] Sugar-sweetened beverages are the main culprit to this shocking finding. Beverages such as juice, soda, sports drinks, energy drinks, sweetened tea, and coffee drinks have been linked to weight gain in both children and adults. After sweetened beverages, the top sources of added sugars for children and teens are sweet pastries, candy, desserts, and sweetened cereal.[2,3]

For children and teens, aiming for less than 10% of daily caloric intake from added sugar is a good starting place. However, because children and teens vary widely in their caloric needs based on size, development, activity level, and growth rate, this can be a challenging number to calculate. The less added sugar the better, so aiming for less than 6 teaspoons a day, or about 25 grams, is a reasonable starting place, especially when considering teenagers are getting close to 20 teaspoons of added sugar daily.

To make sense of the upper limit recommendation when looking at a food label, see the following examples. You may be surprised at how much added sugar is in commonly consumed beverages! Notice how one drink can contain double or even triple the daily recommended limit of added sugar.

Coca-Cola®

12 ounces: 39 grams sugar or 10 teaspoons

Mountain Dew®

20 ounces: 77 grams sugar or 19 teaspoons

Blue Sky® Natural Soda, Cherry Vanilla Cream

12 ounces: 46 grams sugar or 11 teaspoons

Vitaminwater™ Orange-Orange

20 ounces: 32.5 grams sugar or 8 teaspoons

Washington Natural Apple Juice®

16 ounces: 56 grams sugar or 14 teaspoons

Starbucks™ Pumpkin Spice Frappuccino

16 ounces: 65 grams sugar or 16 teaspoons

Gatorade® Cool Blue Sports Drink

20 ounces: 34 grams sugar or 8.5 teaspoons

Pure Leaf Sweet Tea®

18.5 ounces: 42 grams sugar or 10.5 teaspoons

When choosing beverages, it is common to be distracted by the words *natural* or *organic* on a label and to assume incorrectly that it is lower in added sugar. Popular vitamin drinks may have added some extra vitamins, but generally, one of these drinks will put most people above the recommended upper limit of added sugar for the day. 100% fruit juice can provide some important vitamins and antioxidants; however, with the loss of the fiber from the whole fruit, the juice becomes a source of added sugar, one that is very high in fructose. As for soda and energy drinks, the negative effects of the added sweeteners will likely exceed any nutritional benefit of added supplemental vitamins and minerals.

Although the intake of soda has been slowly decreasing in the U.S. since the early 2000s, the intake of sugar-sweetened coffee and tea drinks, energy drinks, and sports drinks has been increasing.[4,5] With larger portion sizes, vending machines everywhere, coffee shops on every corner, and free refills, it is easy to create a society of sweetened beverage drinkers.

Sweetened beverages can significantly add to daily caloric intake while adding little to healthy nutrition in the daily diet. Therefore, limiting or avoiding these beverages is a great way to quickly reduce added sugar in the diet.

More Reasons To Reduce or Avoid Sugar-Sweetened Beverages

Two common sources of added sugar in beverages, refined sugar (table sugar) and high-fructose corn syrup, are composed of different amounts of glucose and fructose, which each affect the metabolism differently. Refined sugar contains sucrose, which consists of 50% glucose and 50% fructose. High-fructose corn syrup (HFCS) contains slightly more fructose than glucose, or 45% glucose and 55% fructose. Glucose directly affects blood sugar regulation and insulin response. Fructose is metabolized in the liver. When consumed in excess, it stimulates energy storage through triglyceride formation, a type of fat that

> *When choosing beverages, it is common to be distracted by the words natural or organic on a label and to assume incorrectly that it is lower in added sugar. Popular vitamin drinks may have added some extra vitamins, but generally, one of these drinks will put most people above the recommended upper limit of added sugar for the day.*

when elevated is a risk factor for heart disease and increases the risk of fatty liver disease.[6] High added sugar intake, in the form of both glucose and fructose, increases the risk of obesity, heart disease, diabetes, and some cancers.[7,8] Here are some additional reasons to limit or avoid added sugar in beverages:

- Excessive intake of soda is associated with an increased risk of osteoporosis and bone fractures in adults. This seems to be partly due to the combination of the added sugar, phosphoric acid, caffeine, and acidity that impacts calcium absorption.[9,10]
- Give the liver a break. The excess intake of sugar-sweetened beverages is strongly associated with the development of non-alcoholic fatty liver disease, or NAFLD, which is a buildup of fat in the liver that can impair its normal functions and increases the risk of heart disease and diabetes.[11]
- Drinking sugar-sweetened beverages can lead to tooth erosion and dental cavities.[12]
- Sweetened beverage consumption distracts people from good hydration. Water is often neglected in place of soda and juices.
- In addition to the added sugars, many drinks contain chemical additives, artificial colors, flavors, preservatives, and caffeine. Additionally, ultra-processed sweeteners, such as HFCS, are often made from genetically modified corn.

Challenge yourself to go an entire week without any sugar-sweetened beverages. Notice if you then drink more water, if sugar cravings decrease, or if you observe other physical or mental changes.

Here are some low- or no-sugar alternatives to sugar-sweetened beverages:

hot or iced herbal teas, such as mint, chamomile, or hibiscus,

water with cucumber, mint, or rosemary,

green or black tea, or black coffee,

water with a squeeze of lemon, lime, or orange,

sparkling or mineral water with lemon, lime, orange, or berries,

plain coconut water,

apple cider vinegar drinks,

kombucha,

sodas or juices partially or fully sweetened with stevia or monk fruit,

diluted fruit juice with at least 50% water, and

pure water.

Natural Versus Added Sugar

Yogurt is a common food that contains both naturally occurring sugars, primarily lactose, and may also contain added sugars such as cane sugar or high-fructose corn syrup. A small, 6-ounce container of plain, unsweetened yogurt (Label 1) shows 7 grams of total sugar on the label, with no added sugar. This means that the 7 grams of sugar is from the naturally occurring milk sugars and not considered added sugar in the diet.

Label 1

Nutrition Facts
Serving size 6 oz (170g)

Amount Per Serving
Calories 120

% Daily Value*
Total Fat 0g	0%
Saturated Fat 0g	0%
Trans Fat 0g	
Cholesterol 10mg	3%
Sodium 55mg	2%
Total Carbohydrate 8g	3%
Dietary Fiber 0g	0%
Total Sugars 7g	
Includes 0g Added Sugars	0%
Protein 22g	44%
Vitamin D 0mcg	0%
Calcium 260mg	20%
Iron 0mg	0%
Potassium 240mg	6%

* The % Daily Value (DV) tells you how much a nutrient in a serving of food contributes to a daily diet. 2,000 calories a day is used for general nutrition advice.

Label 2

Nutrition Facts
Serving size 1 container

Amount per serving
Calories 150

% Daily Value*
Total Fat 2g	3%
Saturated Fat 1.5g	6%
Trans Fat 0g	
Cholesterol 10mg	3%
Sodium 90mg	4%
Total Carbohydrate 28g	10%
Total Sugars 20g	
Includes 14g Added Sugars	28%
Protein 6g	

Vit. D 3mcg 15% • Calcium 260mg 20%
Potas. 270mg 6% • Vit. A 180mcg 20%
Not a significant source of dietary fiber and iron.

* The % Daily Value (DV) tells you how much a nutrient in a serving of food contributes to a daily diet. 2,000 calories a day is used for general nutrition advice.

On the other hand, a vanilla-flavored container of yogurt (Label 2) shows 20 grams of total sugar, with 14 grams from added sugar, which means 6 grams are naturally occuring. That means there are almost 4 teaspoons of added sugar in the 6 ounce container. Because flavored yogurts tend to have a lot of added sugar, we suggest choosing plain yogurt and adding your own chopped fruits, nuts, vanilla extract, cinnamon, and possibly a small amount (1 teaspoon or less) of honey or maple syrup, if needed. This small change can reduce your added sugar intake by over 3 teaspoons. Also, plain greek yogurt (Label 1), which is a strained and thicker yogurt, will contain more protein, 22 grams versus 6 grams.

Exploring Sweeteners

Nature has provided many naturally-occurring sweet foods: vegetables like carrots, bell peppers, sweet potatoes, squash, and snap peas; spices like cinnamon; and of course, the wide variety of available fruits. There is also the option of choosing small amounts of minimally processed sweeteners, such as raw honey, or using alternatives such as stevia or monk fruit when cooking and purchasing food. It is important to consider the amount, quality, and sourcing of the sweetener you choose. Let's explore some of the most common sweeteners:

High-Fructose Corn Syrup (HFCS) is a commonly used, ultra-processed sweetener, which is added to many sugar-sweetened beverages, including soda, juice, and energy drinks. It is also added to many processed foods, including salad dressings, bread, processed pastries, desserts, cereal, and candy. It is a cheap sweetener, hence its high prevalence in ultra-processed foods. However, even if you avoid high-fructose corn syrup and choose less-processed sweeteners like cane sugar or maple syrup, you can still be at risk for the same health consequences of consuming too much sugar in the diet. Ultimately, all added sugar will contribute to excess calories and increased risk of weight gain and diabetes.

Honey is a nutritious sweetener that provides a trace amount of vitamins, minerals, antioxidants, and enzymes. Produced by bees who feed on the nectar from flowers, honey contains both fructose and glucose. Commercial, store-bought honey is often heated, pasteurized, and filtered to make the honey more smooth and clear in the bottle. Raw, unfiltered honey, which hasn't been heated, preserves more of the phytonutrients and enzymes that make honey medicinal. Check your farmers' markets and neighborhood grocers for organic, local, raw honey. Children under 1 year old should not be given honey.

Agave nectar can be made from several species of agave that grow in North and South America, including *Agave tequiliana, the* same plant from which tequila is made. Agave nectar was initially thought to be a good alternative for those with blood sugar issues because of its lower level of glucose. However, because it consists of up to 75% fructose, anyone with concerns regarding liver health or triglyceride level should use agave nectar with caution. In addition, although it does come from a plant and is considered a natural sweetener, agave nectar often undergoes extensive processing.

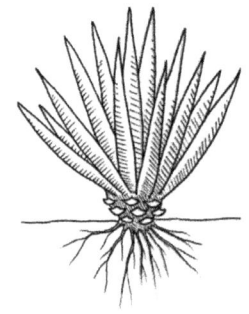

Maple syrup is the collected sap from sugar maple trees, which is then boiled and reduced to create a rich syrup. It is a combination of glucose and sucrose, making it a relatively low fructose sweetener, with trace amounts of potassium, zinc, magnesium, manganese, calcium, and amino acids. On the other hand, "table syrup" is made of highly processed sweeteners, often high-fructose corn syrup. Notice that real maple syrup costs significantly more than the highly processed table syrup. It may take up to 43 gallons of collected sap to make one gallon of syrup!

Cane Sugar comes from the tall, perennial grass native to the Southern tropic regions. It naturally contains sucrose, and in addition to beet sugar, is a main source of refined sugar. Several other sweeteners are derived from the cane plant, including brown sugar, which is refined sugar with some molasses added to provide both color and flavor. Turbinado sugar and evaporated cane juice are minimally processed sweeteners that are crystallized sugar cane juice. Rapadura, also known as sucanat, is made from unrefined whole cane sugar, thus retaining all of the molasses. Molasses is a thick, dark syrup that is removed during the creation of many of the sugars listed above. Molasses can be used as a mild sweetener and provides vitamins and minerals such as iron, calcium, magnesium, and potassium.

Beet sugar, in addition to cane sugar, is another source of refined sugar. Sugar beets are a very sweet root vegetable that naturally contain sucrose and can be grown in more temperate climates, including the U.S. Almost all (about 95%) of the sugar beets grown in the U.S. are genetically modified.[13] Sugar labels may not always indicate if the sugar was sourced from beet sugar or cane sugar.

There are several other sweeteners derived from natural sources, such as **coconut sugar, palm sugar, date sugar, rice syrup,** and even **yacon syrup** which is made from a sweet root vegetable native to the Andes Mountain region. They may all add a distinct flavor or texture for different recipes. While some of these sweeteners may be less processed and contain some additional nutritional value, they should still be limited.

Sugar Alternatives

Stevia is from the leaves of the native South American plant, *Stevia rebaudiana*, commonly referred to as sweet leaf. It is calorie-free and does not contain any sugar. It contains a natural chemical, called glycoside, that creates a strong, sweet reaction on the taste buds, but it does not significantly impact glucose or insulin levels. Therefore, it can safely be used by people with diabetes and blood glucose dysregulation. It is much sweeter to the taste than sugar, so very little is needed in drinks and food. Be sure to check the label for 100% stevia. Some commercially produced stevia products may be combined with dextrose or maltodextrin, which can impact blood sugar, in addition to other additives and fillers. Stevia is also being used as a sugar alternative to make calorie-free sodas and beverages without artificial sweeteners.

Sugar Alcohols include erythritol, xylitol, sorbitol, and mannitol. Small amounts of sugar alcohol are found in raw fruits and vegetables and normally pose no health concerns in this natural state. Sugar alcohols contain very few calories but may be poorly absorbed by the body, potentially causing digestive symptoms. Xylitol has been shown to be protective against cavities and is commonly used in toothpastes and chewing gum for this reason. Erythritol is also found naturally in some fruits, but in the food industry, it is often produced by fermenting the glucose from corn, for example. Erythritol is better absorbed than other sugar alcohols, causing less potential digestive distress, and may be found in "sugar free" drinks and foods. Recently, their safety has come into question with a small study suggesting that elevated blood levels of sugar alcohols may be correlated with an increased risk of cardiovascular events.[14] However, additional research will be needed to understand if this potential risk relates to dietary intake or the natural production of sugar alcohols in the body.

Monk Fruit, also known as Luo Han Guo, is a small, green melon that comes from the fruit of the *Siraitia grosvenorii* plant, native to southern China. The sweet taste comes from mogrosides, an antioxidant in the fruit. Dried monk fruit skin is used traditionally in herbal teas and soups. Monk fruit sweeteners are made by extracting the juice and antioxidants from the monk fruit, which can be made into a liquid sweetener or dried into a powder. Monk fruit sweeteners contain no calories and do not significantly impact glucose or insulin. Commercial products may be combined with erythritol or stevia in some cases.

Allulose is a sugar found in small amounts in fruits like raisin and figs, brown sugar, maple syrup, and wheat. However, the commercial allulose products are not derived from these plants but rather produced artificially through a chemical process that converts sugars into allulose. It is a low calorie sweetener that is less sweet than sugar and does not significantly impact glucose or insulin.

Artificial Sweeteners

Artificial sweeteners are chemical additives that are considered ultra-processed and made to mimic sugar, without the added calories. Artificial sweeteners are sometimes hundreds of times sweeter than table sugar. They are most commonly found in diet soda, sugar-free energy drinks, coffee syrups, and sugar-free gum, but could also be in any product labeled "sugar free," "zero-sugar," or "diet." Many people choose food and drinks with artificial sweeteners to reduce added sugar in the diet. However, long term consumption of artificial sweeteners is associated with an increased risk of obesity, diabetes, heart disease, and all-cause mortality.[15] Unfortunately, many people are choosing to drink artificial sweeteners thinking it may help to prevent these diseases.

Currently, the FDA does not recommend reducing or avoiding artificial sweeteners in the diet. There have been animal research studies observing the relationship of artificial sweeteners and increased risk of cancer, but studies in humans have been inconclusive.[16] However, because they are linked to increased risk of chronic diseases and are chemical additives found in ultra-processed foods, many health professionals and organizations, including the World Health Organization, recommend limiting or avoiding artificial sweeteners.[17]

It is important to become familiar with the common artificial sweeteners found in our food supply.

Saccharin (Sweet N Low®) is about 300 times sweeter than sucrose (table sugar) and has a bitter aftertaste.

Acesulfame potassium (Equal®), another artificial sweetener that resembles saccharin in structure and taste, is found in many diet foods and chewing gum.

Aspartame (NutraSweet® and Equal®) must be avoided for people with phenylketonuria because of their inability to safely metabolize the chemical.

Sucralose (Splenda®) is considered an organochlorine. Other organochlorines include chemicals such as DDT (dichloro-diphenyl-trichloroethane) and PCBs (polychlorinated biphenyls), two pesticides that have been banned due to their negative impacts on human health. Splenda® is made from sucrose with the addition of chlorine, generating 600 times the sweetness of sugar.

Is Diet Soda Better For Weight Loss?

Diet sodas are commonly sweetened with the artificial sweeteners listed above. Drinking diet soda may, in the short term, decrease daily caloric intake. However, the majority of studies show that artificial sweeteners are not beneficial for long-term weight loss and are associated with weight gain and increased risk of cardiometabolic disease. Unfortunately, there is no definitive understanding on why or how a no-calorie artificial sweetener is linked with weight gain and blood sugar imbalances. Some studies suggest artificial sweeteners increase blood sugar levels through changes in the gut microbiome, or that the

Drinking diet soda may, in the short term, decrease daily caloric intake. However, the majority of studies show that artificial sweeteners are not beneficial for long-term weight loss, and are associated with weight gain and increased risk of cardiometabolic disease.

sweet taste of the artificial sweeteners can possibly still impact the body's perception that there is sugar or glucose present.[18] The best strategy would be to decrease any regular consumption of both sugar-sweetened and artificial sweetened beverages and keep them for rare occasions.

> *The FAME series and Dr. Briley weaned me off my diet soda habit. Learning how unhealthy it is for people was very thought-provoking and made me seriously question the value of having it in my home and on the road, enough so to quit the habit.*
>
> —Scott, FAME Series, Charlee's Kitchen

Chapter Ten

Benefits Of Breakfast

We started eating oatmeal every morning and cutting out the sugary cereals. My husband started feeling more energized and more refreshed for his long days of work and school. Oatmeal is now his favorite breakfast.

—Christine, ECO project, Mt. Olivet

THE WORD *BREAKFAST* IS A COMPOUND OF *BREAK* AND *FAST*, DESCRIBING IN ITSELF THE END OF A FAST (ABSTINENCE FROM FOOD or drink) from the night before. A healthy habit is to fast for at least 12 hours between dinner and breakfast. When breakfast is skipped, the fast is lengthened, as are the potential negative side effects of prolonged fasting, which can include blood sugar instability, fatigue, mood changes, and headaches, including migraines.[1] Eating within one to two hours of waking is ideal, to promote a healthier stress response (especially in females), and to jump-start metabolism.[2,3,4,5] While breaking a fast has numerous noted health benefits, it is equally important to have a fast to break: this means avoiding late night eating and snacking. Several studies have shown negative health effects associated with the habit of late night eating, including weight gain, impaired weight loss, and increased risk of cardiometabolic disease.[6]

The habit of eating breakfast can provide numerous benefits for adults:

- Decreased risk of heart disease[7]
- Decreased risk of developing type 2 diabetes[8]

  People who eat breakfast tend to manifest healthier eating patterns for the remainder of the day, decreasing their risk of developing blood sugar imbalances over time.

- Successful maintenance of weight loss

  Eating breakfast is a key habit for people who have achieved long-term, successful weight loss.[9,10]

- Improved memory and stress tolerance[2,11]
- Improved mood—specifically reduced risk of depression[12]

Skipping breakfast can contribute to feelings of fatigue, irritability, or sadness. The body is built to regulate blood sugar levels to the brain, but after a long night of fasting, your brain may not get the fuel it needs to function optimally. Fatigue and irritability may be a sign of low blood sugar. Support your brain by loading up on healthy morning fuels: protein, fats, and fiber-rich foods.

What about Intermittent Fasting?

Intermittent fasting (IF) can be defined as periods of fasting (either completely abstaining or strictly limiting caloric intake) in combination with periods of unrestricted eating. The most common forms of IF are alternate-day fasting (0-500 calories on days of fasting and unrestricted eating on other days), the 5:2 diet (two days of fasting with five days of unrestricted eating), and time-restricted eating (eating for a period of 6-10 hours in a day and then avoiding caloric intake the other hours of the day). The health benefits seem to arise from the reduced caloric intake these dietary patterns create and not necessarily the specific pattern of IF. Research has shown benefits for weight loss in adults with prediabetes, type 2 diabetes, and obesity. One of

The most common forms of IF are alternate-day fasting (0-500 calories on days of fasting and unrestricted eating on other days), the 5:2 diet (two days of fasting with five days of unrestricted eating), and time-restricted eating (eating for a period of 6-10 hours in a day and then avoiding caloric intake the other hours of the day).

> the limitations of this type of research is the short-term nature of the studies and whether this type of eating pattern is sustainable over time.[13,14,15] Because there are also known benefits for eating breakfast and maintaining meal regularity, and because skipping meals can increase the risk of inadequate macro and micronutrient intake, intermittent fasting should be considered on an individual basis and ideally with the support of a qualified healthcare provider.

Breakfast And Children

If you have or care for children, there are many reasons to be a good role model and to encourage them to enjoy a healthy meal in the morning. Lack of breakfast or a nutrient-poor breakfast may result in a nutritionally inadequate diet for some children, negatively influencing learning and health in a number of ways.

Consider these reasons for kids to eat a well-balanced, daily breakfast:[16,17,18]

- Improved nutritional intake, including important minerals and vitamins

  Breakfast provides a strong foundation for healthy children to grow into healthy adults.

- Improved alertness and mood at school
- Reduced risk of developing obesity, diabetes, and cardiovascular disease.

Building The Habit Of Eating Breakfast

These strategies will help you to incorporate this incredibly healthy behavior into your life.

- Go to bed 15 minutes earlier and wake up 15 minutes earlier in the morning so that there is extra time to prepare breakfast.
- Make extra dinner the night before or package up leftovers to eat the next morning.
- Plan ahead for the week. Have quick protein options on hand

like Greek yogurt, cottage cheese, turkey bacon, or smoothie ingredients. Prepare overnight oats, chia seed pudding, or hard-boiled eggs for the week.

- Remember, eating something quick and healthy is better than eating nothing. If you have to grab-and-go, consider a handful of nuts and a piece of fruit, a cup of warmed bone broth, or a couple of hard-boiled eggs until you can eat a more complete meal.

Healthy Breakfast Options

Now, let's list some examples of a healthy, balanced breakfast. Remember that protein, fat, and fiber provide slower energy sources compared to refined carbohydrates or heavily sweetened foods. Think of how common it is to see people eating on the go for breakfast with refined carbs, such as a bagel or pastry, and a coffee (often with added sugar). It is not surprising that many people feel a mid-morning or mid-afternoon crash in energy due to their morning fuel choices.

The following healthy breakfast options include 20–30 grams of protein as well as healthy fat and fiber. If your breakfast has usually been made with sweeter foods, then we encourage some experimentation with more savory options.

- Three **scrambled eggs** cooked in healthy fats (extra virgin olive oil, avocado oil, or butter) with your favorite veggies such as spinach, tomatoes, and garlic. (See recipe, **Egg and Veggie Scramble.**)
- Two-thirds cup of **unsweetened Greek yogurt** with berries, 1 tablespoon of ground flaxseed or chia seed, 1 teaspoon of honey, and 2 tablespoons of slivered almonds.
- Two-thirds cup of **low-fat cottage cheese** with sliced tomatoes, basil, green onions, and 1–2 tablespoons of sunflower or hemp seeds.
- Two slices of **100% whole grain toast** (containing 4–5 grams of protein per slice) with 2 tablespoons of almond butter, 2 tablespoons of pumpkin seeds, 1–2 teaspoons of honey (optional), and some apple slices.

- Two slices of **100% whole grain toast** (containing 4–5 grams of protein per slice) with two fried or scrambled eggs and avocado slices.
- **Oatmeal** (½ cup dried oatmeal, cooked in 1 cup unsweetened dairy, pea, or soy milk) with 2 tablespoons of almond butter or ¼ cup nuts, 1 tablespoon of ground flaxseed or chia seed, and your favorite fruit. (See recipe, **Not Just Oatmeal**.)
- Have **dinner leftovers** for breakfast! This may include 3–4 ounces of cooked chicken, fish, or beef with steamed veggies or a quinoa and bean bowl with cheese and sliced avocado.
- Two slices of **turkey bacon** with two fried eggs and sautéed vegetables in extra virgin olive oil and a piece of fruit.
- **Chia seed pudding** made with unsweetened dairy, pea, or soy milk and with ¼ cup chopped nuts and fruit. (See recipe, **Chia Seed Pudding**.)
- **Smoothies** with frozen berries, dark greens, and Greek yogurt or your preferred protein powder. (See recipe, **Breakfast Smoothie**.)

Enjoy breakfast!

Chapter Eleven

Habits For Health

IN ADDITION TO A NUTRITIOUS DIET, A HEALTHY LIFE IS BUILT UPON A COMBINATION OF HEALTHY HABITS. CONSIDER THE following aspects of a person's lifestyle and how they affect health and well-being: family, friends, sense of community, spirituality, recreation, time in nature, fulfilling work or career, service, play, and laughter. All of these are important to cultivate in addition to the Habits For Health we will discuss here: water, sleep, mindful breathing, movement, and social connection.

Water

The body is composed of 60% to 70% water. Water is essential for human life and helps the body detoxify and eliminate waste, improve circulation and metabolism, maintain alertness, regulate body temperature, and protect and support joints and organs. Symptoms such as fatigue, mental fogginess, headaches, muscle cramps, constipation, and dry skin can be improved and even solved with better hydration.

Water is lost through breathing, sweating, urination, and bowel movements. Food can provide about 20% of your total fluid intake, especially from water-rich fruits and vegetables like cucumbers, tomatoes, and watermelon. The rest must come from the water and fluids you consume. While there is no strict rule for how much water a person needs, a common recommendation is based on body size: as mentioned earlier, drink half your body weight, measured in pounds, in ounces of water each day. For example, if you weigh 150 pounds, you would aim for 75 ounces of water a day. With exercise, pregnancy, illness, and breastfeeding, more water intake is necessary. Consider drinking eight additional ounces with every 30 minutes of exercise. In addition, another simple way to assess if you are well-hydrated is to consider the amount and color of your urine. After your first morning urine, the urine should be pale yellow and clear for the remainder of the day.

Many people are using electrolytes or water enhancers to increase or improve hydration. Electrolytes include minerals such as sodium, chloride, potassium, calcium, magnesium, and phosphate that help maintain the fluid balance in the body. Electrolyte powders and drinks vary widely, and many have significant amounts of added sugar with low amounts of electrolytes, and they may contain chemical additives. If needed, choose a low or no-sugar electrolyte product, and read the label to understand the amount and type of minerals included. However, for most people, sufficient electrolytes are consumed through a diverse diet of whole foods, especially fruits and vegetables. Plain coconut water is also a great source of naturally-occurring electrolytes.

People need access to clean, safe water. Public water systems will make drinking water safe for consumption, but often the water still contains certain chemicals like chlorine, ammonia, and fluoride. Additionally, trace amounts of pesticides, herbicides, pharmaceutical medications, and harmful minerals, such as lead, can make their way into drinking water. The U.S. Environmental Protection Agency sets the standard for limits on contaminants in water for public safety. Keep in mind, consuming bottled water will cost extra money and create more waste without necessarily making your water safer. In addition, the plastic from the bottle can leach additional chemicals into the water including BPA (an endocrine disruptor), microplastics, and nanoplastics. Bottled water is the largest source of ingested microplastics in the diet and contains 22 times more microplastics than tap water.[1,2]

We recommend accessing information about your local drinking water, including where the water is sourced, and the amount of mineral content, including chlorine and fluoride. Consider using a home

If you weigh 150 pounds, you would aim for 75 ounces of water a day. With exercise, pregnancy, illness, and breast-feeding, more water intake is necessary. Consider drinking eight additional ounces with every 30 minutes of exercise.

water filtration unit to help minimize some of the contaminants found in drinking water, including chemicals, heavy metals, microorganisms, and microplastics. Filters can range from pitchers to full home systems using technology such as activated carbon, carbon or ceramic block filters, or reverse osmosis, for example.

What are microplastics?

Microplastics are very small pieces of plastic, less than 5mm, that typically come from the breakdown of larger plastic items, including plastic food packaging, synthetic clothing, car tires, microbeads (used in cosmetic products, some of which are now banned), and from plastic manufacturing. Nanoplastics are even smaller pieces of plastic that are not visible to the naked eye. Microplastics and nanoplastics are ubiquitous in the environment, found in the air, soil, and water. Animals and humans are exposed to these contaminants through the ingestion of food and water that contain microplastics, inhalation, and absorption through the skin. Microplastics have the ability to accumulate in the human body and have been found in the lungs, liver, spleen, colon, blood, placenta, and in feces and breast milk. However, the long term impacts of these accumulated microplastics are not well understood and are currently being studied by government, environmental, and health organizations.[3,4] We recommend limiting your intake of water and other beverages in plastic bottles when possible and generally aiming to reduce overall use of plastics.

Sleep

Sleep is essential to good health. While sleeping, the body recovers from the stress of the day. The immune system becomes active to help fight off infections and to help the body detoxify. Good quality sleep is essential for growth, energy, mood, weight management, memory and brain function, blood sugar balancing, stress management, and heart health. Most adults need around seven to nine hours of sleep a night, while young children and teenagers need more. For children ages 6–12, 9–12 hours is recommended, and for teens ages 13–18, 8–10 hours is recommended. Sleep deprivation is very common in this age group, and it is estimated that more than 70% of adolescents get less than eight hours of sleep a night. Some of the contributing factors include hormonal changes, excessive screen time, early start times at school, extracurricular activities and busy schedules, and caffeine intake.[5]

Insomnia is a form of sleep disturbance characterized by difficulty falling asleep, staying asleep, or waking up too early that results in the impairment of normal daytime functioning. Up to 30% of the U.S. population may suffer from insomnia. Females report more sleep abnormalities than males. Additionally, people tend to report increased insomnia with advanced age. This may be due to changes in the circadian rhythm and sleep cycles as we age, in addition to certain health conditions, medications, and lifestyle factors.

Chronic insomnia is associated with an increased risk of obesity, insulin resistance, and type 2 diabetes. Sleep deprivation leads to an increase in a hormone called ghrelin, which increases hunger and can lead to cravings for carbohydrates. It also leads to an increase in the stress hormone cortisol, which impacts blood sugar balance, and over time can also contribute to insulin resistance and weight gain.[6] Working toward optimizing sleep is essential to support a healthy metabolism.

Here are some strategies to help achieve optimal, restorative sleep:

- **Create a routine around sleep and wake cycles**. This will help you get the most benefits for your health. Go to sleep at a consistent time every night, optimally before midnight, and wake at the same time every morning.
- **Sleep in a cool, dark room**. Melatonin is a hormone that supports healthy sleep and is activated by the brain during darkness. To promote healthy melatonin production, sleep in a completely dark room, and use a sleep mask or black out curtain if needed. In addition, having exposure to bright, natural light during the day for at least 15 to 20 minutes will also help support melatonin production at night.

Sleep is essential to good health. While sleeping, the body recovers from the stress of the day. The immune system becomes active to help fight off infections and to help the body detoxify. Good quality sleep is essential for growth, energy, mood, weight management, memory and brain function, blood sugar balancing, and heart health.

- **Avoid screens before bed.** Screen use before bed is associated with difficulty falling asleep, reduced sleep time and quality, and daytime fatigue.[7] Limit or avoid electronics at least one hour before bed. Additionally, dim your bright house lights in the evening, and reduce the blue light settings on computers and phones, or use blue light blocking filters or glasses. Replace evening screen time with other calming activities, such as reading, stretching, meditation, journaling, or other self-care practices.
- **Avoid caffeine after noon.** Some people may need to avoid caffeine entirely. The effects of caffeine can last up to ten hours for some people. Sources of caffeine include sodas, energy drinks, black or green tea, chocolate, and some over-the-counter drugs.
- **Avoid alcohol.** A glass of wine or a beer may seem to initially aid sleep, but alcohol disrupts the brain's ability to enter deeper levels of restorative sleep.
- **Use the bed for sleeping only.** Try not to watch TV in bed, scroll on your phone, or work in your bed.

Mindful Breathing

When we consider that breathing is essential to life, it is surprising how little emphasis we place on the quality of breathing and its impact on a healthy lifestyle. Breathing is one way the body detoxifies through the exchange of oxygen and carbon dioxide. Mindful breathing is when you bring awareness to your breath and pay attention to your inhale and exhale. This can be a powerful meditation practice by bringing focus to the present moment, and it promotes many mental, emotional and physical health benefits. Deep breathing, also known as diaphragmatic breathing, is an example of mindful breathing, when you focus on deep, quality breaths, which can reduce stress and support healthy blood pressure. With practice, deep breathing is really quite simple.

Find a quiet place to sit down or lie down, whichever is most comfortable. Place one hand on the belly. Begin by exhaling all breath through the nose or mouth. Then, take a deep breath in through the

Breathing is one way the body detoxifies through the exchange of oxygen and carbon dioxide. Focusing on deep, quality breaths (diaphragmatic breathing) can reduce stress and support a healthy blood pressure.

nose, for a count of five. Hold the breath for one more second. Exhale for a count of five and wait for one second before beginning the cycle again. Breathe in this rhythm for several minutes. Try to extend your focused breathing practice to ten minutes a day.

During times of stress, simply do a handful of these deep breaths as a reliable stress reduction technique. Deep, mindful breathing before meals and before sleeping can assist optimal digestion and a more restful night of sleep.

Movement

Just like healthy eating, a habit of daily movement is critical for well-being. In today's fast-paced, technology-driven world, there are many challenges to incorporate movement into our lives. Many adults sit all day at work. Kids sit most of the day at school, and physical education classes and recesses have been shortened or even cut. In addition, many communities are not designed for walking and biking and lack green spaces, further reducing opportunities for movement. With few exceptions, technology (TV, computers, tablets, smart phones) encourages a sedentary lifestyle, as well. Ideally, increased physical activity should be incorporated into daily school and work schedules for children and adults. Until then, it will be up to individuals and families to make sure everyone is physically active.

However, a workout at the gym won't solve it all. It is not just exercise we are promoting: our society is fighting *sitting disease*. The act of sitting for extended periods of time is now recognized as its own risk factor for disease. Long periods of physical inactivity, rather than simply lack of exercise, raises the risk of developing heart disease, high blood pressure, diabetes, cancer, and obesity.[8,9]

What can be done to combat sitting disease? It is essential to integrate movement into your daily routine. Consider the following suggestions based on your abilities:

- Set reminders if needed and move your body every 45 to 60 minutes. Stretch, do a few full body exercises to your ability (squats, planks, or yoga, for example), climb the stairs for five minutes, or go for a short walk. This is not just for work days; do this at home, during travel, or when relaxing on vacation.

The act of sitting for extended periods of time is now recognized as its own risk factor for disease. Long periods of physical inactivity, rather that simply lack of exercise, raises the risk of developing heart disease, high blood pressure, diabetes, cancer, and obesity.

In addition to daily movement and aiming to reduce sitting, people still need focused exercise in addition to the movement suggestions listed above. Exercise can include cardiovascular (aerobic) exercise, stretching, weight-bearing exercise, and resistance or strength training. It also needs to include activities that are enjoyable to help stay motivated.

- Stand more instead of sitting! You can read, talk on the phone, answer emails, have meetings, and watch TV, all while standing. Consider using a standing desk.
- When you can, walk up the stairs instead of using the elevator.
- Park in the back of the parking lot.
- Carry groceries to your car instead of pushing the cart.
- Bike to work or to run errands instead of driving.
- Gardening, yard work, and cleaning contribute to an active lifestyle.
- Reduce screen time. Remember, every hour spent sitting in front of the TV, computer, tablet, or smartphone is one hour less of moving.
- It's important to play and have fun while moving your body: go for a bike ride, dance, play tag, play sports, or swim. There is no limit.
- Remember, the most basic movement—walking—is associated with many health benefits, including improved heart and lung health and a reduced risk of diabetes. It is also a great way to reduce fatigue, improve sleep, and improve mood. It is an inexpensive activity, requiring only time, space, and a pair of comfortable shoes.[10]

In addition to daily movement and aiming to reduce sitting, people still need focused exercise in addition to the movement suggestions listed above. Exercise can include cardiovascular (aerobic) exercise, stretching, weight-bearing exercise, and resistance or strength training. It also needs to include activities that are enjoyable to help stay motivated.

At a minimum, it is recommended that adults engage in at least 150 minutes a week of moderate intensity aerobic activity (or 30 minutes a day, 5 days a week) such as brisk walking, or 75 minutes a week (or 15 minutes a day, 5 days a week) of vigorous aerobic activity, such as jogging or running, for example. In addition, adults need at least 2 days a week of resistance or strength building activities that address all the major muscle groups. If you are sedentary most of the day and are unable to change your environment to include more frequent movement, you can add 15–30 more minutes of moderate to vigorous exercise each day to help offset the negative effects of sitting.[11]

Children and adolescents need at least 60 minutes of moderate aerobic activity every day. As part of the 60 minutes a day, at least 3 days a week should include resistance or strength building exercise, vigorous aerobic activity, and bone building activities including jumping, running, hopping or sports requiring quick changes of direction, such as soccer, basketball, or dance. The benefits of movement and exercise for kids includes improved mental focus, better performance in school, healthier weight and improved body image, and overall increased feelings of wellness. Caregivers are in the best position to serve as healthy, active role models for their children, but so are siblings and friends. If family members are involved, it can be encouraging for others to participate.

Beyond the physical benefits of moving, there are numerous mental and emotional benefits to incorporating movement into your life including reduced anxiety and depression for all ages.[12,13]

Social Connection

There is an epidemic of loneliness and social isolation in the United States, with over half of Americans reporting feeling lonely. Loneliness has become a public health crisis due to its known impact on mental and physical health, including an increased risk of depression, anxiety, heart disease, stroke, dementia, and premature death.[14] Much like the benefits from a healthy diet, regular exercise, and quality sleep, putting effort into staying connected with friends, family, coworkers, and your community is good for your health. Community-based strategies that support social connection can include investing in social infrastructure (such as parks, libraries, and playgrounds), improving public transportation, and increased awareness of screening for loneliness in the healthcare field. Additionally, here are some strategies at the individual level that can improve social connection in our daily lives:

- Connect with people daily. Reach out to friends, family members, coworkers, and neighbors. Engage in phone or video calls, and schedule regular visits and activities.

Much like the benefits of improving your diet, exercise, and sleep, putting effort into staying connected with friends, family, coworkers, and your community is good for your health.

- Spend time in social environments: coffee shops, shopping areas, gyms, and parks, and engage with the people around you.
- Stay involved. Take a new class, join a group or club, volunteer in your community, and attend community events.
- Minimize distractions in conversations. Put the phone away, and engage in active listening.
- Increase your awareness about the practices and activities that make you feel disconnected, and work on strategies to overcome those habits and patterns.
- Limit social media. Although some internet use has the potential to improve social connection, more time spent on social media is associated with increased loneliness. People who limit their social media use to less than 30 minutes a day report less loneliness than people who use social media two or more hours a day.[15,16]

Many of these activities may sound simple: drinking water, sleeping, breathing, moving, and improving social connection. Perhaps because they sound so simple, many people do not put much time into thinking how they incorporate these activities into their daily lives. Unfortunately, the consequences of neglecting these activities have come at a great cost to our long-term health. The full benefits of a highly nutritious diet may not be realized if other lifestyle habits are not in place. For instance, symptoms of dehydration can often appear as hunger, making it more likely to grab a sugary snack. Deep breathing helps to tonify the rest and digest phase of the nervous system, supporting healthy digestion and allowing for optimal nutrient absorption. Without a restful night of seven to nine hours of sleep, it is very difficult to maintain a healthy metabolism and to manage sugar cravings. Regular movement supports the maintenance of lean muscles, which is essential for balancing blood sugar over time. Lack of social connection can impact mental health, making it more challenging to consistently make healthy food choices. These habits for health do require some initial attention and commitment to incorporate into your life, but they are well worth the effort.

Chapter Twelve

Healthy Eating On The Go

Is it possible to eat healthy at a fast food restaurant? The benefit to eating fast food is that it is often conveniently located, and food is served quickly at an affordable cost. Yet, fast food tends to be high in calories, saturated fat, and sodium, and low in important nutrients (for example—calcium, vitamins A and C, and fiber).[1] These foods and beverages are purposely designed by the fast food industry to be hyperpalatable, meaning you get a feeling of reward when eating it and want to consume more.

The average fast food meal contains more than 800 calories and the average beverage contains more than 300 calories.[2] Eating fast food increases the intake of ultra-processed foods and beverages, which ultimately contributes to increased caloric intake. Over time, this can lead to unwanted weight gain.[3] Additionally, the consequences of eating fast food go beyond the excess calories. The concept of fast food challenges all that we have learned about healthy digestion. It can be difficult to remain in a parasympathetic state (rest and digest) while eating on the go. Eating high fat, low fiber foods can lead to digestive distress like bloating and gas. Frequently eating ultra-processed foods, commonly found in fast food, is also associated with a greater risk of depression and anxiety.[4] This can negatively impact motivation for making healthy lifestyle and dietary changes.

More frequent consumption of fast food increases the risk of type 2 diabetes, metabolic syndrome, and heart disease.[5] In spite of the health risks, on any given day, about 36% of adults in the U.S. and one-third of children eat a meal at a fast food restaurant.[6] This is largely due to social determinants of health that negatively impact certain communities' access and resources to pursue healthier options. Racial and ethnic minority communities and low-income communities often have a higher density of fast food restaurants in their neighborhoods.[7]

Think about this: as you move along the dietary spectrum from a highly processed diet to a whole foods based diet, how can you visit a fast food restaurant and make the most nutritious, health-promoting choices?

Making The Most Of Fast Food

Look for whole and minimally processed foods on the menu that may be offered on the side or as part of the meal like whole fruits (apple slices), vegetables (baby carrots, sliced tomatoes, onions, lettuce, grilled peppers), whole grains (brown rice vs white rice), eggs, beans, and grilled (not fried) meat or fish. You can find a few fast food restaurants that source minimally processed, pasture-raised, or hormone-free meat, poultry, and animal products.

Here are some additional strategies to consider:
- Find the fiber! Seek out whole grains, whole fruit, and extra vegetables to improve the fiber content of your meal. Some fast food restaurants offer unsweetened oatmeal with fruit for breakfast instead of a bagel. Fiber-rich legumes in the form of refried beans or black beans can be an option, as well. Add avocado slices or guacamole to meals when available.
- Drink plain water, carbonated water, or unsweetened iced tea or black coffee with your meal. Avoiding sugar-sweetened beverages including soda, juice, and sweetened tea or coffee is one of the best decisions you can make when eating out at fast food restaurants.
- If you do choose to drink sweetened beverages, avoid super-sized and large portions. For instance, a large soda con-

Cooking food at very high temperatures by frying or broiling can create inflammatory compounds called advanced glycation end products (or AGEs). Additionally, frying polyunsaturated oils like soybean oil or vegetable oil can create unhealthy changes in the oil through oxidation, which is then reused, over and over.

Eating a burger without the bun is another way to avoid a highly processed part of a typical fast food meal.

tains 380 calories with 100 grams of added sugar compared to a small soda with 200 calories and 53 grams of added sugar, which is still well above the daily recommended intake of added sugar.[8,9] Remember that drinking diet soda will help decrease your caloric intake in the short term, but regular consumption of diet soda is linked to weight gain and increased cardiovascular disease risk.

- Limit mayonnaise, ketchup, sauces, and dips. They often contain added sugar and unhealthy fats. Remember that salad dressings are often made from highly processed oils, like soy and corn. Mustard can often serve as a healthier condiment because it is lower in added fat and sugar.
- Practice your strategies for healthy digestion, even when eating fast food. Slow down. Eat with intention. Pay attention to the environment and how it makes you feel. Take some deep breaths before eating.
- Limit fried foods. While a golden french fry or a fried chicken sandwich can taste delicious, these foods can contribute not only to excess calories but also to increased inflammation. Cooking food at very high temperatures by frying or broiling can create inflammatory compounds called advanced glycation end products (AGEs). Additionally, frying polyunsaturated oils like soybean oil or vegetable oil can create unhealthy changes in the oil through oxidation, which is then reused, over and over. For these reasons, try to avoid fried or broiled foods when eating at fast food restaurants, or choose smaller portions of these foods. If you do choose to eat fried foods, try to also include antioxidant-rich foods like a colorful side salad, a piece of fruit, or drink unsweetened ice tea or black coffee.[10]
- Reduce refined carbohydrates. Eating a burger without the bun is another way to avoid a highly processed part of a typical fast food meal. Instead, consider asking for a lettuce wrap. In addition to the refined grains, poor-quality oils, and added sugars in a bun, there are added chemicals, preservatives, and artificial flavors. Read the ingredient list below for a bun and beef patty

from a popular fast food restaurant to determine the amount of processing:

100% Beef Patty—*Ingredients*:
100% Pure USDA Inspected Beef; No Fillers, No Extenders. Prepared with Grill Seasoning (Salt, Black Pepper).

Premium Bun—*Ingredients*:
Enriched Flour (Bleached Wheat Flour, Malted Barley Flour, Niacin, Reduced Iron, Thiamin Mononitrate, Riboflavin, Folic Acid), Water, High-fructose Corn Syrup, Yeast, Barley Malt Extract, Soybean Oil, Salt, Wheat Gluten, Contains 2% Or Less: Soybean Oil, Calcium Sulfate, Ammonium Sulfate, Yellow Corn Flour, Conditioners (Sodium Stearoyl Lactylate, DATEM, Ascorbic Acid, Azodicarbonamide, Distilled Monoglycerides, Monocalcium Phosphate, Enzymes, Calcium Peroxide), Turmeric, Annatto and Paprika Extracts (Color), Natural (Plant Source) and Artificial Flavors, Caramel Color, Calcium Propionate (Preservative), Sesame Seed. Contains wheat.

What About Salt And Sodium?

Remember: Salt is a combination of minerals the body depends upon to function. Salt is composed of sodium and chloride which are important electrolytes that influence regulation of blood pressure, fluid balance, and even nerve conduction. One of the concerns with frequent fast food consumption is the excessive amount of salt added to the food. For instance, one popular fast food cheeseburger contains 1050 mg of sodium or 46% of the recommended daily value, and a large fries contains 775 mg of sodium. One serving of a chicken, egg, and cheese biscuit sandwich contains 1870 mg of sodium or 81% of recommended daily value.[11,12]

Recall that the general recommended daily limit of sodium intake for adults is about 2,300 mg of sodium per day, or one teaspoon of table salt, for most people, and possibly lower for those at risk of high

One of the concerns with frequent fast food consumption is the excessive amount of salt added to the food. For instance, one popular fast food cheeseburger contains 1050 mg of sodium or 46% of the recommended daily value, and a large fries contains 775 mg of sodium.

blood pressure, heart, or kidney disease. Avoid adding salt to your food when eating fast food. It is important to balance potassium and sodium intake, especially when eating fast food. A diet that contains about twice as much potassium as sodium helps to support healthy heart function. The best sources of potassium are fresh fruits and vegetables. Including a side salad, piece of fruit, or guacamole is a great way to increase the potassium in a fast food meal. Here's a shout to the mighty avocado, which contains up to 700 mg of potassium!

Final Thoughts On Fast Food

Lack of will-power is not the reason that many people are unable to stop eating fast foods. It is because fast foods are convenient, readily available, cheap, and contain high amounts of sugar, salt, and fat that are all highly addictive.[13] There are no direct numbers about how often is too often to spend eating fast food, although eating more than 1-2 fast food meals a week is associated with a significantly increased risk of developing type 2 diabetes and metabolic syndrome.[14] Thus, reducing the frequency of visits is a good start. Cutting out sweetened beverages will also have a significant impact on your health.

One of the best ways to reduce your fast food frequency is to be prepared with some basic meal and snack planning. Try not to skip meals in order to prevent increased cravings for quick, sugary, and salty food. Consider preparing and having some healthy snacks available, such as hard-boiled eggs or chopped veggies and fruit. Stock your car, bag, or desk with nuts, fruit, trail mix, protein bars, and nut butters. When you make a homemade meal, make extra, so that you can have a healthy option for lunch or dinner the next day. Instead of eating at a fast food restaurant, stop at a grocery store and pick up a premade salad or roasted veggies in addition to a good protein.

Chapter Thirteen

Nutritious Lunches And Snacks

It was so interesting to see what my children would try and how they really wanted to go to ECO workshops. Now that they've learned about eating less sugar, I see them making that choice. How to read food labels, learning about fake sugars, choosing which foods are most important if you want to go organic—you can't go over all that too often. It's kind of like gardening. They can tell you what to do, and maybe you'll do it. But when they give you seeds, all you have to do is plant them.

—Ginean (mom), son, age 6, and daughter, age 4, ECO project, Mt. Olivet

I now know more than most people my age about my overall well-being. Now that I have these strategies of being healthy, I can carry it on throughout my whole life. KALE CHIPS ROCK!

—Claire, age 14, FAME Series, Charlee's Kitchen

SNACKS CAN BE IMPORTANT FOR BOTH ADULTS AND CHILDREN. THEY HELP BALANCE BLOOD SUGAR AND CAN PROVIDE EXTRA nutrition for the day. Meals and snacks can be balanced in the same way, with protein, fat, and fiber. Most conventional and packaged snacks tend to be high in refined carbohydrates; for example, crackers, chips, pretzels, and cookies. They also tend to be high in added sugars, highly processed oils, and chemical additives. Snacks that are from whole foods with minimal processing and no additives are healthier choices.

Some people may not need to snack and can maintain balanced blood sugar by eating three meals a day. For others, five to six smaller meals or a combination of larger meals and smaller snacks may be best. We often think of snacks as being for kids, but adults often benefit from the same healthy snack suggestions.

The key to creating healthy snacks that kids will love is to make them as fun, simple, and engaging as possible. This is true for most adults, too.

Healthy Snacks For Everyone

Check out the following FAME recipes that make healthy snack options with whole food ingredients: **Baked Kale Chips, Breakfast Smoothie, Turkey Avocado Roll-ups, Homemade Hummus, Cocoa Loco Bars, Guacamole, Basic Bone Broth, Spring Herb Crackers, Coconut Berry Bliss, Chia Seed Pudding, Frozen Yogurt Bars,** and **Carrot Zucchini Muffins.**

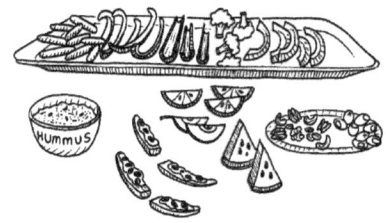

In addition, here are some other tips and creative ways to encourage healthy snacking for kids and adults.

Veggies and Dips

Fresh vegetables should always be on hand for quick snacks. Take some time to prep and chop all of your vegetables so they are ready to grab and go. If time is an issue, there are often pre-chopped, pre-washed veggies available at the grocery store. Adding a dip can also help increase vegetable intake. Carrots, sugar snap peas, celery, red peppers, and cucumbers can be dipped in hummus or guacamole for example.

Fruit and Veggie Kabobs

Use a skewer and create a colorful fruit kabob with strawberry, kiwi, pineapple, grapes, apple, or pear. Or, make vegetable kabobs out of carrots, zucchini, onion, bell peppers, and mushrooms. You can eat vegetable kabobs raw with hummus, or add avocado oil and seasonings and roast them. Kids will love to help make these!

Fresh and Frozen Fruit

Frozen fruit is available year-round, or purchase fresh fruits in season. Try frozen grapes or a bowl of frozen berries for dessert. Add fruit to unsweetened yogurt, chia pudding, or a smoothie.

Freeze-dried fruits and veggies are also great for a crunchy snack. Freeze-dried strawberries, blueberries, mangoes, sweet peas, tomatoes, bananas, and plantains can be found at most grocery stores. Make sure there are no added sugars or preservatives.

Ants on a Log

Take celery sticks and fill them with nut butter. Try peanut, almond, or cashew butter with no added sugar. Then, line raisins across the top. Apples or bananas with nut butter also make a great snack.

Smoothie Bowls

Freeze ripe bananas without the peel. Blend them with frozen fruit and non-dairy milk to make a thick, ice-cream like treat. You can add nut butter for extra protein and ground flaxseeds or chia seeds to add fiber. Top with your favorite fruit, nuts and seeds, or coconut flakes.

Nuts and Trail Mix

Almonds, walnuts, cashews, pecans, pistachios, and hazelnuts are all great snacking choices. Enjoy them raw or lightly roasted and seasoned.

Make your own trail mix by mixing together your favorite nuts, seeds, and dried fruits. The bulk section of the grocery store is a great place to find a variety of ingredients and to purchase the amount needed. Check the labels on pre-made trail mixes to limit added sugar.

Granola and Protein Bars

Read the ingredients. Review the protein and fiber content and the sources and amount of added sugar. Healthier options are those with higher protein and fiber, lower sugar (aim for less than 5 grams per serving), and made from whole food ingredients such as nuts, seeds, whole grains, and dried fruits.

Meat Jerky or Sticks (turkey, beef, pork, salmon, venison, or elk, for example)

Meat and fish that have been cooked and dehydrated can be a great source of protein on the go. However, as with any animal products, aim to choose organic, pasture-raised, or sustainably farmed or fished. Additionally, read the ingredient list before purchasing, as some products may contain high amounts of sodium, added sugars, or preservatives such as sodium nitrite or nitrate.

Beans and Legumes

Edamame (soybeans), either roasted or steamed in the pods, make a great snack that is high in fiber and protein. Any beans can be roasted and seasoned for a crunchy snack. (See recipe **Power Bowls** for instructions for roasted chickpeas.)

Other great snack choices include hard-boiled eggs, whole grain or flaxseed crackers with cheese or hummus, and whole-grain chips and salsa or guacamole.

Healthy Lunches

Along with breakfast, lunch is the meal that provides kids and adults with the energy needed to focus and learn in school or at work. Lunch contributes to balanced blood sugar later in the day, reducing evening cravings.

A balanced lunch will include fiber-rich foods, protein, and healthy fats. A good goal is to include at least one to two servings of vegetables. For kids and adults used to having something sweet in their lunch, try packing their favorite fruit. Limit packing juice, candy, or foods with high amounts of added sugar. For younger kids, getting a special note or a fun sticker can be a fun and healthy alternative to a dessert.

Lunch Ideas To Get You Started

Check out the following FAME Recipes to get you started with healthy, convenient lunch options: **Refried Pinto Beans and Rice, Nut Butter Banana Jam Sandwiches, Turkey Avocado Roll-ups,** and **Basic Green Salad with Protein.**

Any dinner recipe can make a healthy lunch option. Prepare extra, and pack into lunch containers that can be reheated. Many of the FAME recipes work well as leftovers.

Additionally, the following ideas may help inspire other healthy lunch ideas:

Not Just Any Sandwich

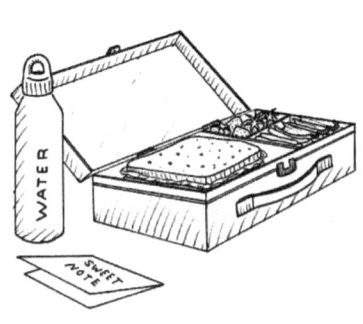

In order to make a nutritious sandwich, start by choosing 100% whole grain bread, as it will contain higher amounts of protein and fiber. Add a good source of protein: chicken, turkey slices, cheese, or pan-fried tofu or tempeh. Add your favorite veggies: lettuce, spinach, onions, tomato, avocado, bell peppers, cucumber, shredded cabbage, or more. Include a healthy spread or dressing: hummus, guacamole, roasted red pepper sauce, tofu tzatziki sauce, or a drizzle of extra virgin olive oil and vinegar.

Sandwich Wrap

Take your favorite sandwich ingredients and roll them in a whole grain tortilla, a lettuce wrap, or a blanched green leafy vegetable, such as collard greens. (See recipe, **Quinoa Veggie Stir-fry in Collard Wraps** for blanching instructions.)

Lox Lunch

Layer lox (fillet of brined salmon) or smoked salmon, spinach, cream cheese, and tomato on a slice of whole-grain bread or on half of a whole grain bagel and enjoy.

Egg Salad

Mix hard-boiled eggs with mayonnaise, made with olive or avocado oil, and mustard and serve over a bed of greens with veggies. You can also spread it on whole grain or flaxseed crackers.

Fun And Tasty Ways To Prepare Veggies

Here are some FAME recipes with creative ways to include more vegetables into the day: **Baked Kale Chips, Breakfast Smoothies, Egg and Veggie Scramble, Carrot Zucchini Muffins, Spaghetti Squash with Hearty Marinara Sauce, Sweet Potato Cornbread, Bean and Veggie Chili,** and **Rainbow Nachos.**

Other ideas include:

Root Vegetable Fries

Yams, sweet potatoes, carrots, and parsnips can be cut into fries and baked to make a delicious addition to meals or as snacks. For a sweeter option, spice with cinnamon or nutmeg. (See recipe **Baked Root Fries**.)

Steamed Carrots

Steam chopped or baby carrots until soft. Add butter, coconut oil, or olive oil and serve.

Cheesy Trees

Steam broccoli until soft, and sprinkle a small amount of grated cheese on top. Or, use another healthy fat like extra virgin olive oil, coconut oil, or butter, and add nutritional yeast and a pinch of salt. This makes a great side dish.

Getting Kids On Board With Healthy Eating

If there are children in your life, teaching them how to eat and enjoy healthy foods is just as important as teaching them to ride a bike, swim, read, and brush their teeth. Food provides them with the nutrients to support their body and their mind. But, that doesn't mean that choosing healthy foods comes naturally to children. Children learn how to eat from their parents, caregivers, schools, and community, and they are influenced by their cultural upbringing. Children are frequently bombarded with extreme marketing of junk food. Many parents and caregivers are resource-stressed, whether by time, finances, nutrition knowledge, or their physical environment, which can create barriers

Fresh vegetables should always be on hand for quick snacks. Take some time to prep and chop all of your vegetables so they are ready to grab-and-go.

to making healthy food available to their children. The time it takes to encourage, model, and empower kids to eat nutritious foods is worth the effort. Healthy eating habits in childhood creates a foundation for healthy adult dietary habits, which will reduce their risk of disease later in life.[1]

Here are some strategies to consider to help children develop a healthy relationship with food:

Positive Reinforcement

Children are given positive reinforcement for learning how to get dressed, tying their shoes, sharing toys, and during potty training. It is just as important, and often overlooked, to give positive acknowledgement when children choose and eat healthy foods. Making healthy choices can be challenging for kids. Let's be honest, it can be hard for adults, too. So, let's acknowledge and encourage each other when we eat our vegetables or try a new food.

Use Positive Language

Tell children how strong and healthy they will be by eating their nutritious meal or how it will help them focus in school or when playing sports. Talk about the foods and habits that are healthy or foods that you eat "occasionally." Try not to label foods as "good" or "bad." Avoid talking about body weight with regards to food choices or making negative comments that could result in a child feeling guilt or shame for their food choices.

Give Options

Have a variety of healthy options available to make healthy eating as easy as possible. Allowing kids to choose between two or three healthy food options, either for a snack or something to pack in their lunch, encourages healthy eating and can be empowering.

Introduce New Foods

A child is more likely to try a food if it is introduced multiple times. It is not uncommon for a child to refuse to even try certain foods at first. Pair new foods with familiar foods, and encourage trying a few bites. Also, texture, flavor, and presentation are important

---

"My 17-year old son and I are taking the ECO project classes for a school health credit. I have learned so much, even if the info is not brand new, it comes at a time when I am making a more focused effort regarding our diet at home. We have definitely increased our intake of vegetables and whole grains. Experimenting with whole grains has been fun. The actual cooking part of the class makes trying new things so do-able. I think this is such an effective way to teach and actually affect changes in everyday life."

—Jody, ECO Project, Mt. Olivet Food As Medicine Everyday

when introducing foods. Experiment with cooking and seasoning in different ways, and know that it will take time and patience.

Include Kids and Let Them Lead

Let children and teens be a part of the process. Encourage age-appropriate ways for them to help with meal planning, creating the grocery list, going shopping, and cooking and preparing the meal. Allow kids to listen to their body cues and to self-regulate their eating at mealtime. Putting pressure on kids to eat or to finish their plates or restricting food can lead to increased emotional eating and overeating in children.[2]

Eat a Shared Family Meal

Schedules can get busy, but eating meals together helps set kids up for success. Eating a shared family meal three or more times a week is associated with children and teens eating more healthy foods and less unhealthy foods, contributes to a healthy weight, and decreases the risk of disordered eating.[3]

Manage Expectations

Every meal doesn't have to be perfect. Aim for an overall lifestyle that prioritizes nutritious ingredients. Accept that children will go through different phases of eating habits, with outside influences and social pressures exerting more of an impact at times.

Understand Emotional Eating

Emotional eating is defined as eating in response to an emotional state, rather than a physiological need. People who are stressed, anxious, depressed, or experience other negative emotions tend to eat less healthy, higher calorie, nutrient poor foods. Positive emotional states are associated with healthier diets and increased fruit and vegetable intake.[4] These patterns are sometimes learned from a very young age and reinforced in our culture. In these cases, it is important to be aware of the underlying emotions in order to help make changes in dietary patterns. Emotional eating can be a complex issue, and modeling healthy eating for children to observe is a great place to start.

Chapter Fourteen

Shopping Guide And Everyday Superfoods

I look at food differently now. I have gratitude for the farmers and stores that take a risk to produce organic, whole foods. I cook differently now with new spices, and lots of them, and better-for-me oils. Bread is NOT a staple anymore. Oatmeal as granola was phenomenal as were the smoothies—what a surprise! Lastly, I look at NDs differently—with greater love and reverence because of your compassion, knowledge, and creativity.

—Susan, FAME Series, Charlee's Kitchen

IT IS TIME TO CONVERT WHAT WE HAVE LEARNED INTO ACTION. LET'S HEAD TO THE GROCERY STORE! THIS CHAPTER FOCUSES ON how to navigate a conventional grocery store. Conventional grocery stores remind us just how ultra-processed our food supply can be, with one study showing that over 70% of products in a large grocery store are ultra-processed.[1] This chapter will highlight strategies to use at the grocery store to make the healthiest and most economical purchases available. As you move toward a whole-foods lifestyle, you may need to begin with small steps.

General Grocery Shopping Tips

Read these tips before you head out to shop:
- Do not go shopping while hungry; buying on impulse and purchasing unhealthy foods or larger portions is more likely.
- Always make a list before going to the grocery store. List the meal ingredients and staple foods needed. You will be less likely to overspend, make impulse purchases, or forget an item.
- Allow for flexibility when buying produce, taking into account what is in season or on sale.
- At the store, start by purchasing food at the periphery—that is often where the most nutritious foods are, such as fruits and vegetables, dairy, fresh meat, poultry, and fish. Then go to the aisles or bulk section where you can locate whole grains, legumes, and nuts. Limit shopping in the aisles, where more highly processed foods are located.
- When products are on sale and can be stored properly, buy extra. Bulk grains and beans last for many months in your pantry and refrigerator.
- Be aware of the placement of less healthy food products that promote impulse buying for adults and children.
- Compare the price per unit for similar products to determine which offers the best value.

How To Shop The Bulk Section

One of the benefits of shopping in bulk is that it allows experimentation of new foods and spices with minimal risk to your wallet. Shopping in bulk can help you stick to a budget. You can buy exactly the amount you need for a specific recipe instead of buying double that amount in pre-packaged items. Proper containers to store your bulk foods will be needed. Clean and reuse bottles or containers (preferably glass ones). Rinse them out, take off the label, and fill them with bulk items. This will prevent food from spilling out of the bags and will keep them free of pests. Designate an area in your pantry and fridge for specific bulk food items.

"The FAME series helped me shop better—I'm not afraid of the bulk section anymore. And who knew I could make my own almond butter, all natural, no added ingredients, to use instead of peanut butter?"
　—Shannon, FAME Series,
　　Mt. Olivet

Common bulk items to purchase

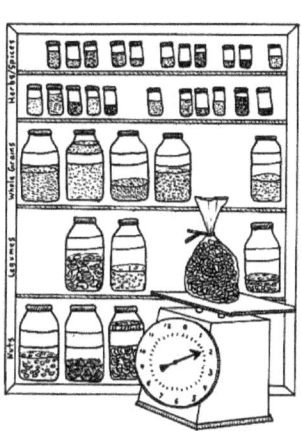

- Dry beans can be up to three times cheaper than canned beans. In addition, preparing beans at home eliminates added salt, sugar, or preservatives found in canned beans.
- Whole grain prices can vary. It's usually beneficial to compare the packaged prices to the bulk prices. Keep in mind that bulk grains allow you to purchase specific amounts. Whole grains can be stored in a cool dark place, like a fridge or freezer.
- Whole grain flour is also available in the bulk section and is often less expensive than packaged flour. Be sure to have a storage plan for the flour at home, since the thin bulk bags at most stores will not allow for proper storage of bulk flour. In particular, store all flour in an airtight container in a cool, dark place, either the fridge or freezer. Since flour is made from ground whole grains, there is more potential for spoilage when exposed to light and heat.
- Herbs and spices can be purchased in small amounts. This is cheaper than paying for the entire jar, and bulk purchasing makes trying a variety of spices easier. If you buy a spice in the jar the first time, save the jar and refill it from the bulk section. Store spices for up to six months, at most, and then replace.
- Dried fruits are often less expensive in the bulk section. Limit dried fruits that have added sugar or sulfites. Sulfites are a preservative that can have negative side effects ranging from hives to aggravation of asthma in some individuals.[2,3]
- Raw nuts may also be less expensive when purchased from the bulk section. You can also soak and roast nuts at home. Make your own trail mix by purchasing nuts, seeds, and dried fruit and mixing them at home.

Everyday Super Foods

Most people hear the word superfood and think of exotic tropical berries like goji, acai, or noni berries. While these berries do pack a punch in terms of antioxidants and can be a great addition to the diet, locally grown whole foods from your region are truly daily superfoods. Below, we list a variety of vegetables, fruits, healthy fats, beans and legumes, herbs and spices, and fermented foods that can serve as everyday foods.

1. Vegetables of all types

- **Dark green leafy vegetables:** Dark green veggies are one of the most nutrient-dense group of foods. They provide minerals, vitamins, antioxidants, and fiber. Eat them raw, lightly steamed, or sautéed. Add a handful or two and blend into a smoothie, or finely chop them and add to soups and sauces. Options include spinach, collards, chard, kale, mustard, and dandelion leaves.

- **Cruciferous vegetables:** Part of the Brassica family, these veggies include cabbage, arugula, Brussels sprouts, broccoli, bok choy, cauliflower, kale, mustard greens, radishes, turnips, and collard greens. They all contain a healthy dose of phytonutrients, vitamins, minerals, and fiber. They also contain sulfur compounds called glucosinolates that can decrease inflammation in the body and reduce oxidative stress. Cruciferous vegetables have been well-studied for their role in cancer prevention.[4] Eating more cruciferous vegetables is associated with a lower risk of breast cancer and colon cancer.[5,6] The best cooking method for these veggies is steaming or sautéing, although some cruciferous vegetables can be enjoyed raw. Enjoy eating one to two cups of these vegetables, several times a week.

- **Garlic and onions:** These members of the allium family aid in balancing blood sugar, keeping a strong immune system, supporting healthy blood pressure, and supporting detoxification pathways in the body.[7,8] They also make your food taste great.

- **Squash:** Look for the orange-fleshed varieties, which pack more beta-carotene, a vitamin A precursor, than almost any other vegetable or fruit. Gain all the nutritional benefits by adding some healthy fat to the squash. Try mashed squash with butter or coconut oil, cinnamon, and nutmeg.

highly processed foods

whole foods

- **Beets:** With their rich, deep color, this root vegetable provides valuable antioxidants and is traditionally known for supporting liver health. Beets are also packed with minerals. As an added bonus, buy beets with the greens attached. Beet greens are edible and can be consumed steamed or substituted for other dark green leafy veggies in a recipe.
- **Mushrooms:** Mushrooms are technically not plants or vegetables. They are fungi. But, they made our vegetable list because they are often prepared like vegetables, whether by sautéing them in olive oil or butter or adding sliced mushrooms to soups or salads. Some of the most popular edible mushrooms include portobello, shiitake, cremini, button, porcini, morel, oyster, and chanterelle. Besides tasting delicious, mushrooms are incredibly medicinal and have been researched for their following properties: anti-inflammatory, antioxidant, anticancer, antidiabetic, antiviral, and antibacterial.[9] They support a healthy immune response and provide a wide variety of nutrients including a plant-based source of Vitamin D2.[10]

2. Fruits

Fruit can provide a uniquely valuable source of vitamins, fiber, and antioxidants in the diet. However, fruit juice does not count as a substitute for a whole fruit.

- **Berries:** Try frozen, fresh, or dried (with no sugar added); any type is great. Berries provide some of our most potent antioxidants. Blackberries and raspberries are two of the most fiber-rich fruits out there, with 8 grams of fiber per cup!
- **Citrus fruits:** Lemons, oranges, and grapefruit are high in immune-stimulating vitamin C, as well as antioxidants that are good for vision and liver health. Grapefruit juice can affect the metabolism of some prescription medications, so check with your doctor for potential interactions.
- **Melons:** Each variety of melon has a different balance of vitamins and minerals, as well as antioxidants. Cantaloupes, in particular, provide a great amount of vitamin C and beta-carotene.

- **Apples or pears:** Take advantage of the many varieties of apples and pears. Each variety has a different flavor and a different complement of health-boosting antioxidants and fiber. Notably, consuming a whole apple, rather than drinking apple juice, has been found to support both balanced blood sugar and cholesterol, due to the apple's soluble fiber content.[11]

3. *Healthy Fats*

   - **Olives and olive oil:** Mainstays of the Mediterranean diet, olives provide a rich source of monounsaturated fats and polyphenols, which are powerful antioxidants. Extra virgin olive oil contains the greatest concentration of polyphenols. Regularly consuming extra virgin olive oil is associated with a reduced risk of cardiovascular disease and type 2 diabetes.[12,13]
   - **Avocados and avocado oil:** This fruit contains a rich source of monounsaturated fat, potassium, and fiber, with one avocado providing up to 14 grams of fiber.
   - **Butter and ghee from pasture-raised cows** will be richer in omega-3 fatty acids, vitamin E, and beta-carotene than conventional butter. Butter can be used for baking and medium-heat cooking, while ghee can be used to stir-fry and sauté at higher heats.
   - **Nuts and seeds:** Consider pecans, almonds, walnuts, cashews, and macadamia nuts. Healthy seeds include pumpkin, sunflower, chia, hemp, and flax. Nuts and seeds provide a nutrient-dense package of protein, fat, and fiber.
   - **Fish:** Salmon, trout, mackerel, tuna, herring, anchovies, and sardines contain a higher content of omega-3 fatty acids compared to other fish. These omega-3 fatty acids help to reduce inflammation and promote cardiovascular health. Fish is also a great source of complete protein.
   - **Coconut oil** provides a stable fat to cook with at higher heat. Refined coconut oil, which often undergoes bleaching, deodorizing, and filtering, has a higher smoke point and more

neutral flavor compared to unrefined coconut oil. This oil contains 13 grams of saturated fat per tablespoon (compared to 7 grams in butter), about half of which are medium-chain fatty acids, which are a specific type of fat that provide rapid energy and can support a healthy metabolism. Coconut oil can be substituted for butter in recipes.

4. Beans and Legumes

Beans are packed with heart-healthy fiber, protein, antioxidants, minerals, and vitamins. The more colorful the bean, typically the higher the antioxidant value.

- **Choose your favorite bean:** black beans, kidney beans, garbanzo, and black-eyed peas, or red, brown, or green lentils.
- **Soybeans:** They can be consumed as edamame, dried soy nuts, tofu, tempeh, or miso. Soybeans serve as a popular, complete plant-based protein, as well as a source of polyunsaturated fat and fiber. Look for organic soy when possible.

5. Herbs, Spices, and Teas

Supplement your diet daily with additional sources of health-promoting phytonutrients, or plant-based compounds, with a variety of herbs, spices, and tea. They have anti-inflammatory and antioxidant properties that benefit cardiovascular and neurological health, as well as additional sources of vitamins and minerals.[14]

- **Turmeric:** Traditionally used in Ayurvedic cooking in combination with black pepper for better absorption, this bright yellow-orange root contains curcumin, which is an antioxidant and has anti-inflammatory effects.
- **Cinnamon:** A naturally sweet spice, cinnamon can be used to help sweeten hot beverages and baked goods. It is made from the inner bark of a variety of *Cinnamonum* trees. Cinnamon has been studied for its role in promoting healthy blood sugar regulation.
- **Ginger:** This spicy root is recognized for its role as a carminative, or its ability to relieve digestive complaints like gas or nausea.

- **Cayenne:** Made from dried, bright orange-red peppers and ground into a powder, this spice contains the active ingredient capsaicin, known for its pain-relieving properties. This herb packs a powerful punch in terms of spice, so measure carefully before adding to recipes.
- **Thyme, Oregano, Rosemary, Basil:** Commonly used in Mediterranean cooking, these spices can be used fresh or dried. They are delightfully aromatic when used in combination. These spices contribute to the heart-healthy benefits attributed to the Mediterranean diet.
- **Cumin:** These earthy, aromatic seeds come from the same family as parsley! Cumin combines well with chili powders in many savory recipes like chili or marinades for meat, poultry, and fish.
- **Cilantro:** Also known as coriander, fresh cilantro is a delicious addition to guacamole and salads! Unless, of course, you are someone who tastes soap when you eat cilantro, which is due to a unique, genetic difference that impacts taste and smell.
- **Non-caffeinated Herbal Teas:** Technically, these "teas" are herbal infusions. Delicious choices include peppermint, chamomile, ginger, raspberry, dandelion, and hibiscus. There is a wide variety of benefits from drinking herbal teas that may benefit digestion, sleep quality, and immune function.
- **Caffeinated Herbal Beverages Green Tea, Black Tea, and Coffee:** Green and black tea come from the same tea plant, *Camellia sinensis*. After water, tea is the most commonly consumed beverage in the world, except in the U.S., where coffee is more popular than tea. Both tea and coffee provide powerful antioxidants with every cup as well as caffeine. Caffeine is a chemical that stimulates the central nervous system and can increase energy and attention for some people and increase symptoms of anxiety in others. Caffeine content varies between these beverages. Comparing an 8-ounce serving of each, green tea contains about 30 mg of caffeine compared to 50 mg and 100 mg for black tea and coffee.

6. Fermented Foods

These foods provide the body with healthy bacteria (probiotics) to support a healthy microbiome, keep the immune system strong, and aid in digestion and bowel health.

- Choose from a variety of options: unsweetened yogurt, kefir (a cultured milk beverage), miso, kimchi, kombucha, tempeh, pickles, and sauerkraut that contain live, active cultures.

A Review Of Foods To Limit Or Avoid

1. Limit excess added sugar and artificial sweeteners

- Aim to avoid or to only drink sparingly all sweetened beverages like sodas, teas, coffees, and energy drinks since they are often highly caloric and provide little nutritional value.
- High-fructose corn syrup (HFCS) is the most common sweetener added to beverages and ultra-processed foods in the U.S. In excess, it can cause unhealthy changes in the liver and lead to blood sugar dysregulation. Common sources are soda, juices, baked goods, candy, ketchup, and other condiments.
- Artificial sweeteners are considered ultra-processed and may contribute to metabolic dysfunction if consumed regularly.

2. Limit refined grains

- If the ingredient list contains enriched or refined flour, this indicates the product contains refined grains, meaning the nutrient-dense parts of the whole grain, the bran and the germ, were removed.
- These simple carbohydrates cause large spikes in blood sugar. Eating these foods frequently can contribute to the development of obesity and diabetes.
- Common sources include bread, bagels, or buns (unless packaging states 100% whole grain), baked goods, pasta, white rice, frozen meals, desserts, and snack foods like chips, crackers, and pretzels.

3. *Limit ultra-processed oils and saturated fats*

   - These will include hydrogenated vegetable oils and margarine. Also, limit omega-6 rich oils found in ultra-processed foods such as corn, soybean, safflower, canola, and sunflower oils.
   - Limit saturated fats found in fatty cuts of meat, processed meat, fast food, and ultra-processed meals such as pizza and pasta dishes.
   - The FDA has ruled trans fats are no longer recognized as safe to consume.[15] In spite of FDA regulations to remove trans fat from our food supply, it may still be possible to find products that contain small amounts.

4. *Limit ultra-processed foods*

   - Ultra-processed foods contain many of the above ingredients that contribute to development of chronic diseases like diabetes, heart disease, and obesity.
   - This includes packaged foods such as canned soups, frozen dinners, boxed foods, chips, candy, and pre-made sauces, gravies, and salad dressing.
   - Ultra-processed foods may contain high amounts of sodium, added sugars, highly processed oils, and chemical additives such as preservatives, thickeners, and artificial colors, flavors, and sweeteners, which are associated with several chronic diseases.

Stocking The Pantry

The following list can help you build your pantry and fridge with foods that are commonly used at home and in the majority of our recipes. Pay attention to what produce is in season. Our recipes are generally very adaptable to substitutions. Please see each individual recipe for a complete list of ingredients.

Herbs and Spices

Black pepper
Cayenne pepper
Chili powder
Cilantro
Cinnamon
Coffee/tea
Cumin
Garlic powder
Ginger (fresh and/or dried)
Herbal teas
Oregano
Rosemary
Sea salt
Turmeric
Thyme

Oils and Fats

Avocado and avocado oil
Butter
Coconut oil
Extra virgin olive oil
Ghee
Olives
Sesame oil

Whole Grains

Amaranth
Brown rice
Brown rice flour
Cornmeal
Millet
Oats
Quinoa

Legumes and Peas

Black beans
Black-eyed peas
Edamame
Garbanzo beans
Kidney beans
Green peas
Lentils
Pinto beans
Tofu or tempeh

Vegetables

Asparagus
Beets
Bell peppers
Bok choy
Broccoli
Brussels sprouts
Carrots
Cauliflower
Cucumber
Dark Greens:
    Chard
    Collards
    Dandelion greens
    Kale
    Mustard greens
    Spinach
Garlic
Mushrooms (fungus)
Onions
Romaine lettuce
Squash
Sweet potato
Tomato (fruit)

Fruits

Apples
Bananas
Berries
Citrus:
    lemon
    lime
    grapefruit
Melons
Pears

Nuts and Seeds

Almonds and almond butter
Cashews
Chia seeds
Flaxseed
Hazelnuts
Hemp seeds
Peanuts and peanut butter
Pecans
Sesame seeds
Sunflower seeds
Walnuts

Dairy and Dairy Alternatives

Almond milk

Cheese

Coconut milk

Unsweetened yogurt

Meat/Fish/Poultry

Chicken

Beef

Fish:

    salmon

    cod

    halibut

Pork

Turkey

Eggs

Other

Honey

Maple syrup

Miso

Mustard

Nutritional yeast

Shredded coconut

Tamari

Vinegar:

    apple cider

    balsamic

    rice

Chapter Fifteen

Kitchen Skills

The FAME series has helped me bridge the gap between wanting to make more whole-foods meals and actually doing it. The fact that my whole family (3 of us) took the class together was really helpful because we encourage each other at home.

—Elizabeth, FAME Series, Charlee's Kitchen

Instructions For Cooking Whole Grains, Beans, and Greens

Soaking whole grains

Whole grains can be soaked for a few hours or even overnight in water with two tablespoons of apple cider vinegar, lemon juice, or plain yogurt to create an acidic environment that begins the breakdown of nutrient inhibitors, such as phytic acid. This process makes the grains more digestible and increases the nutrient availability. Before cooking the grains, simply drain the water, rinse in a colander, and continue with the instructions listed below. Most grains were traditionally prepared this way.

Rinse: Prior to cooking, rinse whole grains thoroughly in cold water until the water runs clear. Then strain to remove any dirt or debris. A fine mesh colander may be needed.

Cook: Boil the water, add the grain, return water to a boil, reduce heat, then cover and simmer until tender.

For ground, whole grains (using meal, grits, or flakes): Combine cold water and grain. Bring to a boil, stirring constantly. Reduce temperature to low, cover, and cook to desired thickness.

Test: Check the cooked grain before removing from heat to ensure it is thoroughly cooked. Whole grains should be slightly chewy when cooked.

Fluff: Remove from the heat, and gently fluff them with a fork. Cover and set aside for 5 to 10 minutes and then serve.

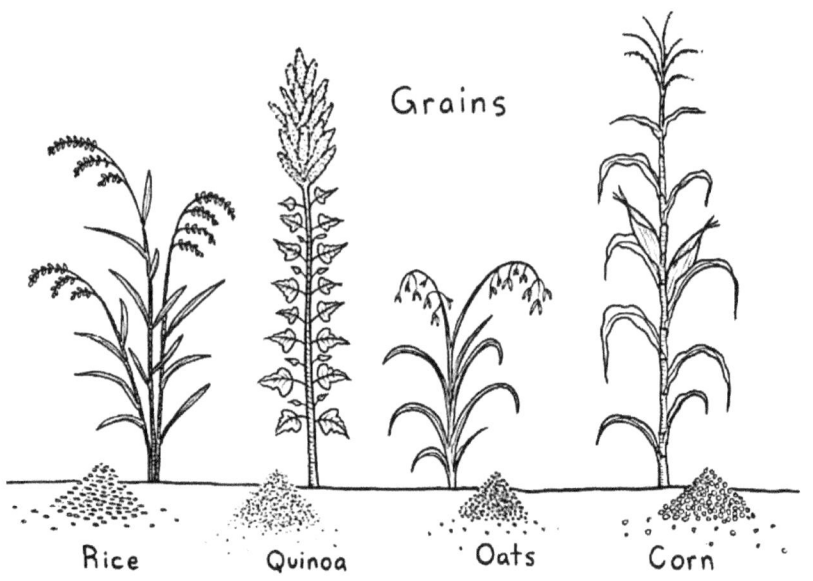

Whole grains can be soaked for a few hours or even overnight in water with two tablespoons of apple cider vinegar, lemon juice, or plain yogurt to create an acidic environment that begins the breakdown of nutrient inhibitors such as phytic acid. This process makes the grains more digestible and increases the nutrient availability of the grain.

Table 15.1 Cooking Guidelines for Common Whole Grains

Grain (1 cup dry)	Cups Water	Estimated Cook Time	Yield (in cups)
Amaranth	2½	20–25 min	2½
Barley, hulled	3	75 min	3½
Buckwheat groats	2	15 min	2½
Cornmeal, coarse ground	4	20 min	2½
Millet, hulled	3	20 min	3½
Oats, rolled	2	15 min	2
Oats, steel cut	3	20 min	3
Quinoa	2	20 min	2 or 3
Rice, brown	2	35–40 min	3
Rice, wild	4	50–60 min	4
Sorghum	3	50–60 min	2½
Teff	4	15 min	3
Wheat, berries	3	50 min	2

Cooking Dried Beans

Rinse: Place dried beans in a colander, and rinse thoroughly in cold until water runs clear.

Soak: Soaking beans before cooking helps to reduce some of the indigestible compounds (saponins) that can cause gas, and it breaks down phytic acid. Depending on time, you can do a regular soak or a quick soak.

Regular soak: Put beans into a large bowl and cover with 2 to 3 inches of cool, clean water. Add 2 tablespoons of apple cider vinegar, lemon juice, or plain yogurt and set aside for at least 8 hours or overnight; then drain and rinse.

Quick soak: Put beans into a large pot and cover with 2 to 3 inches of cool, clean water. Bring to a boil then boil briskly for 2 to 3 minutes. Cover and set aside, off of the heat, for 1 to 2 hours. Then drain and rinse.

Cook: Put soaked beans into a large pot and cover with two inches of water. Don't add salt at this point since that slows the beans' softening. Slowly bring to a boil, skimming off any foam on the surface. Reduce heat, cover, and simmer. Stir occasionally, and add more liquid if necessary, until beans are tender when mashed or pierced with a fork. Cooking times vary based on the beans, generally taking one to two hours. Refrigerate cooked beans in a covered container for up to four days. Alternately, store them in an airtight container and freeze them for up to six months.

Peas and lentils

Split peas and lentils require less preparation than beans since they do not need to be pre-soaked prior to cooking. They are great to consider for including in meals when you have less preparation time. However, whole dried peas should be soaked overnight.

Rinse: Rinse dried peas and lentils as you would dry beans (see above).

Cook: Bring water to a boil, add the lentils or peas, and then return to a boil. Then, reduce the heat and simmer for 30 to 45 minutes, partially covered, until peas or lentils are tender. Red lentils will cook in as little as 15 to 20 minutes.

Cooking tip: Uncooked dried split peas and lentils can be added directly to soups and stews and cooked accordingly.

See Table 15.2 for information about individual cook times and water requirements. This table is for pre-soaked beans. Beans with an asterisk do not require soaking.

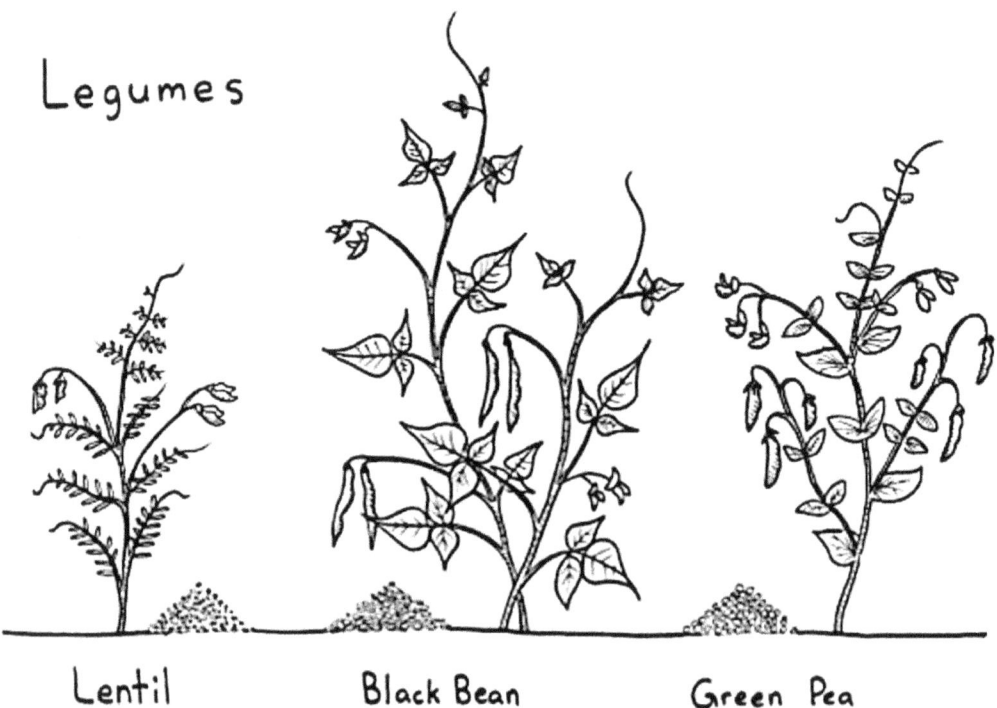

Table 15.2 Cooking Guidelines for Common Beans

Bean (1 cup dry)	Cups Water	Estimated Cook Time	Yield (in cups)
Black beans	4	60–90 min	2½
Black-eyed peas	4	60 min	2
Cannellini	3	45 min	2½
Fava beans	3	40–50 min	2
Garbanzo (chick peas)	4	60–90 min	2
Great northern beans	3	90 min	3
Green split peas*	4	45 min	2
Yellow split peas*	4	60–90 min	2
Kidney beans	3	60 min	2½
Lentils, brown*	3	20–30 min	3
Lentils, red*	3	15–20 min	2 to 2½
Lima beans	4	60 min	2 to 3
Navy beans	3	45–60 min	3
Pinto beans	3	60–90 min	3

* Do not require soaking

Preparing greens

In selecting greens, look for crisp leaves with a bright green color. Signs that greens are no longer at peak nutrition and taste include yellowing or limp leaves, brown spots, and slimy leaves. Check with your grocer or a local farmer's market to learn the best season to purchase certain greens that are harvested locally in your area. In many parts of the country, the growing season for kale and spinach can extend through winter months, while dandelion leaves may appear in many markets only in the spring. Greens are best stored in a higher humidity crisper drawer in the refrigerator. If you find it challenging to store fresh greens, consider purchasing frozen greens to incorporate into meals. Frozen greens can provide a nutrient-dense boost to smoothies, soups, and stews. We encourage you to explore tasting these different greens in a variety of ways to develop a regular habit of eating these superfoods. **See Table 15.3 for preparation tips for common greens.**

Cooking With Oils, A Recap

Many of the recipes included in this book recommend using extra virgin olive oil as your primary, low-heat cooking oil. Extra-virgin olive oil is best used for salad dressings or for low temperature cooking due to its lower smoke point. Unrefined coconut oil, butter, and animal fats (lard, tallow) are minimally processed saturated fats that have a slightly higher smoke point. They work well for medium heat cooking and have a delicious flavor. Refined coconut oil and ghee can tolerate even higher heat cooking. Unrefined avocado oil is high in monounsaturated fats and has a very high smoke point. In general, many of these fats and oils can often be substituted for each other in recipes.

Remember to take into account the type of fat (saturated versus unsaturated), the degree of processing, and the smoke point when choosing fats and oils. Saturated fats, in general, oxidize more slowly due their chemical structure. Polyunsaturated fats are less stable with heat exposure due to their double bonds, and monounsaturated fats are more stable. Aim to choose unrefined oils, as they have not been highly processed with heat and chemicals, and they retain more nutrients and flavor than refined oils. Smoke points are occasionally listed on the food label of the oil and can vary based on the type and quality of the oil and the level of processing. You can also cook many foods at a lower temperature, which will slow the rate of oxidation of the oil.

Limit oils that are highly processed (refined, bleached, and deodorized using high heat and chemicals) such as soy, safflower, sunflower, rapeseed (canola), and corn. Avoid all partially hydrogenated fats and oils.

Use Tables 15.4 and 15.5 as guides to help you choose healthy fats to include in your meals.

Table 15.3 Cooking Guidelines for Dark Green Leafy Vegetables

Variety	What To Expect	Preparation Tips
Arugula	Strong, peppery flavor Soft, tender leaves	Enjoy raw in salad.
Beet greens	Mild flavor, both sweet and bitter Tender leaves	Sauté, stir-fry, or finely chop and add to soups and stews.
Bok Choy	Sweet, mild flavor Firmer, juicy leaves	Sauté, stir-fry, or finely chop and add to soups and stews.
Collards	Mild flavor Tough, thick leaves when raw that soften when cooked	Sauté, stir-fry, or finely chop and add to soups and stews. Blanch and use as a wrap for vegetables or stir-fry; cut away thickest part of stem for wraps.
Dandelion greens	Small leaves, sweet and mild Larger leaves tend toward bitter	Enjoy small leaves raw in salad. Sauté, stir-fry, or finely chop and add to soups and stews.
Kale (Dinosaur/ Italian/ Lacinato, Green, Purple)	Mild flavor Dinosaur/Italian/Lacinato kale: elongated leaves with a curly edge Green kale: softer, very curly Purple kale: softer, delicate leaves	Sauté, stir-fry, or finely chop and add to soups and stews. Finely chop and enjoy in salads. Add to smoothies. Make kale chips.
Mustard greens	Subtle, spicy mustard flavor, bitter	Steam, stir-fry or sauté, and add to soups.
Spinach	Sweet, mild flavor Soft leaves	Enjoy raw in salad. Sauté, stir-fry, or finely chop and add to soups and stews. Add to smoothies.
Swiss chard (Red, Green, Rainbow)	Sweet flavor	Sauté, stir-fry, or finely chop and add to soups and stews.

Table 15.4 Saturated Fats and Their Smoke Points

Fat Or Oil	Things To Know	Type Of Fat	Smoke Point°F
Butter	Organic, pasture-raised/pasture butter is best.	Saturated	350°F
Clarified butter or ghee	Higher smoke point than butter. Commonly used in Ayurvedic cooking. Low in lactose and milk protein.	Saturated	375-485°F (depending on purity)
Coconut oil	Extra virgin/virgin oil (unrefined) is less processed and has a distinct coconut flavor. Refined oil has a neutral flavor. Can also be used for skin and hair care.	Saturated	Extra virgin/virgin (unrefined): 350°F Refined: 400°F
Lard	Rendered fat from a pig. Lard from pasture-raised pigs is the best source.	Saturated	370°F
Palm oil	Increased demand has caused negative environmental impacts. Certified sustainable (CSPO) sources are available.	Saturated	Unrefined: 300°F Refined: 450°F
Tallow	Rendered fat from beef, sheep, deer, and poultry. Tallow from pasture-raised animals is the best source.	Saturated	Beef tallow: 400°F

Table 15.5 Unsaturated Fats and Their Smoke Points

Fat Or Oil	Things To Know	Type Of Fat	Smoke Point°F
Almond oil	Can also be used for skin care.	Monounsaturated	Unrefined: 420°F Refined: 495°F
Avocado oil	Unrefined oil has high smoke point. Can also be used for skin care.	Monounsaturated	Unrefined: 450°F Refined: 520°F
Canola (rapeseed) oil	Mild flavor for cooking. Common genetically modified organism unless organic.	Monounsaturated	400°F
Corn oil	High in omega-6 fatty acids. Common genetically modified organism. Often called *vegetable oil*.	Polyunsaturated	450°F
Cottonseed oil	High in omega-6 fatty acids. Often found in ultra-processed foods.	Polyunsaturated	420°F
Grapeseed oil	High in omega-6 fatty acids. Can be by-product of wine making.	Polyunsaturated	420°F
Olive oil	Extra Virgin has low smoke point. Good for dressings.	Monounsaturated	Extra virgin: 325°F Virgin: 400°F
Peanut oil	Unrefined has distinct peanut flavor.	Monounsaturated	Unrefined: 320°F Refined: 450°F
Safflower oil	Mild flavor for cooking. High in omega-6 fatty acids.	Polyunsaturated	450°F
Sesame oil	Unrefined has distinct sesame flavor.	Monounsaturated	Unrefined: 350°F Refined: 445°F
Soybean oil	High in omega-6 fatty acids. Common genetically modified organism. Often called *vegetable oil*.	Polyunsaturated	450°F
Sunflower oil	Mild flavor for cooking. High in omega-6 fatty acids.	Polyunsaturated	450°F

Table 15.5 Unsaturated Fats and Their Smoke Points (cont'd)

Fat Or Oil	Things To Know	Type Of Fat	Smoke Point °F
Walnut oil	Unrefined oil has mild walnut flavor.	Monounsaturated	Unrefined: 320°F Refined: 400°F

RECIPES

ALL SEASONS
SPRING AND SUMMER
FALL AND WINTER

I have been encouraged to pay more attention to, and become more aware of, what I eat and its effect on my body. I've learned that a beautiful, delicious, and nutritious meal can be made from simple, easy to find whole ingredients, and it can be done quickly.

—Sally, FAME Series, Charlee's Kitchen

All Seasons

Fish Tacos *191*

Carrot Zucchini Muffins *193*

Frozen Yogurt Bars *195*

Marinated Steak Bites *196*

Power Bowls *197*

Baked Kale Chips *199*

FAME Plate Sheet Pan Meal *201*

Chia Pudding 4 Ways *202*

Refried Pinto Beans and Rice *204*

Breakfast Smoothie *207*

Not Just Oatmeal (Rolled Oats) *208*

Healthy Chicken Bites *209*

Colorful Cole Slaw *210*

Baked Root Fries *212*

Savory Salmon Cakes *214*

Quinoa Veggie Stir-Fry in Collard Wraps *215*

Nut Butter Banana Jam Sandwiches *216*

Turkey Avocado Roll-ups *217*

Cocoa Loco Bars *219*

Homemade Hummus *220*

Golden Delicious Granola *221*

Egg and Veggie Scramble *223*

Homemade Almond Milk *224*

Rainbow Nachos *225*

Guacamole *226*

Vegetable Broth *227*

Basic Bone Broth *228*

Fish Tacos

These fish tacos are fresh and flavorful. You can even make your own corn tortillas. If using store-bought tortillas, check the label for simple ingredients such as corn masa or masa harina, lime, and water. Masa harina is a traditionally made corn flour that is cooked and soaked in lime, which is an alkaline solution and not the fruit. This process is referred to as **nixtamalization**. This process makes important nutrients, like niacin, calcium, and protein, more bioavailable, and it improves the texture of the flour to make tortillas. The fish and toppings can also be served over lettuce or greens or with **Refried Pinto Beans and Rice** on the side.

Directions:

1. Preheat the oven to 400°F.
2. Cut fish into approximately 4-ounce portions. Pat dry, and place on a large sheet pan. Brush both sides of each fish filet with avocado oil.
3. In a small bowl, mix together the spices: chili powder, cumin, garlic powder, onion powder, salt, and black pepper. Spread the spices evenly over both sides of the filets.
4. Place the fish in the oven and bake for 12–15 minutes, or until the internal temperature reaches 145°F.
5. While the fish is baking, prepare the mango salsa and avocado dressing. Place all the salsa ingredients in a medium bowl, and stir to combine. Set aside.
6. Place the avocado dressing ingredients in a blender or food processor, and blend until combined and smooth. Set aside.
7. When the fish is done baking, remove it from the oven and let it rest about 5 minutes before serving. To serve, divide fish among warmed tortillas. Top with mango salsa, avocado dressing, shredded cabbage, and pickled red onions.

ingredients

1 pound white fish (cod, halibut, or rockfish)
1 tablespoon avocado oil
1 teaspoon chili powder
1 teaspoon cumin
½ teaspoon garlic powder
½ teaspoon onion powder
½ teaspoon salt
¼ teaspoon black pepper

MANGO SALSA

1 large or 2 small ripe mangos, peeled, and diced
¼ medium red onion, finely diced
¼ cup fresh cilantro, minced
2 tablespoons lime juice
⅛ teaspoon salt
½ jalapeno, finely diced (optional)

AVOCADO DRESSING

1 large ripe avocado, peeled, pitted
¼ cup plain Greek yogurt
¼ cup cilantro
1 clove garlic
1 tablespoon lime juice
¼ teaspoon salt

ingredients

FOR SERVING

8–12 whole grain or corn tortillas

Finely shredded green or red cabbage

Pickled Red Onions (see recipe, Power Bowls)

Servings: 4

Tips:

- Salmon or shrimp can be substituted for the white fish.
- Substitute ripe tomatoes for the mango to make *pico de gallo*, or other ripe fruits, such as pineapple, peach, or nectarine.

Nutrition Facts:

- Fish is a great source of lean protein and healthy fats, including omega-3 fatty acids.

Carrot Zucchini Muffins

Who said veggies and muffins don't mix? These deliciously spiced muffins bring out the sweetness of the zucchini and carrots. They pair well with protein-rich breakfast foods like **Egg and Veggie Scramble**, **Breakfast Smoothies**, and **Chia Pudding**. Or, enjoy them as a snack.

Directions:

1. Preheat the oven to 350°F. Lightly grease a 12-cup muffin pan with some melted butter, or line with muffin cups. Set aside.

2. In a large mixing bowl, combine mashed banana, grated zucchini and carrot, melted butter or oil, maple syrup, eggs, and vanilla extract. Stir until well mixed.

3. Add the remaining dry ingredients to the wet ingredients: almond flour, brown rice flour, baking soda, baking powder, salt, and cinnamon. Stir until combined. Evenly divide batter among the 12 muffin cups. Bake at 350°F for 22–24 minutes, or until a knife or toothpick inserted in the center of a muffin comes out clean.

4. Remove the pan from the oven, and allow the muffins to cool for 10–15 minutes. Then, remove the muffins from the pan, and transfer to a wire rack to cool completely. Store muffins in an airtight container in the refrigerator for up to 4 days.

Tips:

- For a fall variation of this recipe, substitute ½ cup pumpkin puree for the banana, 1 large apple for the zucchini, and pumpkin pie spice for cinnamon.

ingredients

1 ripe banana, mashed

1 medium zucchini, grated

1 large carrot, grated

½ cup melted butter or coconut oil

¼ cup maple syrup

2 eggs

2 teaspoons vanilla extract

1 ½ cups almond flour

½ cup brown rice flour

1 teaspoon baking soda

½ teaspoon baking powder

½ teaspoon salt

2 ½ teaspoons cinnamon

½ cup chopped walnuts (optional)

Servings: 12

Frozen Yogurt Bars

These frozen yogurt bars are fun to prepare and versatile. You can customize the flavors and nutrition depending on what you choose to mix in. Enjoy these as a snack anytime of day, from breakfast to dessert!

Directions:

1. Line a freezer-safe sheet pan with parchment paper, and set aside.
2. In a medium bowl, stir together yogurt, nut butter, maple syrup or honey, and vanilla extract until smooth.
3. Gently fold in additional optional mix-ins, such as berries, banana, cacao nibs, nuts, seeds, or cinnamon.
4. Use a spoon to dollop the yogurt mixture onto the parchment-lined sheet pan, dividing into 8 circular portions. Place a popsicle stick in the center of each dollop, leaving a handle of about 2–3 inches. Alternately, you can spread the mixture evenly across the sheet pan (about ½ inch thickness). Sprinkle any additional toppings on top.
5. Place the sheet pan in the freezer for the bars to set for about 2 hours.

Once the bars are frozen, remove the pan from the freezer and allow bars to thaw for a few minutes, or until the parchment lining can easily be pulled away to remove the frozen bars. If spread evenly on the pan, break into pieces. Serve immediately. Store any remaining frozen yogurt bars in an airtight container in the freezer for up to 2 weeks.

Tips: Our favorite combination of mix-ins and topping include:

- Peanut butter, honey, banana, cinnamon, dark chocolate chips
- Almond butter, maple syrup, raspberries, cacao nibs
- Almond butter, shredded coconut, pumpkin seed, cacao nibs, cinnamon

ingredients

Yogurt base

2 cups plain Greek yogurt

½ cup nut butter (peanut, almond, or cashew)

2 tablespoons maple syrup or honey

1 teaspoon vanilla extract

Mix-ins or Toppings

1 cup fruit: raspberries, blackberries, blueberries or strawberries (mashed, pureed, or sliced)

1 banana, diced

¼ cup nuts or seeds: chopped raw nuts (almond, hazelnut, cashew) or seeds (chia, pumpkin, ground flaxseed)

½–1 teaspoon ground cinnamon (optional)

2 tablespoons cacao nibs, shredded coconut or dark chocolate chips (optional)

Servings: 8

ingredients

1 pound top sirloin, NY strip, tenderloin, or flank steak, cut into 1-inch pieces

¼ cup avocado oil

2 tablespoons lime juice

2 tablespoons lemon juice

2–4 cloves garlic, minced

½ cup minced fresh parsley

1 tablespoon fresh thyme leaves or 2 teaspoons dried thyme

1 teaspoon coarse salt

½ teaspoon ground black pepper

2 tablespoons ghee or avocado oil

Zest of lime and lemon (optional)

Servings: 4

Marinated Steak Bites

Steak bites are a quick and easy way to prepare affordable cuts of beef. They provide an excellent protein source to complement other FAME recipes like **Colorful Cole Slaw**, **Roasted Beet Salad**, or the **Basic Green Salad**.

Directions:

1. In a large bowl, whisk together the marinade ingredients: avocado oil, lemon and lime juice and zest (optional), minced garlic, parsley, thyme, salt, and pepper.

2. Add the steak pieces to the marinade and stir to coat. Cover the bowl with a lid or plastic wrap and place in the refrigerator for at least 1 hour to marinate.

3. Once the meat is marinated, remove from the fridge and let sit for 15–20 minutes to bring to room temperature.

4. Heat a large skillet over medium-high heat. Once hot, add ghee or avocado oil. Place the marinated steak pieces in the skillet. Cook for about 3 minutes on one side, then flip and cook 2-3 minutes on the other. Internal temperature should be at least 145°F. Remove the cooked steak bites from the pan to rest for 3 minutes before serving.

Power Bowls

This ingredient list and directions for this recipe may seem daunting at first. But, these flavor packed bowls are worth it! Each part of the recipe is versatile and can be used for many other dishes. For example, pickled red onions are great for tacos (See **Fish Tacos**), salads, and sandwiches. Both the roasted red pepper and tofu tzatziki sauce are delicious on a salad, a sandwich, or with any fish, meat, or chicken (See **FAME Plate Sheet Pan Meal**). The roasted red pepper sauce also makes a great pasta sauce, and the tofu tzatziki sauce is delicious over roasted veggies or as a dip for raw veggies. You can also choose to make just one of the sauces for the bowls. Roasted chickpeas make a great crunchy salad topping, or enjoy them alone as a healthy snack.

Directions:

1. Make the pickled red onions: Place the sliced onion in a large jar. In a bowl, whisk together the warm water, maple syrup, and salt until the salt dissolves. Whisk in the vinegar. Pour over the sliced onions. Let sit at room temperature for 30 minutes to 1 hour. Store pickled onions in the refrigerator in a sealed container or jar for up to 10 days.

2. Next, make the roasted chickpeas: Preheat the oven to 425°F. Line a large, rimmed sheet pan with parchment paper. Drain and rinse chickpeas. Spread them onto a clean kitchen towel or paper towels and gently pat them dry. Transfer dried beans to a medium mixing bowl and combine chickpeas, avocado oil, cumin, garlic powder, paprika, salt, and pepper. Toss to evenly distribute the oil and spices. Spread the chickpeas in a single layer on the prepared sheet pan, and roast in the oven for 20–25 minutes until crispy, turn them once halfway through.

3. While the chickpeas roast, cook the quinoa (or other whole grain). Bring 2 cups of water to a boil in a medium saucepan. Add quinoa and return to a boil. Reduce heat to simmer, cover, and cook for 12 to 15 minutes, until water is absorbed. Remove from heat. Let the quinoa sit for five minutes and then fluff with a fork.

ingredients

PICKLED RED ONIONS

1 medium red onion, thinly sliced

¾ cup apple cider vinegar

½ cup warm water

1 tablespoon maple syrup

1 teaspoon salt

ROASTED CHICKPEAS

1 can garbanzo beans, drained, rinsed, and dried

1 tablespoon avocado oil

2 teaspoons cumin

1 teaspoon garlic powder

1 teaspoon paprika (or smoked paprika)

½ teaspoon salt

¼ teaspoon black pepper

ROASTED RED PEPPER SAUCE

1 (12-ounce) jar roasted red peppers, drained

1 clove garlic

1 tablespoon extra virgin olive oil

2 teaspoons paprika (or smoked paprika)

2 teaspoons cumin

1 tablespoon lemon juice

Pinch of salt

Pinch of black pepper

ingredients

TOFU TZATZIKI SAUCE

8 ounces firm tofu

1–2 cloves garlic

1 tablespoon lemon juice

¼ cup fresh dill, packed (or 1 tablespoon dried dill)

1 teaspoon apple cider vinegar

¼ cup water

½ English cucumber, grated

½ teaspoon salt

SALAD

1 cup quinoa (or other whole grain)

2 cups water

2 cups baby arugula or baby spinach, packed

½ English cucumber, diced

1 yellow bell pepper, diced

1 cup cherry tomatoes, halved

1 cup artichoke hearts, diced

½ cup Kalamata olives, pitted and sliced

½ cup crumbled feta or goat cheese

½ cup fresh flat-leaf parsley, finely chopped

Extra virgin olive oil, for drizzle

Servings: 4 bowls

4. Prepare roasted red pepper sauce by adding all the ingredients to a blender or food processor. Blend for about 30 seconds, or until pureed. Set aside.

5. Prepare tofu tzatziki sauce by adding all the ingredients to a blender or food processor. Blend for about 30 seconds, or until pureed. Set aside.

6. Begin preparing four bowls by placing a ½ cup of arugula at the bottom of each bowl. Add ½ cup cooked quinoa (or other whole grain) into each bowl. Evenly distribute the cucumber, bell pepper, tomatoes, artichoke hearts, olives, and feta or goat cheese onto each bowl. Add pickled red onions. Top each bowl with a generous spoonful of red pepper sauce, tofu tzatziki sauce, or both, some fresh parsley and a drizzle of olive oil. Serve and enjoy.

Tips:

- Be sure the chickpeas are thoroughly dry prior to roasting. Excess moisture will prevent them from becoming crispy.
- Almost all of the salad ingredients in this recipe can be substituted or changed to try different combinations. Switch the greens, veggies, beans, or grains in these bowls. Try farro, sorghum, or millet for a different whole grain. Add cooked chicken or fish or roasted tempeh to boost the protein.
- Traditional tzatziki sauce is made with Greek yogurt. Sub 1 cup of Greek yogurt for the tofu for another delicious and protein-filled option.

Nutrition Facts:

- Tofu is a plant-based complete protein. 4 ounces of tofu contains about 9 grams of protein.

Baked Kale Chips

Kale chips are a delicious introduction to this amazing dark green leafy vegetable and is a great alternative to potato chips. We find that Italian/lacinato kale works best for these chips, though you can experiment with other varieties.

Directions:

1. Preheat the oven to 325°F.
2. Rinse kale well, and allow the leaves to air dry or pat dry. Peel kale leaves away from thick stems and cut or tear leaves into equal "chip-size" pieces (approximately three inch by three inch).
3. Mix kale pieces, 2 cloves of chopped garlic, salt, and 1 tablespoon of oil into a bowl and massage together. Spread kale chips evenly in one layer onto baking sheets.
4. Bake for 15 minutes. Ovens may vary in their baking time. Move kale around on the baking sheet every 3 to 4 minutes to prevent burning and sticking. Bake until kale is slightly crispy around the edges.

Tips:

- Experiment with various spices for your kale chips. Try adding rosemary, oregano, curry powder, or nutritional yeast.

ingredients

¾ *pound kale (one bunch)*

1 tablespoon avocado oil or extra virgin olive oil

2 cloves garlic, peeled and minced

½ *teaspoon salt*

Cayenne pepper (optional)

Servings: 4 to 6

FAME Plate Sheet Pan Meal

A sheet pan meal allows for protein and vegetables to be cooked together, simplifying meal preparation.

Directions:

1. Preheat the oven to 400°F.
2. Place cubed chicken in a large mixing bowl. Toss with 2 tablespoons avocado oil, 1 tablespoon lemon juice, 2 cloves minced garlic, 1 teaspoon salt, ½ teaspoon black pepper, and 1-2 teaspoons Italian seasoning. Set aside.
3. While the chicken marinates, prepare 2 cups of cooked whole grain of your choice (brown rice, quinoa, polenta, barley). Refer to Table 15.1 for cooking guidelines for common whole grains.
4. Prepare your vegetables. Toss the chopped vegetables with the remaining avocado oil, salt, pepper, spices, and garlic.
5. Spread the vegetables evenly on a large sheet pan, and place the marinated chicken on the remaining quarter of the sheet pan.
6. Place the pan in the oven for 30–45 minutes until the internal temperature of the chicken is 165°F and the vegetables are tender.
7. Serve a portion of the chicken and vegetables over ½ cup of cooked whole grains. For a sauce or dressing: **Basic Vinaigrette** pairs well with all vegetable combinations; Roasted Red Pepper Sauce and Tofu Tzatziki (**Power Bowls**) pair well with Spring/Summer vegetables; **White Miso Vinaigrette** pairs well with Fall/Winter vegetables.

Tips:

- Plant-based option: 1 pound (16 ounces) extra-firm tofu, drained and dried with 1 can of chickpeas (1.5 cups), drained, rinsed, and patted dry. Drain and dry the extra firm tofu prior to baking for the best texture and flavor. Slice tofu block in half. Place tofu halves on a couple layers of paper towels or on a clean kitchen towel. Cover the tofu with additional paper towels or a clean towel. Lay a heavy skillet on top of the covered tofu and wait at least 10 minutes for additional moisture to be pressed out. If you frequently bake tofu, you may want to consider purchasing a tofu press.

ingredients

- 1 cup of dried whole grain (brown rice, quinoa, polenta, barley)
- 2–3 cups water (depending on whole grain)
- 1 pound boneless, skinless chicken (breast or thighs) cubed
- ¼ cup avocado oil
- 1 tablespoon lemon juice
- 1–1 ½ teaspoons salt
- ½–1 teaspoon black pepper
- 1 tablespoon dried Italian seasoning (or spice blend of your choice)
- 2–4 garlic cloves, minced
- 6–8 cups assorted seasonal vegetables, chopped

Spring/Summer: asparagus, snap peas, cauliflower, broccoli, mushrooms, zucchini, bell peppers, eggplants, cherry tomatoes, green beans, onions

Fall/Winter: delicata or butternut squash, Brussels sprouts, onions, parsnips, carrots, sweet potatoes, beets, onions

Servings: 4

Chia Pudding 4 Ways

ingredients

CHOCOLATE

2 tablespoons chia seeds

½ cup milk (unsweetened non-dairy or dairy milk)

2 teaspoons maple syrup

¼ teaspoon vanilla extract

1 teaspoon cocoa powder

PUMPKIN PIE

2 tablespoons chia seeds

½ cup milk (unsweetened non-dairy or dairy milk)

2 teaspoons maple syrup

¼ teaspoon vanilla extract

2 tablespoons pumpkin puree

½ teaspoon cinnamon or pumpkin pie spice

RASPBERRY

2 tablespoons chia seeds

½ cup milk (unsweetened non-dairy or dairy milk)

1-2 teaspoons maple syrup

¼ teaspoon vanilla extract

½ cup fresh or frozen raspberries

Chia seeds are packed with fiber, protein, and healthy fats, including omega-3 fatty acids. Two tablespoons of chia seeds contain 10 grams of fiber and 6 grams of protein. These individual chia pudding recipes are easy to prepare ahead of time, and the base and topping combinations are endless. Or, you can easily double or triple this recipe to make a larger batch. We've included four different flavors to help you enjoy chia pudding all year round for breakfast, a snack, or dessert.

Directions:

1. Combine all ingredients in a small jar or other glass container with a lid (minimum 8 ounces capacity). Stir or whisk until mixed. Refrigerate for a minimum of 4 hours, or overnight, until thickened. For the raspberry recipe only, add the raspberries, milk, vanilla extract, and maple syrup to a blender and blend for 30 seconds prior to adding to the container and mixing with chia seeds.

2. Add desired toppings before serving.

Tips:

- Whole milk, full fat coconut milk, or using ¼ cup plain Greek yogurt for the milk will make thicker, richer chia pudding. Soy milk, pea milk, and dairy milk and yogurt help increase the protein content.
- **Homemade Almond Milk** can be used as a non-dairy option for this recipe.
- Sugar alternatives, such as monk fruit or stevia, can replace the maple syrup.

Nutrition Facts:

- The raspberry chia pudding contains 14 grams of fiber, almost halfway to the daily goal of 30 grams!

i n g r e d i e n t s

VANILLA

2 tablespoons chia seeds

½ cup (unsweetened non-dairy or dairy milk)

1–2 teaspoons maple syrup

½ teaspoon vanilla extract or vanilla bean paste

OPTIONAL TOPPINGS

Fruit: berries, mango, kiwi, peaches, pears, apples

Nuts: almonds, walnuts, hazelnuts

Seeds: pumpkin, hemp, ground flaxseed

Almond or peanut butter

Servings: 1 for each

ingredients

1 cup brown rice

2 cups water for rice

3 cups cooked or canned pinto-beans

2 tablespoons avocado oil

½ yellow onion, diced

4 cloves garlic, peeled and minced

1 tablespoon cumin

½ to 1 teaspoon salt

¼ teaspoon black pepper

1 cup water, broth, or stock

2 medium avocados, diced

2 medium tomatoes, diced

¼ cup chopped cilantro

¼ teaspoon cayenne (optional)

1 finely chopped fresh jalapeno (optional)

Servings: 4

Refried Pinto Beans and Rice

Perfecting brown rice and beans provides you and your family with a wholesome and adaptable meal option that provides plant-based protein as well as fiber. The addition of diced tomatoes, avocados, and cilantro provide vibrant color, antioxidants, and healthy fat.

Directions for rice:

1. Add rice and water to a saucepan and bring to a boil.
2. Cover, reduce heat to a gentle simmer, and cook for about 35 to 40 minutes until the rice is tender. Do not lift the lid frequently or stir the rice while cooking.
3. Remove from heat and fluff with a fork before serving.

Directions for refried beans:

1. If using dried beans, refer to soaking and cooking methods in Chapter Fifteen, **Kitchen Skills**. If using canned beans, drain and rinse.
2. Heat a large saucepan over medium heat and add 2 tablespoons of oil.
3. Sauté onions until translucent, then add garlic and finely chopped jalapeno (optional). Add salt, black pepper, cumin, and cayenne (optional).
4. Add beans and ½ cup water, broth, or stock. Allow to heat thoroughly. Then, mash beans well with a potato masher or fork. Add additional water or broth as needed for desired consistency.
5. Serve beans over rice and top with diced avocado, chopped tomato, and cilantro.

Nutrition Facts:

- A half a cup of cooked pinto beans, which is a typical serving size, provides about 7 grams of fiber and 8 grams of protein, and may contribute to lowering total and LDL cholesterol.[1]
- Combining beans with a whole grain like brown rice provides a

complete protein.

- One serving size of cooked whole grain rice is 1/2 cup. Brown rice contains fiber, B-vitamins, and trace minerals such as manganese and selenium.

Tip:

- Increase the protein content of your meal by adding one pound of cooked ground turkey, chicken, or lean or extra lean ground beef to the meal. This can add up to 24–30 grams of protein to each of the four servings.

Breakfast Smoothie

Smoothies provide a delicious opportunity to get whole fruit, greens, nuts, and seeds into your diet. Building a nutritionally-balanced smoothie that contains protein, fat, and fiber can be a creative process, and there is no exact science.

Directions:

1. Place all ingredients into a blender. Blend at high speed until smooth. Add more liquid (water or milk) for a thinner smoothie.
2. Pour in glasses and enjoy.

Tips:

- Try the following options: Milk (unsweetened hemp milk, pea milk, soy milk, or cow milk); Fruit (blackberries, raspberries, apples, or pears); Greens (chard or kale); Nut butters (peanut, cashew, walnut, or sunflower seed butter).

- Experiment with adding spices like cinnamon, ginger, or turmeric.

- Keep in mind that many protein powders can be highly processed supplements. Review the ingredients lists for artificial colors, flavors, excessive sweeteners, or artificial sweeteners. Look for protein powders that contain ingredients that you can understand clearly.

ingredients

1 cup frozen berries

½ banana

1 cup milk (unsweetened non-dairy or dairy milk)*

1 tablespoon ground flaxseed

1 tablespoon almond or peanut butter

½ cup spinach

2–4 tablespoons protein powder (optional)

*sub ½ cup Greek yogurt for ½ cup milk

Serving Size: 1 serving (16 ounces)

ingredients

2 cups rolled oats

4 cups water

¼ teaspoon salt

½ cup chopped nuts or 4 tablespoons almond or peanut butter

4 teaspoons raw honey

½ teaspoon cinnamon

1 cup berries or chopped fruit

¼ cup ground flaxseed

Servings: 4

Not Just Oatmeal (Rolled Oats)

The soluble fiber found in oats has numerous health benefits, including reducing risk factors for heart disease and diabetes, as well as supporting a healthy gut microbiome.[2] Both rolled oats and steel cut oats offer similar nutrition to start your day. If you substitute steel cut oats for this recipe, use 1 cup of steel cut oats to 3 cups of water and cook for 15 to 20 minutes.

Directions:

1. Bring water and salt to a boil.
2. Add oats and simmer over low heat for approximately 10 minutes, depending upon desired consistency. Stir occasionally.
3. Take the pot off the heat and let cool.
4. Serve cooked oats with healthy toppings: chopped nuts or almond butter, honey, cinnamon, berries or chopped fruit, and ground flaxseeds.

Tips:

- One serving size of oats is 1 cup cooked oats.
- Increase the protein content of your meal by adding plain Greek yogurt or your favorite protein powder to the cooked oats. You can also add more nuts and seeds like hemp, chia, sunflower, or pumpkin seeds.
- Cooked and cooled oats store well in the fridge for up to five days. Divide your cooked oats into single portions and have a healthy breakfast ready to go for the rest of your week.
- Make overnight oats! Mix the following ingredients into a mason jar, cover, and place in the refrigerator overnight: ½ cup of rolled oats, ½ cup of milk, ¼ cup of Greek yogurt, ½ teaspoon of vanilla, 1-2 teaspoons of honey or maple syrup, and 1-2 teaspoons of chia seed. Top with fresh fruit before eating.

Nutrition Facts

- Cooked and cooled oats as well as overnight oats help create more resistant starch, a prebiotic, that supports gut health.

Healthy Chicken Bites

Are you looking for a delicious and fun way to bring a healthier version of chicken nuggets and French fries into your home? The following three recipes provide alternatives to popular fast food items. Chicken is an excellent source of lean protein and B-vitamins for balanced energy throughout the day. If possible, choose chicken that is organic and pasture-raised.

Directions:

1. Preheat the oven to 400°F.
2. Grease bottom of 9" x 13" baking dish with 2 tablespoons of oil. Set aside remaining oil.
3. Cut chicken into nugget-sized pieces, and set aside.
4. Add milk and egg to a bowl, and whisk together.
5. Place cornmeal and flour with mixed herbs and salt in another bowl, and mix together.
6. Dunk chicken pieces first into liquid mixture, and then dredge through cornmeal and flour mixture until well coated. Place chicken evenly into a baking dish and lightly drizzle remaining oil on top of battered chicken bites. Place the dish into a preheated oven and bake for 10 minutes. Flip the chicken bites and bake for an additional 10 minutes.
7. After 20 minutes, check that the chicken is fully cooked. The internal temperature should reach 165°F.

ingredients

4 tablespoons avocado or coconut oil

1½ pounds chicken breasts (3 to 4 ounces per person)

¾ cup milk (unsweetened non-dairy or dairy milk)

1 egg

¾ cup brown rice flour

¼ cup fine or medium ground cornmeal

2 tablespoons mixed, dried herbs (rosemary, garlic, thyme, oregano)

1 teaspoon salt

Servings: 6

ingredients

8 to 10 cups finely chopped or shredded green or red cabbage (1 small or 1/2 medium head)

½ cucumber, diced

1 carrot, diced or shredded

3 asparagus, finely sliced

4 green onions, finely sliced

Cole Slaw Dressing

½ cup extra virgin olive oil

2 tablespoons apple cider vinegar

2 tablespoons fresh lime juice

1 tablespoon raw honey

¼ cup cilantro, finely chopped

1 to 2 cloves garlic, minced

¼ teaspoon salt

¼ teaspoon black pepper

Servings: 6 to 8

Colorful Cole Slaw

We are sure you will enjoy every bite of this zesty and colorful salad. Make a balanced FAME plate by serving with the **Healthy Chicken Bites** and **Baked Root Fries**.

Directions:

1. In a large serving bowl, combine cabbage, cucumber, carrots, asparagus, and green onions.
2. For the dressing, add all ingredients into a bowl and whisk.
3. Add dressing to cabbage salad so that it is lightly coated and mixes well. Allow salad to marinate for at least 60 minutes before serving. Store any excess dressing in the refrigerator and use for other meals.

ingredients

2 medium sweet potatoes

2 large carrots

2 medium parsnips

2–3 tablespoons avocado oil

1 teaspoon salt

½ teaspoon black pepper

Cayenne pepper, cinnamon, cumin, rosemary, garlic powder (optional)

Servings: 6 to 8

Baked Root Fries

When baking fries, think beyond the white potato. Add more colors and variety with other tasty root veggies, and bring a power-packed nutritional punch to this favorite finger food.

Directions:

1. Preheat the oven to 400°F.
2. Slice potatoes, carrots, and parsnips into thin wedges or "fries" and place in a bowl.
3. Massage root vegetables with oil. Add salt, pepper, and other spices of choice.
4. Spread evenly on a baking sheet and bake for 30 to 45 minutes. Be sure to stir the root fries every 15 minutes. Remove from the oven when slightly brown and crispy.

Tips:

- Experiment with adding different combinations of spices to your baked root fries; combine cumin, garlic and cayenne, or rosemary and garlic powder. For sweet and spicy flavors, combine cinnamon and cayenne.

ingredients

¾ cup mashed, cooked sweet potato (2 medium sweet potatoes)

14-16 ounces cooked or canned salmon

1 egg

⅓ cup medium-grind cornmeal or almond meal

3 tablespoons fresh parsley, finely chopped

2 tablespoons yellow onion, finely chopped

¾ teaspoon paprika

½ teaspoon cumin

½ teaspoon salt

½ teaspoon black pepper

2 tablespoons avocado oil

Servings: 4 patties

Savory Salmon Cakes

These sweet and savory cakes are a delicious way to enjoy salmon throughout the year. They provide a rich source of healthy protein and fat and pair well with a **Basic Green Salad**.

Directions:

1. Cut the sweet potatoes into 2 to 3 inch pieces. Steam until they are soft (about 10 minutes). Or, pierce the sweet potatoes with a fork 3-4 times and microwave for about 5-7 minutes, until soft. Then, puree or mash them.

2. Add cooked or canned salmon (remove excess water) to a bowl. Separate salmon with a fork.

3. Mix together cornmeal or almond meal, parsley, onion, paprika, cumin, salt, and pepper. Add salmon and mashed sweet potato, and mix together. Whisk egg in a small bowl, and gently combine with all ingredients. Shape into four patties.

4. Heat a frying pan over medium heat and add oil. Cook patties for about 3-4 minutes on each side until lightly browned.

Nutrition Facts:

- Canned salmon will often contain small, delicate, and edible bones that provide an excellent source of calcium. We recommend keeping these mineral-rich additions in your recipe. Salmon skin may also be present, which can be a source of omega-3 fatty acids.

Quinoa Veggie Stir-Fry in Collard Wraps

This is a great recipe for getting a variety of vegetables into the diet. Additionally, blanched collard greens make a sturdy wrap for this stir-fry. They can be used as a wrap for burritos, spring rolls, chicken salad, or burgers, for example.

Directions:

1. Add quinoa and water to a saucepan and bring to a boil. Cover and reduce heat to a gentle simmer. Cook for 12 to 15 minutes until water is absorbed. Remove from heat, uncover, and let quinoa cool for 5 to 10 minutes.

2. Whisk eggs in a bowl. Heat 1 tablespoon of oil in a pan or wok, and fry the eggs over medium heat. Set aside in a small bowl.

3. Heat a large pan or wok over medium heat and add 1 tablespoon of oil. Add garlic and ginger and sauté for 2 to 3 minutes. Add the remaining vegetables, mushrooms, and cashews. Sauté for an additional 3 to 4 minutes.

4. Gently fold quinoa into the mixture. Add tamari, vinegar, and scrambled eggs. Continue stirring until the liquid is absorbed, approximately 3 to 5 minutes.

5. Remove from heat and serve in a bowl or prepare as Collard Wraps.

Collard Wraps:

To blanch collard leaves, begin by cutting off the thick stem just below the bottom of the leaf. Heat water in a medium pot (not boiling). Use tongs to dip each leaf into the hot water for 5 to 10 seconds. The leaf should turn a bright green color and soften. Next, dip the leaf into a cold-water bath, or rinse under cold running water. Lay a leaf out flat, and spoon stir-fry ingredients onto one end of the leaf. Begin to roll, fold in the sides, and then finish rolling.

ingredients

1 cup quinoa

2 cups water

6 eggs

2 tablespoons sesame oil

2 cloves garlic, peeled and minced

2 tablespoons ginger, peeled and minced

6 asparagus stalks, finely chopped

1 red bell pepper, finely chopped

1 medium carrot, finely chopped

4 green onions, chopped

1 cup sliced mushrooms (any variety)

1½ cup cashews, whole or chopped

¼ cup low-sodium tamari

¼ cup rice vinegar

6 to 8 large collard greens leaves

Servings: 6

ingredients

Nutritional Facts:

- Mushrooms such as crimini, shiitake, portobello, and button can support a healthy immune system. These amazing fungi provide a unique plant-based source of vitamin D2 as well as numerous other immune-stimulating chemicals.[3] Mushrooms also contain powerful anti-inflammatory compounds.[4]

- Quinoa is one of a few whole grains that is a complete protein. A half cup of cooked quinoa contains up to 4 grams of fiber and 6 grams of protein as well as minerals such as manganese, magnesium, iron, copper, and phosphorus.

- Collard greens are one of the best non-dairy sources of calcium. A cup of cooked collards provides 268 mg of calcium.

Nut Butter Banana Jam Sandwiches

2 bananas

1 teaspoon cinnamon

8 tablespoons nut butter (peanut, almond, cashew)

8 slices 100% whole grain bread

Serving Size: 4

Peanut butter and jelly sandwiches are loved by many. This recipe reminds us that simple substitutions can improve the nutritional value of some of our favorite meals. Substituting a whole fruit like banana for sweetened jelly is a healthy alternative. Remember to check your nut butter labels, and try to avoid added oils, sugars, and preservatives.

Directions:

1. Mash bananas in a bowl and add cinnamon.
2. Spread nut butter on bread slices followed by banana jam. Pair up slices. Cut into halves or quarters.

Turkey Avocado Roll-ups

Directions:

1. Spread a spoonful of hummus on a slice of turkey. Lay a few pieces of spinach flat on the hummus. Place avocado and cucumber at one end of the turkey slice and roll it up. Use a toothpick to hold the roll together, if needed.
2. You may also choose to place a blanched collard green leaf under the turkey slice, and follow the directions above.

Tips:

- To blanch collard leaves, begin by cutting off the thick stem just below the bottom of the leaf. Heat water in a medium pot (not boiling). Use tongs to dip each leaf into the hot water for 5 to 10 seconds. The leaf should turn a bright green color and soften. Next, dip the leaf into a cold-water bath, or rinse under cold running water. Lay a leaf out flat, and add ingredients onto one end of the leaf. Begin to roll, fold in the sides, and then finish rolling.

ingredients

8 slices of turkey

½ cup hummus

1 cup baby spinach

1 medium avocado, thinly sliced

1 cucumber, julienned

4 collard green leaves (optional)

Servings: 4

Cocoa Loco Bars

These delicious bars are energy-dense and very satisfying. The bars provide several sources of dietary fat through a variety of nuts, seeds, chocolate, and butter or coconut oil.

Directions:

1. Grease a 9 x 9 inch baking pan.
2. Mix together dry ingredients (walnuts, sunflower seeds, ground flaxseed, and pumpkin seeds) in a medium bowl.
3. Melt together dark chocolate chips, nut butter, and butter or coconut oil over a double boiler, stirring regularly.
4. Add the dry ingredients to the bowl of melted ingredients and stir until mixed.
5. Press into the baking pan. Chill for 15-20 minutes in the freezer or one hour in a refrigerator until the bars are solid. Cut into 24 bars.

Tips:

- These bars can be stored in the fridge for up to five days.

ingredients

1 cup walnuts, chopped

1 cup sunflower seeds, raw

1 cup ground flaxseed

¼ cup pumpkin seeds

1¼ cup dark chocolate chips

1 cup almond or peanut butter

¼ cup butter or coconut oil

Servings: 24 bars

ingredients

1 ½ cups cooked or canned garbanzo beans

¼ cup water

2 tablespoons extra virgin olive oil

1 to 2 teaspoons lemon juice

1 teaspoon tahini (ground sesame seeds)

2 cloves garlic, minced

¼ teaspoon salt

Servings: 4

Homemade Hummus

Hummus highlights the rich flavor of garbanzo beans while providing a simple, delicious way to include protein, fat, and fiber in your meal. Dipping chopped vegetables of any kind (peppers, carrots, celery, or cucumber) in hummus can be an excellent snack for adults and children.

Directions:

1. Prepare garbanzo beans. (See Chapter Fifteen, **Kitchen Skills** for preparing from dry beans.) If using canned beans, drain and rinse.
2. Add cooked beans, lemon juice, garlic, tahini, salt, olive oil, and half the water in a blender or food processor. Blend for one minute on medium speed until thoroughly mixed and smooth. Add more water as needed for desired consistency.

Tips:

- Hummus can be served immediately or stored in the refrigerator for 3–5 days. Enjoy as a dip for fresh vegetables or the **Spring Herb Crackers,** or use as a spread for the **Turkey Avocado Roll-ups**. For additional flavors of the hummus, add fresh greens (spinach or kale), roasted red peppers, jalapeno, or cayenne pepper.

Golden Delicious Granola

Store-bought granola can be expensive and full of refined sweeteners and highly processed oils. Save money and enjoy this homemade version using your favorite healthy nuts and seeds. Serve as a topping to plain Greek yogurt or in a smoothie bowl. Pay attention to serving size with this sweet treat, since granola contains added sweeteners.

Directions:

1. Preheat the oven to 350°F.
2. Combine all the dry ingredients, except dried coconut, in one bowl (oats, nuts, seeds, salt, cinnamon).
3. Melt the oil or butter in a saucepan. Add vanilla and maple syrup to the melted oil and mix.
4. Pour the wet ingredients slowly into the dry ingredients and mix thoroughly.
5. Spread the granola on a baking sheet in a thin, even layer and bake for 30 to 40 minutes. Stir the granola every 5 to 10 minutes to prevent burning around the edges. After 20 minutes of baking, gently fold in the dried coconut for the final 10 to 15 minutes of baking.
6. Remove granola from the oven and let cool.
7. Leftovers can be stored in an airtight container for up to two weeks.

Tips:

- Experiment with other combinations of nuts, seeds, and spices.

ingredients

2 cups rolled oats

½ cup raw nuts *(slivered almonds, chopped walnuts or hazelnuts)*

¼ cup raw seeds *(pumpkin or sunflower)*

1 ½–2 teaspoons cinnamon

¼ teaspoon salt

¼ cup coconut oil or butter

3 tablespoons maple syrup

1 teaspoon vanilla extract

¼ cup unsweetened shredded coconut

Servings: 6

Egg and Veggie Scramble

Finding creative ways to include veggies in a meal can be especially challenging for breakfast. With a few minutes of chopping and a few minutes of cooking, you can have a delicious, nutritious scramble to start your day. Use any fresh vegetable in your fridge.

Directions:

1. Chop all veggies into 1/2-inch pieces.
2. Crack eggs into a mixing bowl and whisk together.
3. Heat oil or butter in a skillet on medium heat and sauté onions until translucent. Add garlic and vegetables and sauté for 3 to 4 minutes, until slightly softened.
4. Lower the heat to low-medium and add the eggs to the skillet. Season with salt and pepper.
5. Stir mixture occasionally, turning the eggs and veggies in the pan. Continue until the eggs are set and no longer runny—approximately 5 minutes.
6. Add optional toppings, avocado and/or tomato, and enjoy your morning veggies.

Nutrition Facts:

- Organic, pasture-raised eggs provide a complete protein, as well as B-vitamins and choline, an important nutrient for healthy brain function.

ingredients

4 cups chopped vegetables (broccoli, bell peppers, mushrooms, zucchini, Brussels sprouts, and greens such as spinach and chard)

8 eggs

2 tablespoons avocado or coconut oil, or butter

¼ cup diced onion

1 clove garlic, peeled and minced

½ teaspoon salt

¼ teaspoon black pepper

½ avocado, diced (optional)

1 tomato, diced (optional)

Servings: 4

ingredients

1 cup raw almonds

3 cups water for soaking

2 to 3 cups water for blending

salt, a pinch

½ teaspoon vanilla extract (optional)

1 teaspoon cinnamon (optional)

Servings: 2 to 3 cups

Homemade Almond Milk

Store-bought almond milk is hard to find without added sugar and almost always contains natural or artificial flavors, as well as gums and thickeners. Avoid unnecessary additives and enjoy a big difference in taste with this homemade almond milk.

Directions:

1. Place the raw almonds in a large bowl and cover with two inches of water. Loosely cover the bowl, and keep it in the fridge or on your countertop. Let the almonds soak for at least 6 hours, and up to 24 hours.

2. After soaking, drain the water and rinse the almonds. Add 1 cup soaked almonds and 2 to 3 cups of fresh water (the less water, the more creamy the almond milk will be) to a blender. Add salt and optional ingredients, vanilla extract and/or cinnamon. Blend on high for 1 to 2 minutes.

3. Once blended, pass the mixture through a fine cheesecloth placed within a strainer over a bowl or pitcher. Press out as much of the almond milk through the cheesecloth as possible. You may use a nut-milk bag, which is a reusable fine mesh bag used for straining. Alternatively, don't strain the milk and use it for smoothies.

Tips:

- Store your homemade almond milk in an airtight container for up to 3 or 4 days. It will settle and separate but can be shaken to remix.

Rainbow Nachos

Rainbow Nachos are a fun and delicious way to get vegetables into the diet and can help make nachos a quick and healthy meal choice.

Directions:

1. Preheat the oven to 375°F.
2. If using canned beans, drain and rinse. In a bowl, mix beans with cumin, cayenne pepper, and salt.
3. Grate the cheese.
4. Spread chips out on a baking sheet. Layer first with beans. Then, add the chopped onions, bell pepper, kale, and tomatoes. Top with grated cheese.
5. Place nachos in the oven and bake for approximately 10 minutes until the cheese is melted.
6. Top with guacamole, chopped cilantro, diced tomatoes, or fresh salsa.

Tips:

- Add an additional layer to your nachos of cooked and diced chicken breast or cooked lean ground beef, chicken, or turkey for more protein.

Nutrition Facts:

- Black beans are a good source of fiber and protein. Black beans provide folate. Folate is an important B vitamin that is protective against cardiovascular disease.
- Kale is a source of beta-carotene (a precursor to vitamin A), vitamin K, and folate. In addition, kale is a great way to include a plant-based source of calcium in your diet.
- Tomatoes contain immune-supporting vitamin C and the powerful antioxidant, lycopene.
- Tomatoes are often excluded in many anti-inflammatory diets because they are in the nightshade family, which is a group of

ingredients

- 3 cups cooked or canned black beans
- ½ teaspoon cumin
- ¼ teaspoon cayenne pepper
- ¼ teaspoon salt
- 1 to 1½ cups grated cheddar cheese (optional)
- 8 to 10 ounce bag whole grain corn chips
- ½ cup diced onion
- 1 bell pepper, diced
- ½ bunch kale, finely chopped
- 1 to 2 tomatoes, diced

Servings: 4 to 6

ingredients

2 to 3 ripe avocados

2 tablespoons finely diced red onion

1 clove garlic, peeled and minced

1 tomato, diced

¼ cup cilantro, finely chopped

2 tablespoons lime juice

¼ to ½ teaspoon salt

1 jalapeno, minced (optional)

Servings: 4 to 6

plants that contain chemicals called alkaloids. There is anecdotal evidence that shows for certain individuals, consuming alkaloids from nightshades can lead to a worsening of their arthritis and digestive symptoms. Most people tolerate these chemicals without issue.

Guacamole

Directions:

1. Peel the avocados, remove the pit, and mash with a fork or potato masher to a smooth texture. Mix in onions, garlic, tomato, cilantro, lime juice, salt, and jalapeno (optional).
2. Serve immediately.

Tips:

- Serve with **Rainbow Nachos**, **Egg and Veggie Scramble** or with **Refried Beans and Rice**.

Nutrition Facts:

- People are often surprised to learn that avocados can provide more potassium than bananas. One medium banana contains 422 mg of potassium while one medium avocado contains up to 700 mg of potassium (and 12 grams of fiber). Potassium is a critical mineral for healthy heart function. Our bodies work best with a potassium-to-sodium ratio of greater than two parts potassium to one part sodium. A lower ratio puts us at risk for cardiovascular disease. In the Standard American Diet, people generally are over-consuming sodium and under-consuming potassium. Reducing added salt in the diet from processed foods and eating fresh fruits and vegetables will improve your potassium to sodium ratio.

Vegetable Broth

Vegetable broth delivers vitamins and minerals as well as delicious flavor to many recipes. To make vegetable broth, you can use any vegetables available, even your veggie scraps from other recipes. Save your scraps from chopped carrots, bell pepper, mushrooms, fennel, celery, onion skins, and stems and leaves from all dark green leafy veggies. Freeze the scraps and when you have saved enough, make a broth. Use the directions below as a guideline.

Directions:

1. Chop all vegetables into 1-inch or smaller pieces.
2. Heat a large pot over medium heat and add oil. Add onion and sauté until translucent, about 3 to 5 minutes.
3. Add garlic, carrots, and celery. Sauté for another 3 to 5 minutes until softened.
4. Add water, herbs, and additional vegetables and bring to a boil. Add salt if desired. Lower heat and simmer, uncovered, for at least 60 minutes. You can strain the vegetables or blend all ingredients together with an immersion blender, creating a thicker broth.

ingredients

1 tablespoon avocado oil

1 onion, diced

8 cloves garlic, peeled and minced

2 carrots, chopped

2 stalks celery, including leaves, chopped

4 sprigs fresh rosemary

2 sprigs fresh thyme

2 bay leaves

1 teaspoon salt (optional)

8 cups water

2 cups additional vegetable scraps (optional)

Servings: Makes 8 cups

Basic Bone Broth

ingredients

- 4 pounds bones from organic, pasture-raised chicken, cow, lamb, or turkey
- 1 carrot, diced
- 1 onion, diced
- 4 cloves garlic, peeled and minced
- 2 tablespoons apple cider vinegar
- 16 cups of water (or enough to cover the bones)

Servings: Makes 16 cups

The health benefits of nutrient-dense bone broth are numerous! Bone broth and stock both involve simmering animal bones, however bone broth typically indicates a longer cooking duration at a lower temperature. The extended cooking process allows for more nutrient extraction. Bone broth promotes strong bones and healthy skin and hair because of its mineral content, collagen, and gelatin. While some planning is required, preparing bone broth at home is an investment in your health.

Directions:

1. Add all ingredients in a large stockpot and simmer on low heat for at least 8 to 12 hours.
2. Occasionally skim foam that collects on the surface.
3. After 8 to 12 hours, strain the bones and vegetables from the liquid. Enjoy the bone broth by itself, or use it as a base for other soups.

Tips:

- The broth can be stored in the refrigerator for three days or in the freezer for three months.

Nutrition Facts:

- The addition of vinegar allows for the extraction of the healthy minerals and amino acids from the bones.

SPRING AND SUMMER

Spring Lentil Soup *230*
Spring Herb Crackers *231*
Hearty Salmon Salad *233*
Basic Vinaigrette Dressing *235*
Garden-fresh Summer Squash Salad *236*
Lemon Rice *237*
Coconut Berry Bliss *238*
Rainbow Quinoa Salad *240*
Sautéed Seasonal Greens *242*
Summer Tomato Avocado Salad *243*
Basic Green Salad with Protein *244*

ingredients

2 tablespoons avocado oil, ghee, or butter

1 yellow onion, diced

2 stalks celery, finely diced

2 carrots, finely diced

5 cloves garlic, peeled and minced

2 cups red lentils

8 cups vegetable or chicken broth or stock

1 cup fresh parsley, chopped

1 cup fresh basil, chopped

5 cups spinach, finely chopped

½ cup lemon juice

1 teaspoon salt

Servings: 6 to 8

Spring Lentil Soup

Soup is a delicious way to add more greens to the diet. Lentils provide an excellent, plant-based protein and have a short cooking time. In springtime, this herb-rich lentil soup pairs wonderfully with **Spring Herb Crackers**.

Directions:

1. Heat a large pot over medium heat and add oil or butter. Add onions and sauté for 3 to 4 minutes. Then add celery, carrots, and garlic. Sauté for an additional 3 to 4 minutes.

2. Rinse and drain red lentils and add to the pot along with the broth.

   Bring to a boil and cover. Reduce heat and simmer for 20 to 25 minutes, until lentils are soft and thoroughly cooked.

3. Remove the pot from heat and add parsley, basil, spinach, lemon juice, and salt. Stir until well combined and serve.

Spring Herb Crackers

These simple, savory gluten-free crackers are a FAME favorite. They pair well with the **Homemade Hummus**.

Directions:

1. Preheat the oven to 350°F.
2. Combine almond meal, salt, and fresh chopped herbs in a bowl.
3. Whisk together melted oil or butter and egg in a separate bowl.
4. Stir wet ingredients into almond meal mixture until thoroughly combined.
5. Roll the dough into a ball. On a baking sheet, press dough between two sheets of parchment paper to ⅛ to ¼ inch thickness. Use a rolling pin, if available.
6. Remove the top piece of parchment paper.
7. Cut dough into 2-inch squares or other desired shape with a knife or pizza cutter.
8. Bake for 10-15 minutes, until lightly golden. Watch carefully.
9. Let crackers cool on the baking sheet for 10 minutes, then serve.

ingredients

1¾ cups almond meal

½ teaspoon salt

2 tablespoons fresh rosemary or thyme, finely chopped without the stem

1 teaspoon fennel seed, finely chopped (optional)

1 tablespoon avocado oil, melted coconut oil, butter, or ghee

1 egg

Servings: 24

Hearty Salmon Salad

This colorful, fresh salad is nutrient-packed. Salmon, fresh veggies, herbs, and a zesty dressing make this one of the most popular meals in the FAME community cooking classes.

Directions:

1. In a large bowl, add salmon and use a fork to pull the fish apart.
2. Add olive oil, lemon juice, carrots, celery, onion, dill, tarragon, and parsley to the bowl and mix. Set aside.
3. In a large salad bowl, add lettuce or mixed greens with chopped cucumbers, tomatoes, and hazelnuts.
4. Place salmon salad mixture on top of green salad. Drizzle dressing of choice onto the salad and salmon. See recipe for **Basic Vinaigrette Dressing**. Serve immediately.

Tips:

- Use canned salmon or leftover baked or grilled salmon. The small, delicate bones found in canned salmon can be eaten, and they are an excellent food source of calcium. The salmon salad can be stored in an air-tight container for 3 to 4 days in the refrigerator. It makes a great to-go lunch.

Nutrition Facts:

- Omega-3 fatty acids are essential fatty acids that must be obtained from the diet. Omega-3 fatty acids help to reduce inflammation and to support a healthy heart. They are found in cold-water, oily fish such as salmon, mackerel, tuna, herring, sardines, and anchovies.

ingredients

Salmon Salad

12 to 24 ounces canned or cooked salmon (3-4 ounces per person)

2 tablespoons extra virgin olive oil

¼ cup lemon juice

1 carrot, finely grated

2 stalks celery, finely diced

½ medium red onion, finely diced

1 teaspoon finely chopped fresh dill

1 teaspoon finely chopped fresh tarragon

2 tablespoons finely chopped fresh parsley

Green Salad

1 head red or green leaf lettuce, chopped, or 6 to 8 cups mixed greens

1 cucumber, sliced

2 tomatoes, sliced or 1 cup cherry tomatoes

1 cup hazelnuts, chopped

Servings: 4 to 6

Basic Vinaigrette Dressing

Directions:

1. Combine these ingredients in a small bowl and whisk together.

ingredients

- ½ cup extra virgin olive oil
- ¼ cup vinegar (balsamic, apple cider)
- 1 teaspoon maple syrup or raw honey
- 1 teaspoon yellow or dijon mustard
- ¼ teaspoon salt or to taste
- ⅛ teaspoon black pepper
- 1 tablespoon finely chopped fresh or dried herbs (parsley, tarragon, dill)

Servings: 12

ingredients

3 cups cooked or canned garbanzo or white beans

1 cup diced zucchini (about ½ inch)

1 tomato, diced

1 clove garlic, peeled and minced

½ cup finely chopped fresh basil leaves

2 tablespoons finely chopped fresh oregano, without stems

2 tablespoons finely chopped fresh parsley

½ teaspoon salt

¼ teaspoon black pepper

Dressing Ingredients

½ cup extra virgin olive oil

¼ cup apple cider vinegar

1 clove garlic, peeled and minced

1 teaspoon finely chopped fresh herbs, (oregano, parsley, basil, or combination)

1 teaspoon finely diced onion

1 teaspoon Dijon mustard

¼ teaspoon salt

⅛ teaspoon black pepper

Servings: 6

Garden-fresh Summer Squash Salad

If you have a garden, you may be able to supply most of the ingredients for this colorful, herb-filled recipe. Enjoy the inspiring scents provided by the spring herbs.

Directions:

1. In a medium bowl, combine beans, zucchini, tomato, garlic, basil, oregano, and parsley. Add salt and pepper. Toss gently.
2. Combine all dressing ingredients in a bowl and whisk together.
3. Add dressing to the salad mixture and mix. Let the salad marinate for at least 30 minutes in the refrigerator before serving.

Tips:

- You can also enjoy this salad over greens or as a side dish with a lean protein source such as baked fish or chicken.

Lemon Rice

Brighten your brown rice with lemon and herbs!

Directions:

1. Combine broth, butter or oil, and rice into a medium saucepan.
2. Bring to a boil, then reduce heat.
3. Cover the pot, and allow it to simmer for 40 to 45 minutes, or until liquid is absorbed.
4. Remove from heat. Stir in lemon juice and basil. Fluff with a fork before serving.

ingredients

2½ cups vegetable or chicken broth or stock

2 teaspoons butter or coconut oil

1 cup brown rice

¼ cup lemon juice

1 teaspoon finely chopped fresh basil

Servings: 4

ingredients

1 cup full-fat canned coconut milk

1 tablespoon maple syrup

½ teaspoon cinnamon

⅛ teaspoon salt

½ teaspoon vanilla extract

4 cups fresh or frozen berries (raspberries, blueberries, strawberries)

4 tablespoons ground flaxseed

4 tablespoons chopped nuts (optional)

Servings: 4

Coconut Berry Bliss

This naturally sweet treat is made with fresh berries and spiced coconut milk. Coconut Berry Bliss is a great alternative to typical desserts with high amounts of sugar and refined carbohydrates.

Directions:

1. Mix coconut milk with maple syrup, cinnamon, salt, and vanilla extract in a small bowl.
2. Add one cup of berries into each of four small bowls. Add ¼ cup of coconut mixture plus 1 tablespoon of ground flaxseed and 1 tablespoon chopped nuts (optional) on top of each bowl. Serve immediately.

Rainbow Quinoa Salad

ingredients

1 cup quinoa (red or white)

2 cups water

2 cups finely chopped spinach

2 to 3 cups cooked or canned black beans

1 cup frozen corn, thawed

1 red or orange bell pepper, diced

2 medium tomatoes, diced

5 green onions, chopped

¼ cup chopped cilantro

1 avocado, diced

Dressing ingredients

½ cup extra virgin olive oil

¼ cup apple cider vinegar

¼ cup lime juice

1 teaspoon salt

1 teaspoon cumin

⅛ teaspoon chili powder

black pepper to taste

Servings: 4 to 6

This is a colorful recipe to add to your cooking repertoire, and it has an abundance of flavor! Colorful meals ensure you are consuming a wide range of vitamins, minerals, and antioxidants. This quinoa salad can be served warm or cold or enjoyed in a collard green wrap.

Directions:

1. To prepare the quinoa: bring two cups of water to a boil in a medium saucepan. Add 1 cup quinoa and return to a boil. Reduce heat to simmer, cover, and cook for 12 to 15 minutes, until water is absorbed. Remove from heat. Add chopped spinach on top of quinoa, cover with a lid, and steam for 3 minutes. Let the quinoa sit for an additional five minutes, and then fluff with a fork.

2. If using canned beans, drain and rinse. While quinoa is cooking, mix the black beans, corn, bell pepper, tomatoes, green onion, and cilantro in a separate bowl and gently stir.

3. In a separate bowl, whisk together the dressing ingredients.

4. Fold the quinoa into the bean mixture. Slowly add the dressing. Stir until mixed well.

5. Add diced avocado and enjoy.

Nutrition Facts:

- Quinoa adds a plant-based, complete protein to the recipe. The beans add protein and fiber. Tomatoes are an excellent source of vitamin C and the antioxidant, lycopene.

ingredients

¾ pound (1 bunch) dark green leafy greens (rainbow chard, mustard greens, dandelion greens, kale)

2 tablespoons healthy fat or oil

6 cloves garlic, finely chopped

3 teaspoons yellow onion, finely chopped

2 tablespoons apple cider vinegar

Servings: 6

Sautéed Seasonal Greens

A delicious and simple way to enjoy dark green leafy veggies is to sauté them in a healthy fat or oil, such as butter or ghee, coconut oil, avocado oil, extra virgin olive oil, or animal fats, such as lard and tallow. The recipe below can be adapted to include your favorite spices.

Directions:

1. Chop or tear greens into smaller pieces. Remove thick stems if present.
2. Heat a pan over medium heat (or low-medium heat if using extra virgin olive oil), and add a healthy fat or oil of your choosing.
3. Add onion and sauté for 2 to 3 minutes.
4. Add the garlic and the greens and gently stir until the leaves are wilted but still a bright green color.
5. Add apple cider vinegar and enjoy.

Nutrition Facts:

- Green leafy vegetables are a good source of antioxidants, beta-carotene, a precursor to vitamin A, and many minerals including calcium.

Summer Tomato Avocado Salad

This salad incorporates several summer garden favorites like tomato, cucumber, red pepper, and fresh herbs. It makes a refreshing side salad to any summer meal.

Directions:

1. Add all the vegetables to a bowl and set aside.
2. To a small bowl add the dressing ingredients, olive oil, vinegar, garlic, salt, and fresh herbs. Stir or whisk.
3. Add the dressing to the vegetables and gently mix. Serve immediately or store in the refrigerator.

Tips:

Add 1 cup of garbanzo beans for some extra protein and fiber!

ingredients

- 4 medium tomatoes, medium diced
- 1 English cucumber, halved and sliced
- ½ red pepper, medium diced
- ¼ red onion, finely diced
- 1 large avocado, diced
- 2 tablespoons extra virgin olive oil
- 2 tablespoons apple cider vinegar
- 1 clove garlic, finely minced
- ½ teaspoon salt
- 2 tablespoons fresh herbs, chopped (basil or parsley)

Servings: 4

ingredients

8 cups chopped dark green salad leaves (romaine, green or red lettuce, mixed greens, spinach)

12-16 ounces cooked turkey, chicken, fish, steak, or tofu or tempeh

2 eggs, hard-boiled

1 cucumber, diced

2 tomatoes, diced

½ cup sunflower seeds

1 carrot, finely chopped

1 avocado, sliced

Basic Vinaigrette Dressing

½ cup extra virgin olive oil

¼ cup vinegar (balsamic or apple cider)

1 teaspoon raw honey

1 teaspoon yellow or dijon mustard

¼ teaspoon salt

⅛ teaspoon black pepper

Servings: 4

Basic Green Salad with Protein

Add a healthy source of protein to this salad for a balanced meal. Include cooked chicken, fish, turkey, steak, tofu, or tempeh. A simple salad and leftover cooked meat or poultry make for a quick, healthy dinner or lunch. The dressing can be made ahead of time and used throughout the week.

Directions:

1. Chop or tear green leaves into small pieces. Chop vegetables into 1-inch cubes. Slice hard-boiled eggs. Chop cooked meat, fish, or poultry into small pieces. Add all ingredients into a large salad bowl.

2. Whisk dressing ingredients together.

3. Drizzle dressing on the salad and enjoy.

Tips:

- To hard-boil eggs, place 6 eggs in a single layer at the bottom of a saucepan. Cover with 2 inches of cold water. Heat the pot on high heat and bring the water to a full rolling boil for 1 to 2 minutes. Turn off the heat, keep the pan on the hot burner, and let sit for 10 to 12 minutes. Carefully pour off the hot water from the pan and run very cold water over the eggs to cool them quickly and stop them from cooking further. Crack and peel away the shells of two eggs for the recipe and store the extra hard boiled eggs in a covered container in the refrigerator. Eat as a healthy snack within 5 days.

Nutrition Facts:

- The protein, fat, and fiber found in this basic green salad support healthy blood sugar regulation.

FALL AND WINTER

Spaghetti Squash Pasta with Hearty Marinara Sauce   247

Roasted Beet Salad with White Miso Vinaigrette   249

Bean and Veggie Chili   250

Easy Cornbread   252

Ginger Tempeh Stir Fry with Quinoa   253

Black-eyed Peas and Collard Greens Soup   254

Sweet Potato Cornbread   255

Pumpkin Pie Amaranth Porridge   256

Delicata Squash Over Broccoli and Quinoa   258

Baked Acorn Squash   259

Spiced Red Lentils (dal) with Spinach   260

Black Bean Pumpkin Soup   261

Roasted Brussels Sprouts   262

Spaghetti Squash Pasta with Hearty Marinara Sauce

You can reimagine a spaghetti dinner of noodles and red sauce with this nutrient-packed recipe. It is filled with a variety of colorful vegetables, healthy protein, and uses spaghetti squash for the noodles instead of refined pasta. It also includes a healthy, dairy-free cheese alternative.

Directions:

1. Preheat the oven to 400°F. Using a large, sharp knife, cut the spaghetti squash in half lengthwise. Scoop out the seeds using a spoon. Brush each half using 1 tablespoon of avocado oil, and sprinkle with ½ teaspoon of salt and pinch of pepper. Place the spaghetti squash halves cut-side down on a sheet pan. Roast for about 40 minutes, or until easily pierced with a fork. Remove the squash from the oven, flip the halves upright, and let cool for several minutes. Use a fork to gently scrape and fluff the strands from the sides of the cooked squash.

2. While the squash is roasting, cook the ground meat or crumbled tofu. (See *Tips* below for how to crumble tofu.) Heat a large skillet over medium heat and add 1 tablespoon of oil. Add the ground meat or crumbled tofu and cook, regularly stirring until the meat is no longer pink. Cooked ground beef should have an internal temperature of 160°F and cooked poultry 165°F. Set aside.

3. Next, make the marinara sauce. Heat a large saucepan over medium-high heat. Add the remaining 2 tablespoons of avocado oil. Add the onion, carrots, bell pepper, and garlic. Sauté for about 5 minutes or until they start to become tender. Add the grated zucchini, finely diced mushrooms, 1 teaspoon salt, and Italian seasoning. Sauté for about 5 more minutes, or until zucchini and mushrooms become tender.

4. Add the tomato paste, stir to coat the vegetable mixture, and cook for about 2 minutes. Then add the crushed tomatoes and vegetable broth to the pot, making sure to scrape the bottom of the pot.

ingredients

- 1 large spaghetti squash
- 3-4 tablespoons avocado oil
- 1 medium yellow onion, finely chopped
- 2 large carrots, finely chopped
- 1 red bell pepper, finely chopped
- 8 ounces cremini mushrooms, finely chopped
- 1 medium zucchini, grated
- 2 teaspoons salt, divided
- 4 cloves garlic, minced
- 1 tablespoon dried Italian seasoning
- 3 tablespoons tomato paste
- 28-ounces crushed tomatoes
- 1 cup low-sodium vegetable or chicken broth or stock
- 2 tablespoons balsamic vinegar
- 2 cups baby spinach, finely chopped
- ½ cup fresh basil, finely chopped
- 1 pound cooked lean ground beef, chicken or turkey, or 16 ounces of extra-firm tofu
- Grated parmesan (optional)

ingredients

NON-DAIRY CHEESE BLEND

½ cup hemp hearts

½ cup nutritional yeast

½ teaspoon garlic powder

½ teaspoon onion powder

½ teaspoon salt

Servings: 4-6

5. Add the cooked meat or tofu. Bring the mixture to a boil, reduce heat and simmer for 15 minutes.
6. Add the balsamic vinegar, chopped spinach and basil. Cook for 2-3 minutes, or until spinach is wilted.
7. Serve the marinara sauce over cooked spaghetti squash. Mix together ingredients and top with the non-dairy cheese blend or parmesan cheese if desired. Store leftovers in an airtight container in the refrigerator for up to 4 days.

Tips:

- Crumbled, extra-firm tofu can serve as a plant-based alternative to ground meat in many dishes.

  Drain and dry the extra firm tofu prior to cooking in order to get the best texture and flavor. Slice tofu block in half. Place tofu halves on a couple layers of paper towels or on a clean kitchen towel. Cover the tofu with additional paper towels or a clean towel. Lay a heavy skillet on top of the covered tofu and wait at least 10 minutes for additional moisture to be pressed out. If you frequently bake tofu, you may want to consider purchasing a tofu press. Break tofu apart with your hands into small pieces. Cook the tofu on a heated skillet with oil. The crumbled tofu should brown and become a little crispy.

Roasted Beet Salad with White Miso Vinaigrette

This hearty winter salad is a great way to pair greens, root veggies, fruit, and nuts with a savory miso dressing. Miso is a fermented soybean paste that adds a delicious and savory flavor to the dressing. You can pair this salad with the **Marinated Steak Bites**, **Baked Salmon Cakes** or other roasted fish or chicken.

Directions:

1. Preheat the oven to 400°F.
2. Place peeled and diced beets on a large sheet pan, and toss with avocado oil, salt, and pepper. Roast for 40–45 minutes or until tender and easily pierced with a fork. Remove from the oven, and set aside to cool while preparing the rest of the salad.
3. Add 1–2 tablespoons of white miso and 1–2 tablespoons of warm water to a bowl and mix until smooth. Add olive oil, vinegar, honey, garlic, and black pepper. Set aside.
4. In a large bowl, toss arugula with about half the vinaigrette. Arrange diced beets, sliced pears, and almonds over the dressed greens. Drizzle a few tablespoons of remaining vinaigrette over the top, top with crumbled goat cheese or feta, and serve.

Tips:

- You can sub other greens, root veggies, fruit, or nuts in this recipe. For example, finely chopped kale, roasted sweet potato, apple, and chopped hazelnuts are another great combination.

ingredients

4 medium beets, peeled and diced (about ½ inch)

1 tablespoon avocado oil

½ teaspoon salt

¼ teaspoon black pepper

5 ounces baby arugula (about 5 packed cups)

2 ripe pears, sliced

½ cup slivered or sliced almonds

4 ounces crumbled goat cheese or feta

WHITE MISO VINAIGRETTE

¼ cup extra virgin olive oil

¼ cup apple cider vinegar

1–2 tablespoons white miso

1–2 tablespoons warm water

1–2 teaspoons raw honey

1 clove garlic, finely minced or grated

¼ teaspoon black pepper

Servings: 4

ingredients

1 tablespoon avocado or coconut oil, or butter

½ yellow onion, diced

4 cloves garlic, peeled and minced

1 red bell pepper, diced

4 cups diced tomatoes, with liquid, or 1 can (32 ounces) diced tomatoes

4 cups cooked or canned beans (kidney, black, pinto or combination)

1 cup frozen whole corn

1 cup vegetable or chicken broth or stock

1 teaspoon salt

½ teaspoon black pepper

2 tablespoons cumin

2 tablespoons chili powder

⅛ teaspoon cayenne pepper

⅛ teaspoon cinnamon

1½ cups finely chopped spinach or kale

Toppings

2 avocados, diced

½ cup chopped fresh cilantro

Serving size: 8

Bean and Veggie Chili

This recipe is a healthy twist on a common fall and winter comfort food. It's a wholesome, one pot meal and can be made in double batches to freeze leftovers. Use this recipe to avoid the excessive sodium, artificial flavors, and ultra-processed meat often found in canned chili. Any veggies can be added, especially dark leafy greens. Add ground turkey, chicken, or lean beef for an extra protein. The **Easy Cornbread** recipe accompanies this recipe well.

Directions:

1. Heat a large pot over medium heat and add oil. Sauté onions until translucent, about 3-5 minutes.
2. Add garlic and red pepper and sauté for an additional 3 minutes.
3. Add diced tomato, beans (rinse and drain canned beans, if needed), corn, and vegetable or chicken broth. Add spices and bring to a boil.
4. Reduce heat and simmer for 20–30 minutes. Add additional broth if needed.
5. Add the spinach in the last 5 minutes of cooking.
6. Top each bowl of chili with chopped cilantro and diced avocado.

Tips:

- If using canned tomatoes or beans, look for these items in glass jars or in cans or packaging that is BPA-free.
- Check the bulk section of grocery stores for a premixed chili blend, which will often contain cumin, chili pepper, garlic powder, oregano, coriander, cloves, and allspice.

ingredients

1½ cups cornmeal, medium or fine grind

1½ cups brown rice flour

1 teaspoon baking powder

½ teaspoon baking soda

1 teaspoon salt

1½ cups milk (unsweetened non-dairy or dairy milk)

3 tablespoons maple syrup

2 eggs

½ cup coconut oil or butter, melted

Servings: 16

Easy Cornbread

Directions:

1. Preheat the oven to 375°F.
2. Grease a 9 x 13 inch baking pan.
3. In a large bowl, mix together the cornmeal, brown rice flour, baking powder, baking soda, and salt.
4. In a second bowl, whisk together the milk, maple syrup, eggs, and melted oil or butter.
5. Add dry and wet ingredients and stir—just until combined.
6. Pour batter into the pan and bake until golden brown, 25 to 30 minutes. A knife or toothpick inserted in the middle should come out clean. Serve while warm.

Tips:

- If you are avoiding eggs, consider the following egg substitutions for baking:

    1 egg = ¼ cup unsweetened applesauce = 1 tablespoon ground-flaxseed with ¼ cup hot water; let sit for 5 minutes to create a gelatinous consistency.

Ginger Tempeh Stir-Fry with Quinoa

The dressing with sesame oil, ginger, and garlic help create this flavorful dish. Tamari is a fermented, gluten-free soy sauce, making it an ideal option for those avoiding wheat or gluten in the diet. This is a terrific recipe with which to practice creating your healthy FAME plate with appropriate portion sizes.

Directions:

1. Add the dressing ingredients—sesame oil, rice vinegar, tamari, raw honey or maple syrup, ginger root, and garlic, to a small bowl and whisk.
2. Prepare the tempeh: Cut the tempeh into 2-inch cubes, or slice into ½ inch strips. Marinate the tempeh in ½ cup of the ginger tamari dressing for 10 to 15 minutes prior to sautéing.
3. While the tempeh is marinating, prepare the quinoa. Bring 2 cups of water to a boil in a medium saucepan. Add 1 cup quinoa and return to a boil. Reduce heat to simmer, cover, and cook for 12 to 15 minutes, until water is absorbed. Remove from heat. Let the quinoa sit for five minutes and then fluff with a fork.
4. Dice the vegetables and cut the broccoli into florets. Heat 2 tablespoons of sesame oil over medium heat in a large frying pan or wok and add the vegetables. Pour remaining dressing onto vegetables and cook for 5 to 10 minutes until vegetables are softened but still brightly colored. Add the cashews for the last few minutes.
5. In a large skillet, add the tempeh with marinade sauce and cook it for 5 to 10 minutes, turning frequently, until the tempeh is lightly browned.
6. Create a healthy FAME plate: Serve 1 to 2 cups of cooked vegetables on half of the plate. Place ½ cup of quinoa on one quarter of the plate. Add 3 to 4 ounce serving of tempeh on one quarter of the plate.

Nutritional Facts:

- Soybeans provide a complete plant-based protein and are a good

ingredients

12–16 ounces organic tempeh

2 cups water

1 cup quinoa

2 tablespoons sesame oil

6 to 8 cups chopped vegetables, including onion, broccoli, carrots, celery, bok choy, snow peas, and/or cabbage

¾ cup of cashews

GINGER TAMARI DRESSING

½ cup sesame oil

¼ cup rice vinegar

¼ cup low-sodium tamari

1 tablespoon maple syrup or raw honey

1 teaspoon peeled and minced ginger root

1 clove garlic, peeled and minced

Servings: 4

source of fiber. A three-ounce serving of tempeh contains about 16 grams of protein and 7 grams of fiber.

- Broccoli is a cruciferous vegetable that is high in carotenoids and antioxidants, which can be protective against cancer and inflammation.[5] It is also a good source of vitamin C, A, K, folate, calcium, and fiber.
- Cashew nuts are a rich source of monounsaturated fats, like olive oil and avocados, which contribute to its heart-healthy benefits.[6]

Black-eyed Peas and Collard Greens Soup

ingredients

- 3 tablespoons avocado or coconut oil, or butter
- 1 yellow onion, chopped
- 4 cloves garlic, peeled and minced
- 6 stalks celery, chopped
- 4 carrots, chopped
- 3 cups cooked or canned black-eyed peas
- 6 cups low-sodium chicken stock
- 2 teaspoons cumin
- 1 teaspoon chili powder
- 1 teaspoon salt
- ½ teaspoon black pepper
- ⅛ teaspoon cayenne pepper (optional)
- ¾ pound (1 bunch) collard greens, stems removed, finely chopped

Serving size: 6

Black-eyed peas and collard greens are a traditional southern United States dish. Collards are often boiled over a long period of time with a ham hock, and the black-eyed peas are served separately. This variation is a soup that brings together the greens and the beans with extra veggies and can save you some time in the kitchen. The **Sweet Potato Cornbread** recipe makes a great side dish for this soup.

Directions:

1. Heat a large pot over medium heat and add oil or butter. Add onion and sauté until translucent, about 3 to 5 minutes.
2. Add garlic, carrots, and celery. Sauté for another 3 to 5 minutes until softened.
3. Add the cooked black-eyed peas, broth, and seasonings—cumin, chili powder, salt, pepper, cayenne (optional). Bring to a boil. Reduce heat and simmer for about 20 minutes.
4. Add the chopped collard greens, and simmer for 10 more minutes.
5. Remove from heat and enjoy immediately.

Sweet Potato Cornbread

Sweet potato cornbread is a delicious and sweet side dish. We recommend using the brightly-colored orange sweet potatoes, often labeled as jewel or garnet yams, to make a beautiful cornbread that is also high in antioxidants, specifically beta-carotene. Make this recipe a gluten-free cornbread by choosing brown rice flour.

Directions:

1. Preheat the oven to 350°F.
2. Cut the sweet potatoes into 2 to 3 inch pieces. Steam until they are soft (about 10 minutes). Or, pierce the sweet potatoes with a fork 3–4 times and microwave for about 5–7 minutes, until soft. Then, puree or mash them, adding 2 to 4 tablespoons of water if needed to make them smooth.
3. Mix together the dry ingredients, cornmeal, flour, baking powder, baking soda, and salt in a bowl.
4. In a separate bowl mix together the sweet potato puree, egg, maple syrup, and melted coconut oil or butter.
5. Add the dry ingredients to the wet ingredients and gently mix. Batter should be thick.
6. Grease a 9" x 13" pan and pour batter into the pan. Bake for 25 to 30 minutes or until a knife or toothpick inserted in the middle comes out clean.

Tips:

- If you are avoiding eggs, consider the following egg substitutions for baking:

    1 egg = 1/4 cup unsweetened applesauce = 1 tablespoon ground-flaxseed with 1/4 cup hot water; let sit for 5 minutes to create a gelatinous consistency.

ingredients

- 1 cup pureed or mashed sweet potato
- 1½ cups cornmeal, fine or medium-grind
- 1½ cups brown rice flour
- 1 teaspoons baking powder
- ½ teaspoon baking soda
- ½ teaspoon salt
- 1 egg
- ¼ cup maple syrup
- ⅓ cup butter, melted or coconut oil

Servings: 24

ingredients

1 cup amaranth

2½ cups water

1 cup full-fat canned coconut milk

¾ cup pureed pumpkin (fresh or canned)

½ teaspoon salt

½ teaspoon cinnamon

¼ teaspoon ginger, dried

¼ teaspoon nutmeg

⅛ teaspoon ground cloves

1 teaspoon vanilla extract

2 tablespoons maple syrup (optional)

4 tablespoons pumpkin seeds (optional)

¾ cup coconut flakes (optional)

Servings: 4 to 6

Pumpkin Pie Amaranth Porridge

Amaranth, like quinoa, provides a complete, plant-based protein. Amaranth is actually a very tiny seed that dates back 8,000 years as a traditional staple grain of the Aztecs in Mexico. This porridge is delicious for a cool day with its sweet, warming spices. The addition of pumpkin puree and seeds adds flavor and texture.

Directions:

1. Combine amaranth with water in a medium pot and bring to a boil. Reduce heat to simmer, cover, and cook for 20 to 25 minutes, until water is absorbed.

2. Add the pumpkin puree, coconut milk, salt, spices, and vanilla extract and stir. Then, turn the heat off. Let the porridge sit and thicken for a few minutes with the lid on.

3. Sweeten with maple syrup if desired. Sprinkle with ground pumpkin seeds and coconut flakes.

Tips:

- Sweet potato puree can be substituted for the pumpkin.
- Use a pre-blended "pumpkin pie spice" to simplify the spices.
- To modify this recipe for the summer season, cook the amaranth. After removing from the heat, add coconut milk and fresh berries and let porridge sit for 5 to 10 minutes. Add maple syrup along with cinnamon or ginger to sweeten as desired.

Nutrition facts:

- One cup of cooked amaranth contains over 9 grams of protein and 5 grams of fiber.

Ingredients

3 cups water

1½ cups quinoa

3 to 4 delicata squash

¼ cup avocado or coconut oil

1 medium onion, diced

3 cloves garlic, peeled and minced

6 cups chopped broccoli florets

¼ cup sunflower seeds

¾ teaspoon salt

½ teaspoon black pepper

Dressing ingredients:

½ cup extra virgin olive oil

¼ cup balsamic vinegar

1 teaspoon maple syrup

1 teaspoon dijon mustard

2 teaspoons dried herbs (sage, thyme or rosemary)

¼ teaspoon salt

⅛ teaspoon black pepper

Servings: 4 to 6

Delicata Squash Over Broccoli and Quinoa

Enjoy this savory dish in the fall and winter when delicata squash is generally in season. Delicata squash is oblong and yellow colored with distinct bright green stripes. It is considered the delicata, or delicate squash, because its outer skin is easier to cut through. The skin can even be eaten, unlike most other winter squash. Also, it doesn't take quite as long to cook. If you are new to eating squash, the delicata is a great introduction to this vitamin-rich food. Yet, any variety of squash (see **Baked Acorn Squash**) pairs well with broccoli and quinoa, along with this tasty dressing.

Directions:

1. To prepare the quinoa: Bring 3 cups of water to a boil in a medium saucepan. Add 1½ cups of quinoa and return to a boil. Reduce heat to simmer, cover, and cook for 12 to 15 minutes, until water is absorbed. Remove from heat. Let the quinoa sit for five minutes and then fluff with a fork.

2. Mix dressing ingredients together in a bowl and whisk.

3. Cut the delicata squash lengthwise, remove seeds with a spoon and cut squash into 1-inch cubes with the skin on.

4. Heat 2 tablespoons of oil in a pan on low-medium heat. Add squash to the pan and cook until soft, approximately 10 minutes.

5. Heat a separate pan over medium heat and add 2 tablespoons of oil. Sauté the onions until translucent, about 3 to 5 minutes.

6. Add the garlic and broccoli florets. Sauté for another 5 minutes until broccoli is softened, yet still brightly colored. Add a small amount of the dressing to help steam the broccoli. Add sunflower seeds in the last few minutes. Add salt and pepper to taste.

7. Serve 1 to 2 cups of broccoli on top of ½ cup quinoa. Add ½ to 1 cup of cooked squash. Drizzle dressing over plate.

Tips:

- Serve with baked chicken, fish, or **Marinated Steak Bites** to increase the protein content of this meal.

- Oven alternative: Spread 1-inch cubes of delicate squash onto a baking sheet or baking pan and coat with avocado oil or melted coconut oil, salt, and pepper. Bake at 350°F for 20 to 30 minutes until softened.
- Save your squash seeds. Remove squash strings, rinse the seeds and pat them dry. Coat in a small amount of coconut oil or extra virgin olive oil, salt, and add your favorite spices. Bake at 275°F for approximately 15 minutes or until seeds are crisp. Sprinkle on top of this meal, or save for a tasty snack.

Baked Acorn Squash

Acorn squash, a dark green squash in the shape of an acorn, is a delicious alternative to the delicata squash, and is best prepared baked in the oven. Its skin is tougher than a delicata squash, so the cooked squash is often removed from the skin. Most squash tends to be in season in the fall and winter, which is the perfect time to enjoy them due to their immune-supporting nutrients. Squash provides a good source of beta-carotene, a precursor to vitamin A, which supports a healthy immune system.

Directions:

1. Preheat the oven to 375°F.
2. Carefully cut acorn squash in half and remove inner seeds.
3. Rub the open face of each squash with a mixture of 1 teaspoon of coconut oil or avocado oil and 1 teaspoon of maple syrup.
4. Cut a flat edge on the underside of the squash to keep it upright and even. Place squash into a baking dish. Add a pinch of salt to the face of each squash.
5. Prior to putting the baking dish in the oven, add water to cover the bottom of the dish to a depth of approximately ¼ inch.
6. Bake for approximately 45 minutes. Check squash every 10 to 15 minute and add water if needed. When fully cooked, scoop out the squash with a spoon for serving.

ingredients

2 acorn squash

2 teaspoons avocado or melted coconut oil

2 teaspoons maple syrup

salt to taste

Servings: 4 to 6

Spiced Red Lentils (dal) with Spinach

ingredients

4 cups water

2 cup brown rice

2 tablespoons avocado or coconut oil

1 yellow onion, chopped

4 cloves garlic, peeled and minced

2 tablespoons peeled and minced ginger

1 tablespoon cumin

2 tablespoons curry powder

¼ teaspoon ground cardamom

1 jalapeno pepper, finely chopped (optional)

2 cups red lentils

6–8 cups chicken stock

1½ cups diced tomatoes (fresh or canned)

5 ounces or 5 cups finely chopped spinach leaves

1 teaspoon salt

½ cup chopped fresh cilantro

Servings: 8 to 10

Dal is a traditional Indian dish, commonly made with lentils. Nothing compares to this warming, spicy dish on a cool fall or winter day. Cardamom is an uniquely aromatic spice that is also used in chai tea. Cardamom can be expensive, but a small amount can be purchased in the bulk spice section at the grocery store. Curry powder is a spice mixture that contains turmeric, which gives it a bright yellow-colored base. Turmeric contains curcumin, which has very potent anti-inflammatory properties. Be creative and add other vegetables to this dal such as sweet potato, cauliflower, or green peas. The addition of finely chopped dark green leafy vegetables complements this tasty dal.

Directions:

1. Place water and rice into a pot and bring to a boil. Reduce heat to simmer and allow rice to cook for 35 to 40 minutes until water is absorbed. Remove from heat, and fluff with a fork.

2. Heat a large pot over medium heat and add oil. Add onions and sauté until translucent, about 3 to 5 minutes.

3. Add garlic, ginger, cumin, curry powder, cardamom, and jalapeno (optional) to the onions, stirring often, until fragrant, about 2 minutes.

4. Add lentils, 6–8 cups of stock, and diced tomatoes to the pot and bring to a boil. Reduce heat to medium-low. Cover and simmer, stirring often, until lentils are soft (about 15 to 20 minutes). Add spinach and salt during the last 3 minutes of cooking. Add more broth, if needed, for desired consistency.

5. Serve dal over brown rice. Add chopped cilantro if desired.

Tips:

- If you substitute green lentils, they take longer to cook, around 30 to 40 minutes. If adding other ingredients like sweet potato, peas, or cauliflower, add them with the lentils and broth.

- Using chicken stock for this recipe helps increase the protein content, but vegetable broth can also be used.

Black Bean Pumpkin Soup

Many of us feel inspired to include pumpkin in our meals during the fall months. This creamy soup brings together pumpkin, coconut, and black beans with all the right spices to create a very satisfying flavor. While canned pumpkin will suffice in this soup, consider baking a pumpkin and creating homemade pumpkin puree. Be sure to use a pie or baking pumpkin for this recipe; the traditional Halloween pumpkins won't be very tasty.

Directions:

1. Carefully slice the pumpkin in half, scoop out seeds, and chop the pumpkin into large pieces. Steam the pumpkin pieces until soft, about 10 minutes. Let pumpkin cool, remove the skin, and mash well or puree in a food processor or a blender until smooth.
2. Heat a large pot over medium heat and add oil. Sauté onions until translucent, about 3 to 5 minutes.
3. Add garlic, cumin, salt, cayenne, and cinnamon and stir for 2 minutes.
4. Add the black beans, pumpkin, tomatoes, coconut milk and broth into the pot. Simmer for 10 minutes allowing flavors to combine and ingredients to soften.
5. If you prefer a smooth soup, use an immersion blender in the pot or pour soup into a blender and blend to desired consistency.
6. Garnish with cilantro, roasted pumpkin seeds, and avocado.

Tips:

- If you are using canned pumpkin puree, coconut milk, or diced tomato, look for these items in glass jars or in cans or packaging that are BPA-free.
- To increase the protein, add 1 pound of cooked ground turkey or chicken to the soup.
- To cook the pumpkin seeds for a topping, preheat the oven to 275°F. Clean the seeds, and pat them dry. Coat them in a small

ingredients

- 2 cups pureed pumpkin (canned or steamed and pureed)
- 1 tablespoon avocado or coconut oil, or butter
- 1 yellow onion, chopped
- 2 cloves garlic, peeled and minced
- 1 tablespoon cumin
- 1 teaspoon salt
- ½ teaspoon cayenne (optional)
- ½ teaspoon cinnamon
- 3 cups cooked or canned black beans
- 2 large tomatoes, diced or 1 can (14.5 ounces) diced tomatoes
- 1 cup full-fat canned coconut milk
- 3 cups vegetable or chicken broth or stock
- ¼ cup chopped fresh cilantro
- Pumpkin seeds, sliced avocado, plain Greek yogurt, or sour cream (optional toppings)

Servings: 6 to 8

amount of oil and salt, and then spread them evenly on a baking-sheet. Bake for 15 to 20 minutes until crispy.

Nutrition Facts:

- Pumpkin pulp is a rich source of magnesium and vitamins (Bs and C). Pumpkin seeds are a rich source of immune-boosting zinc, as well as tryptophan, the precursor to the feel good neurotransmitter, serotonin.

Roasted Brussels Sprouts

ingredients

4 cups quartered Brussels sprouts

2 tablespoons avocado or melted coconut oil

1 cup pecans

4 cloves garlic, peeled and minced

¼ teaspoon salt

¼ teaspoon cinnamon

¼ teaspoon cumin

¼ teaspoon cayenne pepper (optional)

Servings: 4

There are so many tasty ways to cook and season these cruciferous vegetables, which are known for their cancer-fighting properties. Brussels sprouts are a good source of fiber, with almost 5 grams in 1 cup.

Directions:

1. Preheat the oven to 400°F.
2. Trim the hard ends off the sprouts and remove discolored leaves. Then, chop Brussels sprouts into quarters and place in a bowl.
3. Massage or stir the oil into Brussels sprouts. Add garlic, salt, cumin, cinnamon, and cayenne (optional) to the Brussels sprouts and stir.
4. Spread ingredients onto baking pan. Cover with aluminum foil.
5. Place in the oven, and bake for 30 minutes. Remove aluminum foil and turn sprouts with a spatula and add the pecans. Return to the oven for an additional 10 to 15 minutes, or until Brussels sprouts are soft. Check with a fork.

Tips:

- Try different nuts, such as hazelnuts or pine nuts.
- Add optional toppings after removing the Brussel sprouts from the oven. Fresh squeezed lemon juice and parmesan cheese or nutritional yeast are a great combination, or balsamic vinegar and honey.

References

Preface

1. "Regulated states and regulatory authorities". *American Association of Naturopathic Physicians.* naturopathic.org/page/RegulatedStates. Accessed 15 April 2025.
2. "Naturopathy." National Center for Complementary and Integrative Health. nccih.nih.gov/health/naturopathy#. Accessed 14 April 2025.
3. Ridberg, Ronit A et al. "Food is Medicine National Summit: Transforming Health Care". *The American Journal of Clinical Nutrition*, Volume 120, Issue 6, 1441–1456.

Introduction

1. Araújo J, Cai J, Stevens J. "Prevalence of Optimal Metabolic Health in American Adults: National Health and Nutrition Examination Survey 2009-2016." *Metab Syndr Relat Disord.* 2019 Feb;17(1):46-52.
2. "National diabetes statistics report." *Centers for Disease Control.* cdc.gov/diabetes/php/data-research/index.html. Accessed 10 March 2025.
3. "1 in 3 Americans born in 2000 will develop diabetes." *National Education Policy Center.* nepc.colorado.edu/publication/1-3-americans-born-2000-will-develop-diabetes. Accessed 10 March 2025.
4. "Estimated hypertension prevalence, treatment, and control among US adults". *Million Hearts.* millionhearts.hhs.gov/data-reports/hypertension-prevalence.html. Accessed 10 March 2025.
5. "Obesity and overweight". *National Center for Health Statistics.* www.cdc.gov/nchs/fastats/obesity-overweight.htm. Accessed 10 March 2025.
6. "Social determinants of health (SDOH)". *Centers for Disease Control.* www.cdc.gov/about/priorities/why-is-addressing-sdoh-important.html. Accessed 16 May 2025.
7. "Social determinants of health." *World Health Organization.* www.who.int/health-topics/social-determinants-of-health#tab=tab_1. Accessed 16 May 2025.
8. "Doctoring or diet II- nutrition education for physicians is overdue." *Food Law and Policy Clinic Harvard Law School.* chlpi.org/wp-content/uploads/2024/06/Doctoring-Our-Diet-II_FINAL_6.10.24.pdf . Accessed 10 March 2025.
9. Lane MM, Gamage E, Du S, Ashtree DN, McGuinness AJ, Gauci S, Baker P, Lawrence M, Rebholz CM, Srour B. Touvier M, Jacka FN, O'Neil A, Segasby T, Marx W. "Ultra-processed food exposure and adverse health outcomes: umbrella review of epidemiological meta-analyses." *BMJ.* 2024 Feb 28;384:e077310.
10. Wang L, Martínez Steele E, Du M, Pomeranz JL, O'Connor LE, Herrick KA, Luo H, Zhang X, Mozaffarian D, Zhang FF. "Trends in Consumption of Ultra-processed Foods Among US Youths Aged 2-19 Years, 1999-2018." *JAMA.* 2021 Aug 10;326(6):519-530.
11. Juul, Filippa et al. "Ultra-processed food consumption among US adults from 2001 to 2018." *The American Journal of Clinical Nutrition.* Vol 115, Issue 1, January 2022, pages 211-221.
12. Menichetti G, Ravandi B, Mozaffarian D, Barabási AL. "Machine learning prediction of the degree of food processing." *Nat Commun.* 2023 Apr 21;14(1):2312
13. "The NOVA food classification system". ecuphysicians.ecu.edu/wp-content/pv-uploads/sites/78/2021/07/NOVA-Classification-Reference-Sheet.pdf. Accessed 5 May 2025.
14. Tippens KM, Erlandsen A, Hanes DA, Graybill R, Jackson C, Briley J, Zwickey H. "Impact of a Short-Term Naturopathic Whole-Foods-Based Nutrition Education Intervention on Dietary Behavior and Diabetes Risk Markers: A Pilot Study." *J Altern Complement Med.* 2019 Feb;25(2):234-240.

Chapter 1: The Wisdom of Traditional Diets

1. "Noncommunicable Diseases" *World Health Organization*. n.d. https://www.who.int/news-room/fact-sheets/detail/noncommunicable-diseases. Accessed 3 February 2025.
2. Luciani, Silvana et al. "Prioritizing noncommunicable diseases in the Americas region in the era of COVID-19." *Pan American journal of public health* vol. 46 e83. 20 Jul. 2022.
3. Araújo, Joana et al. "Prevalence of Optimal Metabolic Health in American Adults: National Health and Nutrition Examination Survey 2009-2016." *Metabolic syndrome and related disorders* vol. 17,1 (2019): 46-52.
4. Mercader J. "Mozambican grass seed consumption during the middle stone age." *Science*. 2009 Dec 18;326(5960):1680-3.
5. Hotz C, Gibson R. "Traditional food-processing and preparation practices to enhance the bioavailability of micronutrients in plant- based diets". *J. Nutr*. April 2007; vol. 137 no. 4 1097-1100.
6. González, Neus et al. "Meat consumption: Which are the current global risks? A review of recent (2010-2020) evidences." *Food research international (Ottawa, Ont.)* vol. 137 (2020): 109341.
7. Conceição, Sara et al. "Antimicrobial Resistance in Bacteria from Meat and Meat Products: A One Health Perspective." *Microorganisms* vol. 11,10 2581. 17 Oct. 2023.
8. Nogoy, Kim Margarette C et al. "Fatty Acid Composition of Grain- and Grass-Fed Beef and Their Nutritional Value and Health Implication." *Food science of animal resources* vol. 42,1 (2022): 18-33.
9. Daley C, Abbot A, Doyle P, Nader G, Larson S. "A review of fatty acid profiles and antioxidant content in grass-fed and grain-fed beef." *Nutr J*. 2010 Mar 10; 9:10.
10. Fang, Zhe et al. "Association of ultra-processed food consumption with all cause and cause specific mortality: population based cohort study." *BMJ (Clinical research ed.)* vol. 385 e078476. 8 May. 2024.
11. Gharby, Said. "Refining Vegetable Oils: Chemical and Physical Refining." *The Scientific World Journal* vol. 2022 6627013. 11 Jan. 2022.
12. Tuck, Caroline J et al. "Food Intolerances." *Nutrients* vol. 11,7 1684. 22 Jul. 2019.

Chapter 2: Nourish Yourself with Fat

1. DiNicolantonio JJ, O'Keefe JH. "Monounsaturated Fat vs Saturated Fat: Effects on Cardio-Metabolic Health and Obesity." *Mo Med*. 2022 Jan-Feb;119(1):69-73.
2. Rimm EB, Appel LJ, Chiuve SE, Djoussé L, Engler MB, Kris-Etherton PM, Mozaffarian D, Siscovick DS, Lichtenstein AH; American Heart Association Nutrition Committee of the Council on Lifestyle and Cardiometabolic Health; Council on Epidemiology and Prevention; Council on Cardiovascular Disease in the Young; Council on Cardiovascular and Stroke Nursing; and Council on Clinical Cardiology. "Seafood Long-Chain n-3 Polyunsaturated Fatty Acids and Cardiovascular Disease: A Science Advisory From the American Heart Association." *Circulation*. 2018 Jul 3;138(1):e35-e47.
3. Ganesan et al. "Impact of consumption and cooking manners of vegetable oils on cardiovascular risk- A critical review." *Trends in Food Science and Technology*. 2018 Jan; Vol 71: 132-154.
4. Simopoulos AP, DiNicolantonio JJ. "The importance of a balanced -6 to -3 ratio in the prevention and management of obesity". *Open Heart*. 2016 Sep 20;3(2):e000385. Added updated reference.
5. DiNicolantonio JJ, O'Keefe JH. "Omega-6 vegetable oils as a driver of coronary heart disease: the oxidized linoleic acid hypothesis." *Open Heart* 2018;5:e000898.
6. Jakobsen MU, O'Reilly EJ, Heitmann BL, et al. "Major types of dietary fat and risk of coronary heart disease: a pooled analysis of 11 cohort studies." *Am J Clin Nutr*. 2009;89:1425-1432.

7. Sacks et all. "Dietary Fats and Cardiovascular Disease: A Presidential Advisory From the American Heart Association." *Circulation*. 2017; Vol 136, Issue 3, pages e1-e23.
8. Wang Q, Imamura F, Lemaitre RN, Rimm EB, Wang M, King IB, Song X, Siscovick D, Mozaffarian D. "Plasma phospholipid trans-fatty acids levels, cardiovascular diseases, and total mortality: the cardiovascular health study." *J Am Heart Assoc*. 2014 Aug 27;3(4).
9. "Trans Fat." U.S Food and Drug Administration. fda.gov/food/food-additives-petitions/trans-fat. Accessed 23 May 2025.
10. "Trans Fat." *World Health Organization*. who.int/news-room/fact-sheets/detail/trans-fat. Accessed 23 March 2025.
11. Mozaffarian D. "Natural trans fat, dairy fat, partially hydrogenated oils, and cardiometabolic health: the Ludwigshafen Risk and Cardiovascular Health Study." *Eur Heart J*. 2016 Apr 1;37(13):1079-81.
12. "Facts about trans fat." *National Library of Medicine*. medlineplus.gov/ency/patientinstructions/000786.htm. Accessed 1 May 2025.
13. Gharby S. Refining Vegetable Oils: "Chemical and Physical Refining." *ScientificWorldJournal*. 2022 Jan11; 2022:6627013.
14. Przybylski O, Aladedunye FA. "Formation of trans fats during food preparation" *Can J Diet Pract Res*. 2012; 73(2): 98-101.
15. Borén J et al. "Low-density lipoproteins cause atherosclerotic cardiovascular disease: pathophysiological, genetic, and therapeutic insights: a consensus statement from the European Atherosclerosis Society Consensus Panel." *Eur Heart J*. 2020 Jun 21;41(24):2313-2330.
16. Feingold KR. "The Effect of Endocrine Disorders on Lipids and Lipoproteins." www.ncbi.nlm.nih.gov/books/NBK409608. Accessed 11 January 2025.
17. Fernandez ML. "Effects of eggs on plasma lipoproteins in healthy populations." *Food Funct*. 2010 Nov;1(2):156-60.
18. Jones, PJ. "Dietary cholesterol and the risk of cardiovascular disease in patients: a review of the Harvard Egg Study and other data." *International Journal of Clinical Practice*. 2009 October; Vol 63, Issue Supplement s163, pp. 1-8.
19. Soliman GA. "Dietary Cholesterol and the Lack of Evidence in Cardiovascular Disease. Nutrients." *Nutrients*. 2018 Jun 16;10(6):780.
20. Antoni R. "Dietary saturated fat and cholesterol: cracking the myths around eggs and cardiovascular disease". *J Nutr Sci*. 2023 Sep 11;12:e97.
21. "Choline" *National Institutes of Health*. https://ods.od.nih.gov/factsheets/Choline-HealthProfessional/. Accessed 4 June 2025.
22. Li Y, Hruby A, Bernstein AM, Ley SH, Wang DD, Chiuve SE, Sampson L, Rexrode KM, Rimm EB, Willett WC, Hu FB. "Saturated Fats Compared With Unsaturated Fats and Sources of Carbohydrates in Relation to Risk of Coronary Heart Disease: A Prospective Cohort Study." *J Am Coll Cardiol*. 2015 Oct 6;66(14):1538-1548.
23. Hamdy, Osama and OM P. Ganda. "Chapter 2. Clinical Nutrition Guideline for Overweight and Obese Adults with Type 2 Diabetes (T2D) or Prediabetes, or Those at High Risk of Developing T2D." *Evidence-Based Diabetes Management*. June 2018. Volume 24. Issue 7.

Chapter 3: Nourish Yourself with Carbohydrates

1. Reynolds, Andrew et al. "Carbohydrate quality and human health: a series of systematic reviews and meta-analyses." *Lancet (London, England)* vol. 393,10170 (2019): 434-445.
2. Aune, Dagfinn et al. "Dietary fibre, whole grains, and risk of colorectal cancer: systematic review and dose-response meta-analysis of prospective studies." *BMJ (Clinical research ed.)* vol. 343 d6617. 10 Nov. 2011.
3. Farvid, Maryam S et al. "Fiber consumption and breast cancer incidence: A systematic review and meta-analysis of

prospective studies." *Cancer* vol. 126,13 (2020): 3061-3075.

4. Ghavami, Abed et al. "Soluble Fiber Supplementation and Serum Lipid Profile: A Systematic Review and Dose-Response Meta-Analysis of Randomized Controlled Trials." *Advances in nutrition (Bethesda, Md.)* vol. 14,3 (2023): 465-474.
5. Reynolds, Andrew N et al. "Dietary fibre and whole grains in diabetes management: Systematic review and meta-analyses." *PLoS medicine* vol. 17,3 e1003053. 6 Mar. 2020
6. Reynolds, Andrew N et al. "Dietary fibre in hypertension and cardiovascular disease. management: systematic review and meta-analyses." *BMC medicine* vol. 20,1 139. 22 Apr. 2022.
7. Jovanovski, Elena et al. "Can dietary viscous fiber affect body weight independently of an energy-restrictive diet? A systematic review and meta-analysis of randomized controlled trials." *The American journal of clinical nutrition* vol. 111,2 (2020): 471-485.
8. Quagliani, Diane, and Patricia Felt-Gunderson. "Closing America's Fiber Intake Gap: Communication Strategies From a Food and Fiber Summit." *American journal of lifestyle medicine* vol. 11,1 80-85. 7 Jul. 2016.
9. "Food Sources of Select Nutrients" *Dietary Guidelines for America.* n.d. https://www.dietaryguidelines.gov/resources/2020-2025-dietary-guidelines-online-materials/food-sources-select-nutrients#. Accessed 3 February 2025.

Chapter 4: Nourish Yourself with Protein

1. Westerterp-Plantenga MS, Lemmens SG, Westerterp KR. "Dietary protein - its role in satiety, energetics, weight loss and health." *Br J Nutr.* 2012 Aug;108 Suppl 2:S105-12.
2. Mariotti F, Gardner CD. "Dietary Protein and Amino Acids in Vegetarian Diets-A Review." *Nutrients.* 2019 Nov 4;11(11):2661.
3. Fedewa MV, Spencer SO, Williams TD, Becker ZE, Fuqua CA. "Effect of branched-Chain Amino Acid Supplementation on Muscle Soreness following Exercise: A Meta-Analysis." *Int J Vitam Nutr Res.* 2019 Nov;89(5-6):348-356.
4. Kawai N, Sakai N, Okuro M, Karakawa S, Tsuneyoshi Y, Kawasaki N, Takeda T, Bannai M, Nishino S. "The sleep-promoting and hypothermic effects of glycine are mediated by NMDA receptors in the suprachiasmatic nucleus." *Neuropsychopharmacology.* 2015 May;40(6):1405-16.
5. Bauer J, Biolo G, Cederholm T, Cesari M, Cruz-Jentoft AJ, Morley JE, Phillips S, Sieber C, Stehle P, Teta D, Visvanathan R, Volpi E, Boirie Y. "Evidence-based recommendations for optimal dietary protein intake in older people: a position paper from the PROT-AGE Study Group." *J Am Med Dir Assoc.* 2013 Aug;14(8):542-59.
6. Jäger R, Kerksick CM, Campbell BI, Cribb PJ, Wells SD, Skwiat TM, Purpura M, Ziegenfuss TN, Ferrando AA, Arent SM, Smith-Ryan AE, Stout JR, Arciero PJ, Ormsbee MJ, Taylor LW, Wilborn CD, Kalman DS, Kreider RB, Willoughby DS, Hoffman JR, Krzykowski JL, Antonio J. "International Society of Sports Nutrition Position Stand: protein and exercise." *J Int Soc Sports Nutr.* 2017 Jun 20;14:20.
7. Hamdy, Osama and OM P. Ganda. "Chapter 2. Clinical Nutrition Guideline for Overweight and Obese Adults with Type 2 Diabetes (T2D) or Prediabetes, or Those at High Risk of Developing T2D." *Evidence-Based Diabetes Management.* June 2018. Volume 24. Issue 7.
8. "Soy- Intake Does Not Increase Risk for Breast Cancer Survivors." *American Institute for Cancer Research.* www.aicr.org/cancer-prevention/food-facts/soy/. Accessed 9 June 2024.
9. Boutas I, Kontogeorgi A, Dimitrakakis C, Kalantaridou SN. "Soy Isoflavones and Breast Cancer Risk: A Meta-analysis". *In Vivo.* 2022 Mar-Apr;36(2):556-562.
10. Doerge DR, Sheehan DM. "Goitrogenic and estrogenic activity of soy isoflavones." *Environ Health Perspect.* 2002 Jun;110 Suppl 3(Suppl 3):349-53.

11. Otun J, Sahebkar A, Östlundh L, Atkin SL, Sathyapalan T. "Systematic Review and Meta-analysis on the Effect of Soy on Thyroid Function". *Sci Rep*. 2019 Mar 8;9(1):3964.
12. "Iodine: Fact Sheet for Consumers." *National Institutes of Health*. ods.od.nih.gov/factsheets/Iodine-Consumer/. Accessed July 6, 2024.
13. Petroski W, Minich DM. "Is There Such a Thing as "Anti-Nutrients"? A Narrative Review of Perceived Problematic Plant Compounds". *Nutrients*. 2020 Sep 24;12(10):2929.
14. Rizzo G, Baroni L. "Soy, Soy Foods and Their Role in Vegetarian Diets". *Nutrients*. 2018 Jan 5;10(1):43.
15. Sheffield, Sydney et al. "Nutritional importance of animal-sourced foods in a healthy diet." *Frontiers in nutrition*. vol. 11 1424912. 25 Jul. 2024.
16. Fang, Zhe et al. "Association of ultra-processed food consumption with all cause and cause specific mortality: population based cohort study." *BMJ (Clinical research ed.)* vol. 385 e078476. 8 May. 2024.
17. Li, Chunxiao et al. "Meat consumption and incident type 2 diabetes: an individual-participant federated meta-analysis of 1·97 million adults with 100 000 incident cases from 31 cohorts in 20 countries." *The Lancet. Diabetes & endocrinology* vol. 12,9 (2024): 619-630.
18. Mendoza, Kenny et al. "Ultra-processed foods and cardiovascular disease: analysis of three large US prospective cohorts and a systematic review and meta-analysis of prospective cohort studies." *Lancet regional health. Americas* vol. 37 100859. 2 Sep. 2024.
19. "Per Capita Consumption of Poultry and Livestock, 1965 to Forecast 2022, in Pounds." *National Chicken Council*. www.nationalchickencouncil.org/about-the-industry/statistics/per-capita-consumption-of-poultry-and-livestock-1965-to-estimated-2012-in-pounds. Accessed 19 March 2025.
20. Spencer, Terrell. "Pastured poultry nutrition and forages." *ATTRA (attra. ncat. org)* (2013): 1-20.
21. Nogoy, Kim Margarette C et al. "Fatty Acid Composition of Grain- and Grass-Fed Beef and Their Nutritional Value and Health Implication." *Food science of animal resources* vol. 42,1 (2022): 18-33.
22. Wang, Dong D et al. "Red Meat Intake and the Risk of Cardiovascular Diseases: A Prospective Cohort Study in the Million Veteran Program." *The Journal of nutrition* vol. 154,3 (2024): 886-895.
23. Zhong, Victor W et al. "Associations of Processed Meat, Unprocessed Red Meat, Poultry, or Fish Intake With Incident Cardiovascular Disease and All-Cause Mortality." *JAMA internal medicine* vol. 180,4 (2020): 503-512.
24. Lauren E O'Connor, Jung Eun Kim, Wayne W Campbell. "Total red meat intake of ≥0.5 servings/d does not negatively influence cardiovascular disease risk factors: a systemically searched meta-analysis of randomized controlled trials" 12, *The American Journal of Clinical Nutrition*, Volume 105, Issue 1, 2017, Pages 57-69.
25. Aykan, Nuri Faruk. "Red Meat and Colorectal Cancer." *Oncology reviews* vol. 9,1 288. 28 Dec. 2015.
26. "Omega-3 Fatty Acids" *National Institutes of Health*. ods.od.nih.gov/factsheets/Omega3FattyAcids-HealthProfessional/#alzheimer. Accessed 19 March 2025.
27. Jensen, Ida-Johanne et al. "An Update on the Content of Fatty Acids, Dioxins, PCBs and Heavy Metals in Farmed, Escaped and Wild Atlantic Salmon (*Salmo salar* L.) in Norway." *Foods (Basel, Switzerland)* vol. 9,12 1901. 19 Dec. 2020, doi:10.3390/foods9121901.
28. Inan-Eroglu, Elif, Aylin Ayaz, and Zehra Buyuktuncer. "Formation of Advanced Glycation Endproducts in Foods during Cooking Process and Underlying Mechanisms: A Comprehensive Review of Experimental Studies." *Nutrition Research Reviews* 33.1 (2020): 77–89. Web.
29. Zheng, Wei, and Sang-Ah Lee. "Well-done meat intake, heterocyclic amine exposure, and cancer risk." *Nutrition and cancer* vol. 61,4 (2009): 437-46.
30. Srivastava, Shweta. "Effects of Environmental Polycyclic Aromatic Hydrocarbons Exposure and Pro-Inflammatory Activity on Type 2 Diabetes Mellitus in US Adults." *Open journal of air pollution* vol. 11,2 (2022): 29-46.

Chapter 5: Reading Food Labels

1. Sambu, Saseendran et al. "Toxicological and Teratogenic Effect of Various Food Additives: An Updated Review." *BioMed research international* vol. 2022 6829409. 24 Jun. 2022.
2. Rinninella, Emanuele et al. "Food Additives, Gut Microbiota, and Irritable Bowel Syndrome: A Hidden Track." *International journal of environmental research and public health* vol. 17,23 8816. 27 Nov. 2020.
3. Trasande, Leonardo et al. "Food Additives and Child Health." *Pediatrics* vol. 142,2 (2018): e20181408.
4. Miller, Mark D et al. "Potential impacts of synthetic food dyes on activity and attention in children: a review of the human and animal evidence." *Environmental health: a global access science source* vol. 21,1 45. 29 Apr. 2022.
5. "Brominated Vegetable Oil". *U.S. Food and Drug Administration.* https://www.fda.gov/food/food-additives-petitions/brominated-vegetable-oil-bvo. Accessed 3 February 2025.
6. Wang, Yi-Jie et al. "Dietary Sodium Intake and Risk of Cardiovascular Disease: A Systematic Review and Dose-Response Meta-Analysis." *Nutrients* vol. 12,10 2934. 25 Sep. 2020.
7. Mente, Andrew et al. "Sodium Intake and Health: What Should We Recommend Based on the Current Evidence?." *Nutrients* vol. 13,9 3232. 16 Sep. 2021.
8. "Use of the "Healthy" Claim on Food Labeling" U.S.Food and Drug Administration. https://www.fda.gov/food/nutrition-food-labeling-and-critical-foods/use-healthy-claim-food-labeling#Criteria. Accessed 14 May 2025.
9. Barański, Marcin et al. "Higher antioxidant and lower cadmium concentrations and lower incidence of pesticide residues in organically grown crops: a systematic literature review and meta-analyses." *The British journal of nutrition* vol. 112,5 (2014): 794-811.
10. Rahman, Azizur et al. "A Comprehensive Analysis of Organic Food: Evaluating Nutritional Value and Impact on Human Health." *Foods (Basel, Switzerland)* vol. 13,2 208. 9 Jan. 2024.
11. Nogoy, Kim Margarette C et al. "Fatty Acid Composition of Grain- and Grass-Fed Beef and Their Nutritional Value and Health Implication." *Food science of animal resources* vol. 42,1 (2022): 18-33.
12. Daley C, Abbot A, Doyle P, Nader G, Larson S. "A review of fatty acid profiles and antioxidant content in grass-fed and grain-fed beef." *Nutr J.* 2010 Mar 10; 9.
13. Vom Saal, Frederick S, and Laura N Vandenberg. "Update on the Health Effects of Bisphenol A: Overwhelming Evidence of Harm." *Endocrinology* vol. 162,3 (2021): bqaa171.
14. Gao, Hui et al. "Bisphenol A and hormone-associated cancers: current progress and perspectives." *Medicine* vol. 94,1 (2015): e211.

Chapter 6: The FAME Plate

1. Livingstone MB, Pourshahidi LK. "Portion size and obesity." *Adv Nutr.* 2014 Nov 14;5(6):829-34.
2. Robinson E, McFarland-Lesser I, Patel Z, Jones A. "Downsizing food: a systematic review and meta-analysis examining the effect of reducing served food portion sizes on daily energy intake and body weight." *British Journal of Nutrition.* 2023;129(5):888-903.
3. Ello-Martin JA, Ledikwe J, Rolls B. "The influence of food portion size and energy density on energy intake: implications for weight man-agement." *Am J Clin Nutr.* 2005 Jul;82(1 Suppl):236S-241S.
4. Hall et al. "Ultra-Processed Diets Cause Excess Calorie Intake and Weight Gain: An Inpatient Randomized Controlled Trial of Ad Libitum Food Intake. Cell Metab." 2019 Jul 2;30(1):67-77.e3.
5. Young LR, Nestle M. "Portion Sizes of Ultra-Processed Foods in the United States, 2002 to 2021." *Am J Public Health.* 2021 Dec;111(12):2223-2226.

6. Offringa LC, Stanton MV, Hauser ME, Gardner CD. "Fruits and Vegetables Versus Vegetables and Fruits: Rhyme and Reason for Word Order in Health Messages." *Am J Lifestyle Med.* 2018 May 2;13(3):224-234
7. "Lactose intolerance". *National Library of Medicine,* National Center for Biotechnology Information. www.ncbi.nlm.nih.gov/books/NBK532285. Accessed 31 August 2024.
8. Stewart and Kuchler. "Fluid milk consumption continues downward trend, proving difficult to reverse". *USDA Economic Research Service.* www.ers.usda.gov/amber-waves/2022/june/fluid-milk-consumption-continues-downward-trend-proving-difficult-to-reverse. Accessed 7 July 2024.
9. Alothman M, Hogan SA, Hennessy D, Dillon P, Kilcawley KN, O'Donovan M, Tobin J, Fenelon MA, O'Callaghan TF. "The "Grass-Fed" Milk Story: Understanding the Impact of Pasture Feeding on the Composition and Quality of Bovine Milk." *Foods.* 2019 Aug 17;8(8):350.
10. Guo J, Astrup A, Lovegrove JA, Gijsbers L, Givens DI, Soedamah-Muthu SS. "Milk and dairy consumption and risk of cardiovascular diseases and all-cause mortality: dose-response meta-analysis of prospective cohort studies." *Eur J Epidemiol.* 2017 Apr;32(4):269-287.
11. Feskanich D, Willet WC, Stampfer MJ, Colditz GA. "Milk, dietary calcium, and bone fractures in women: a 12-year prospective study." *Am J Public Health.* 1997;87:992-7.
12. Mishra S, Baruah K, Malik VS, Ding EL. "Dairy intake and risk of hip fracture in prospective cohort studies: non-linear algorithmic dose-response analysis in 486,950 adults." *J Nutr Sci.* 2023 Sep 11;12:e96.
13. Rizzoli R. "Dairy products and bone health." *Aging Clin Exp Res.* 2022 Jan;34(1):9-24.
14. Ratajczak AE, Zawada A, Rychter AM, Dobrowolska A, Krela-Kaźmierczak I. "Milk and Dairy Products: Good or Bad for Human Bone? Practical Dietary Recommendations for the Prevention and Management of Osteoporosis." *Nutrients.* 2021 Apr 17;13(4):1329.
15. Shkembi B, Huppertz T. "Calcium Absorption from Food Products: Food Matrix Effects." *Nutrients.* 2021 Dec 30;14(1):180.

Chapter 7: Strategies for Healthy Digestion

1. Wang, Xiaoxiao, and Chunli Song. "The impact of gratitude interventions on patients with cardiovascular disease: a systematic review." *Frontiers in psychology* vol. 14 1243598. 21 Sep. 2023.
2. Peterson, Christine T et al. "Prebiotic Potential of Culinary Spices Used to Support Digestion and Bioabsorption." *Evidence-based complementary and alternative medicine : eCAM* vol. 2019 8973704. 2 Jun. 2019.
3. Shishehbor, Farideh et al. "Vinegar consumption can attenuate postprandial glucose and insulin responses; a systematic review and meta-analysis of clinical trials." *Diabetes research and clinical practice* vol. 127 (2017): 1-9.
4. Hadi, Amir et al. "The effect of apple cider vinegar on lipid profiles and glycemic parameters: a systematic review and meta-analysis of randomized clinical trials." *BMC complementary medicine and therapies* vol. 21,1 179. 29 Jun. 2021.
5. Rezaie, Peyman et al. "Effects of Bitter Substances on GI Function, Energy Intake and Glycaemia-Do Preclinical Findings Translate to Outcomes in Humans?." *Nutrients* vol. 13,4 1317. 16 Apr. 2021.
6. Hassan, Luke et al. "The effect of gastrointestinal bitter sensing on appetite regulation and energy intake: A systematic review." *Appetite* vol. 180 (2023).
7. Rinninella, Emanuele et al. "What is the Healthy Gut Microbiota Composition? A Changing Ecosystem across Age, Environment, Diet, and Diseases." *Microorganisms* vol. 7,1 14. 10 Jan. 2019.
8. Thursby, Elizabeth, and Nathalie Juge. "Introduction to the human gut microbiota." *The Biochemical journal* vol. 474,11 1823-1836. 16 May. 2017.

9. Goodrich, Julia K et al. "Human genetics shape the gut microbiome." *Cell* vol. 159,4 (2014): 789-99.
10. Monda, Vincenzo et al. "Exercise Modifies the Gut Microbiota with Positive Health Effects." *Oxidative medicine and cellular longevity* vol. 2017 (2017): 3831972.
11. Wan, Yating, and Tao Zuo. "Interplays between drugs and the gut microbiome." *Gastroenterology report* vol. 10 goac009. 8 Apr. 2022.
12. Sjöstedt, Peter et al. "Serotonin Reuptake Inhibitors and the Gut Microbiome: Significance of the Gut Microbiome in Relation to Mechanism of Action, Treatment Response, Side Effects, and Tachyphylaxis." *Frontiers in psychiatry* vol. 12 682868. 26 May. 2021.
13. Singh, Rasnik K et al. "Influence of diet on the gut microbiome and implications for human health." *Journal of translational medicine* vol. 15,1 73. 8 Apr. 2017.
14. Wang, Xiaofei et al. "Dietary Polyphenol, Gut Microbiota, and Health Benefits." *Antioxidants (Basel, Switzerland)* vol. 11,6 1212. 20 Jun. 2022.
15. McDonald, Daniel et al. "American Gut: an Open Platform for Citizen Science Microbiome Research." *mSystems* vol. 3,3 e00031-18. 15 May. 2018.

Chapter 8: Balancing Blood Sugar

1. "Diabetes Prevention Program DPP." *National Institute of Diabetes and Digestive and Kidney Diseases.* niddk.nih.gov/about-niddk/research-areas/diabetes/diabetes-prevention-program-dpp Accessed 1 March 2025.
2. "NWCR Facts". *The National Weight Control Registry.* nwcr.ws/default.htm. Accessed 31 August 2024.
3. Zia, Meng et al. "Breakfast skipping and traits of cardiometabolic health. "A mendelian randomization study." *Clinical Nutrition ESPEN.* Vol 59, Feb 2024, Pages 328-333.
4. XIU M. MA, YONG XU. "The Association between Breakfast Skipping and the Risk of Obesity, Diabetes, Hypertension, or Dyslipidemia—A Meta-analysis from 44 Trials Including 65,233 Cases and 381,051 Controls." *Diabetes* 1 July 2018; 67 (Supplement_1): 1356–P.
5. Lundqvist M, Vogel NE, Levin LÅ. "Effects of eating breakfast on children and adolescents: A systematic review of potentially relevant outcomes in economic evaluations." *Food Nutr Res.* 2019 Sep 12;63.
6. Monzani A, Ricotti R, Caputo M, Solito A, Archero F, Bellone S, Prodam F. "A Systematic Review of the Association of Skipping Breakfast with Weight and Cardiometabolic Risk Factors in Children and Adolescents. What Should We Better Investigate in the Future?" *Nutrients.* 2019 Feb 13;11(2):387.
7. Witbracht M, Keim NL, Forester S, Widaman A, Laugero K. "Female breakfast skippers display a disrupted cortisol rhythm and elevated blood pressure." *Physiol Behav.* 2015 Mar 1;140:215-21.
8. Vasim I, Majeed CN, DeBoer MD. "Intermittent Fasting and Metabolic Health." *Nutrients.* 2022 Jan 31;14(3):631.
9. Yan B, Caton SJ, Buckland NJ. "Exploring factors influencing late evening eating and barriers and enablers to changing to earlier eating patterns in adults with overweight and obesity." *Appetite.* 2024 Nov 1;202:107646.
10. Vujović N, Piron MJ, Qian J, Chellappa SL, Nedeltcheva A, Barr D, Heng SW, Kerlin K, Srivastav S, Wang W, Shoji B, Garaulet M, Brady MJ, Scheer FAJL. "Late isocaloric eating increases hunger, decreases energy expenditure, and modifies metabolic pathways in adults with overweight and obesity." *Cell Metab.* 2022 Oct 4;34(10):1486-1498.e7.
11. Harris C, Czaja K. "Can Circadian Eating Pattern Adjustments Reduce Risk or Prevent Development of T2D?" *Nutrients.* 2023 Apr 4;15(7):1762.
12. Wang P, Tan Q, Zhao Y, Zhao J, Zhang Y, Shi D. "Night eating in timing, frequency, and food quality and risks of all-cause, cancer, and diabetes mortality: findings from national health and nutrition examination survey." *Nutr Diabetes.* 2024 Feb 27;14(1):5.

13. "Alcohol use and your health". *Centers for Disease Control.* cdc.gov/alcohol/about-alcohol-use/index.html. Accessed 2 March 2025.
14. Zhao J, Stockwell T, Naimi T, Churchill S, Clay J, Sherk A. "Association Between Daily Alcohol Intake and Risk of All-Cause Mortality: A Systematic Review and Meta-analyses." *JAMA Netw Open.* 2023 Mar 1;6(3):e236185.
15. Kang DO, Lee DI, Roh SY, Na JO, Choi CU, Kim JW, Kim EJ, Rha SW, Park CG, Kim YS, Kim Y, You HS, Kang HT, Jo E, Kim J, Lee JW, Jung JM. "Reduced Alcohol Consumption and Major Adverse Cardiovascular Events Among Individuals With Previously High Alcohol Consumption." *JAMA Netw Open.* 2024 Mar 4;7(3):e244013.
16. "Recommendation- limit alcohol to reduce cancer risk." *American Institute for Cancer Research.* aicr.org/cancer-prevention/recommendations/limit-alcohol-consumption. Accessed 1 March 2025.
17. "Alcohol use and your health." *Centers for Disease Control.* cdc.gov/alcohol/about-alcohol-use/index.html. Accessed 1 March 2025.
18. Barbería-Latasa M, Bes-Rastrollo M, Pérez-Araluce R, Martínez-González MÁ, Gea A. "Mediterranean Alcohol-Drinking Patterns and All-Cause Mortality in Women More Than 55 Years Old and Men More Than 50 Years Old in the "Seguimiento Universidad de Navarra" (SUN) Cohort." *Nutrients.* 2022 Dec 14;14(24):5310.
19. Engeroff T, Groneberg DA, Wilke J. "After Dinner Rest a While, After Supper Walk a Mile? A Systematic Review with Meta-analysis on the Acute Postprandial Glycemic Response to Exercise Before and After Meal Ingestion in Healthy Subjects and Patients with Impaired Glucose Tolerance." *Sports Med.* 2023 Apr;53(4):849-869.
20. O'Keefe et al. "Dietary Strategies for Improving Post-Prandial Glucose, Lipids, Inflammation, and Cardiovascular Health". *Journal of the American College of Cardiology.* Vol 51, Issue 3, 22 Jan 2008, pages 249-255.
21. Nishi SK, Viguiliouk E, Kendall CWC, Jenkins DJA, Hu FB, Sievenpiper JL, Atzeni A, Misra A, Salas-Salvadó J. "Nuts in the Prevention and Management of Type 2 Diabetes." *Nutrients.* 2023 Feb 9;15(4):878.
22. Kizilaslan N, Erdem NZ. "The Effect of Different Amounts of Cinnamon Consumption on Blood Glucose in Healthy Adult Individuals." *Int J Food Sci.* 2019 Mar 4;2019:4138534.
23. Zelicha H, Yang J, Henning SM, Huang J, Lee RP, Thames G, Livingston EH, Heber D, Li Z. "Effect of cinnamon spice on continuously monitored glycemic response in adults with prediabetes: a 4-week randomized controlled crossover trial." *Am J Clin Nutr.* 2024 Mar;119(3):649-657.
24. Shukla AP, Iliescu RG, Thomas CE, Aronne LJ. "Food Order Has a Significant Impact on Postprandial Glucose and Insulin Levels." *Diabetes Care.* 2015 Jul;38(7):e98-9.
25. Shukla AP, Dickison M, Coughlin N, Karan A, Mauer E, Truong W, Casper A, Emiliano AB, Kumar RB, Saunders KH, Igel LI, Aronne LJ. "The impact of food order on postprandial glycaemic excursions in prediabetes." *Diabetes Obes Metab.* 2019 Feb;21(2):377-381.

Chapter 9: Exploring Sweeteners

1. Park, Sohyun et al. "Children and Adolescents in the United States with Usual High Added Sugars Intake: Characteristics, Eating Occasions, and Top Sources, 2015-2018." *Nutrients* vol. 15,2 274. 5 Jan. 2023.
2. Ricciuto, Laurie et al. "Sources of Added Sugars Intake Among the U.S. Population: Analysis by Selected Sociodemographic Factors Using the National Health and Nutrition Examination Survey 2011-18." *Frontiers in nutrition* vol. 8 687643. 17 Jun. 2021.
3. Nguyen, Michelle et al. "Sugar-sweetened beverage consumption and weight gain in children and adults: a systematic review and meta-analysis of prospective cohort studies and randomized controlled trials." *The American journal of clinical nutrition* vol. 117,1 (2023): 160-174.
4. Dai, Jane et al. "Trends and patterns in sugar-sweetened beverage consumption among children and adults by race and/or ethnicity, 2003-2018." *Public health nutrition* vol. 24,9 (2021): 2405-2410.

5. Larson, Nicole et al. "Sports and energy drink consumption are linked to health-risk behaviours among young adults." *Public health nutrition* vol. 18,15 (2015): 2794-803.
6. Jung, Sunhee et al. "Dietary Fructose and Fructose-Induced Pathologies." *Annual review of nutrition* vol. 42 (2022): 45-66.
7. Huang, Yin et al. "Dietary sugar consumption and health: umbrella review." *BMJ (Clinical research ed.)* vol. 381 e071609. 5 Apr. 2023.
8. Llaha, Fjorida et al. "Consumption of Sweet Beverages and Cancer Risk. A Systematic Review and Meta-Analysis of Observational Studies." *Nutrients* vol. 13,2 516. 4 Feb. 2021.
9. Ahn, Hyejin, and Yoo Kyoung Park. "Sugar-sweetened beverage consumption and bone health: a systematic review and meta-analysis." *Nutrition journal* vol. 20,1 41. 5 May. 2021.
10. Chen, Li et al. "High Consumption of Soft Drinks Is Associated with an Increased Risk of Fracture: A 7-Year Follow-Up Study." *Nutrients* vol. 12,2 530. 19 Feb. 2020.
11. Jensen, Thomas et al. "Fructose and sugar: A major mediator of non-alcoholic fatty liver disease." *Journal of hepatology* vol. 68,5 (2018): 1063-1075.
12. Valenzuela, Maria Josefina et al. "Effect of sugar-sweetened beverages on oral health: a systematic review and meta-analysis." *European journal of public health* vol. 31,1 (2021): 122-129.
13. "Sugar and Sweeteners: Background". *United State Department of Agriculture.* https://www.ers.usda.gov/topics/crops/sugar-and-sweeteners/background. Accessed 4 February, 2025.
14. Witkowski, Marco et al. "Xylitol is prothrombotic and associated with cardiovascular risk." *European heart journal* vol. 45,27 (2024): 2439-2452.
15. Diaz, Cristina et al. "Artificially Sweetened Beverages and Health Outcomes: An Umbrella Review." *Advances in nutrition (Bethesda, Md.)* vol. 14,4 (2023): 710-717.
16. Debras, Charlotte et al. "Artificial sweeteners and cancer risk: Results from the NutriNet-Santé population-based cohort study." *PLoS medicine* vol. 19,3 e1003950. 24 Mar. 2022.
17. Ruiz-Ojeda, Francisco Javier et al. "Effects of Sweeteners on the Gut Microbiota: A Review of Experimental Studies and Clinical Trials." *Advances in nutrition (Bethesda, Md.)* vol. 10,suppl_1 (2019): S31-S48. doi:10.1093/advances/nmy037.
18. Rios-Leyvraz M, Montez J. "Health effects of the use of non-sugar sweeteners: a systematic review and meta-analysis." *Geneva: World Health Organization*; 2022.

Chapter 10: Benefits of Breakfast

1. Dalkara T, Kiliç K. "How does fasting trigger migraine? A hypothesis." *Curr Pain Headache Rep.* 2013 Oct;17 (10): 368.
2. Witbracht M, Keim NL, Forester S, Widaman A, Laugero K. "Female breakfast skippers display a disrupted cortisol rhythm and elevated blood pressure." *Physiol Behav.* 2015 Mar 1;140:215-21.
3. Chawla S, Beretoulis S, Deere A, Radenkovic D. "The Window Matters: A Systematic Review of Time Restricted Eating Strategies in Relation to Cortisol and Melatonin Secretion." *Nutrients.* 2021 Jul 23;13(8):2525.
4. Adafer, R., Messaadi, W., Meddahi, M., Patey, A., Haderbache, A., Bayen, S., & Messaadi, N. (2020). "Food timing, circadian rhythm and chrononutrition: A systematic review of time-restricted eating's effects on human health." *Nutrients*, 12(12), 3770.
5. Lopez-Minguez J, Gómez-Abellán P, Garaulet M. "Timing of Breakfast, Lunch, and Dinner. Effects on Obesity and Metabolic Risk." *Nutrients.* 2019 Nov 1;11(11):2624.

6. Dashti HS, Gómez-Abellán P, Qian J, Esteban A, Morales E, Scheer FAJL, Garaulet M. "Late eating is associated with cardiometabolic risk traits, obesogenic behaviors, and impaired weight loss." *Am J Clin Nutr*. 2021 Jan 4;113(1):154-161.
7. Ofori-Asenso R, Owen AJ, Liew D. "Skipping Breakfast and the Risk of Cardiovascular Disease and Death: A Systematic Review of Prospective Cohort Studies in Primary Prevention Settings." *J Cardiovasc Dev Dis*. 2019 Aug 22;6(3):30.
8. Bi H, Gan Y, Yang C, Chen Y, Tong X, Lu Z. "Breakfast skipping and the risk of type 2 diabetes: a meta-analysis of observational studies." *Public Health Nutr*. 2015 Nov;18(16):3013-9.
9. Wyatt HR, Grunwald GK, Mosca CL, Klem ML, Wing RR, Hill JO. "Long-term weight loss and breakfast in subjects in the National Weight Control Registry." *Obes Res*. 2002 Feb;10(2):78-82.
10. "NWCR Facts". The National Weight Control Registry. nwcr.ws/default.htm. Accessed 31 August 2024.
11. Galioto R, Spitznagel MB. "The Effects of Breakfast and Breakfast Composition on Cognition in Adults." *Adv Nutr*. 2016 May 16;7(3):576S-89S.
12. Wang F, Sun M, Wang X, Wu Z, Guo R, Yang Y, Wang Y, Liu Y, Dong Y, Wang S, Li B. "The mediating role of dietary inflammatory index on the association between eating breakfast and depression: Based on NHANES 2007-2018." *J Affect Disord*. 2024 Mar 1;348:1-7.
13. Elortegui Pascual P, Rolands MR, Eldridge AL, Kassis A, Mainardi F, Lê KA, Karagounis LG, Gut P, Varady KA. "A meta-analysis comparing the effectiveness of alternate day fasting, the 5:2 diet, and time-restricted eating for weight loss." *Obesity (Silver Spring)*. 2023 Feb;31 Suppl 1(Suppl 1):9-21.
14. Chair SY, Cai H, Cao X, Qin Y, Cheng HY, Ng MT. "Intermittent Fasting in Weight Loss and Cardiometabolic Risk Reduction: A Randomized Controlled Trial." *J Nurs Res*. 2022 Feb 1;30(1):e185.
15. Welton S, Minty R, O'Driscoll T, Willms H, Poirier D, Madden S, Kelly L. "Intermittent fasting and weight loss: Systematic review." *Can Fam Physician*. 2020 Feb;66(2):117-125.
16. "Breakfast for learning—why the morning meal matters." *American Academy of Pediatrics*. healthychildren.org/English/healthy-living/nutrition/Pages/Breakfast-for-Learning.aspx Accessed 2 October 2024.
17. "Dietary Data Brief No. 58 Breakfast Consumption by U.S. Children and Adolescents.
18. What We Eat in America, NHANES 2017-March 2020." *National Library of Medicine*.

Chapter 11: Habits for Health

1. Cox, Kieran D et al. "Human Consumption of Microplastics." *Environmental science & technology* vol. 53,12 (2019): 7068-7074.
2. N. Qian, X. Gao, X. Lang, H. Deng, T.M. Bratu, Q. Chen, P. Stapleton, B. Yan, W. Min. "Rapid single-particle chemical imaging of nanoplastics by SRS microscopy" *Proc. Natl. Acad. Sci.* U.S.A. 121 (3) e2300582121.
3. Sun, Anqi, and Wen-Xiong Wang. "Human Exposure to Microplastics and Its Associated Health Risks." *Environment & health (Washington, D.C.)* vol. 1,3 139-149. 2 Aug. 2023.
4. "Dietary and inhalation exposure to nano- and microplastic particles and potential implications for human health." *World Health Organization*. 30 Aug. 2022.
5. Kansagra, Sujay. "Sleep Disorders in Adolescents." *Pediatrics* vol. 145,Suppl 2 (2020): S204-S209.
6. Antza, Christina et al. "The links between sleep duration, obesity and type 2 diabetes mellitus." *The Journal of endocrinology* vol. 252,2 125-141. 13 Dec. 2021.
7. Hale, Lauren et al. "Youth Screen Media Habits and Sleep: Sleep-Friendly Screen Behavior Recommendations for Clinicians, Educators, and Parents." *Child and adolescent psychiatric clinics of North America* vol. 27,2 (2018): 229-245.

8. Levine, James A. "Sick of sitting." *Diabetologia* vol. 58,8 (2015): 1751-8.
9. Park, Jung Ha et al. "Sedentary Lifestyle: Overview of Updated Evidence of Potential Health Risks." *Korean journal of family medicine* vol. 41,6 (2020): 365-373.
10. Ungvari, Zoltan et al. "The multifaceted benefits of walking for healthy aging: from Blue Zones to molecular mechanisms." *GeroScience* vol. 45,6 (2023): 3211-3239.
11. Gao W, Sanna M, Chen Y, Tsai M, Wen C. "Occupational Sitting Time, Leisure Physical Activity, and All-Cause and Cardiovascular Disease Mortality." *JAMA Netw Open.* 2024;7(1):e2350680.
12. Kandola, Aaron, and Brendon Stubbs. "Exercise and Anxiety." *Advances in experimental medicine and biology* vol. 1228 (2020): 345-352.
13. Noetel, Michael et al. "Effect of exercise for depression: systematic review and network meta-analysis of randomised controlled trials." *BMJ (Clinical research ed.)* vol. 384 e075847. 14 Feb. 2024.
14. "Our Epidemic of Loneliness and Isolation." The U.S. Surgeon General's Advisory on the Healing Effects of Social Connection and Community. 2023.
15. Primack, Brian A et al. "Social Media Use and Perceived Social Isolation Among Young Adults in the U.S." *American journal of preventive medicine* vol. 53,1 (2017): 1-8.
16. Bonsaksen, Tore et al. "Associations between social media use and loneliness in a cross-national population: do motives for social media use matter?." *Health psychology and behavioral medicine* vol. 11,1 2158089. 1 Jan. 2023.

Chapter 12: Healthy Eating on the Go

1. Paeratakul S, Ferdinand DP, Champagne CM, Ryan DH, Bray GA. "Fast-food consumption among US adults and children: dietary and nutrient intake profile". *J Am Diet Assoc.* 2003 Oct;103(10):1332-8.
2. Block JP, Condon SK, Kleinman K, Mullen J, Linakis S, Rifas-Shiman S, Gillman MW. "Consumers' estimation of calorie content at fast food restaurants: cross sectional observational study." *BMJ.* 2013 May 23;346:f2907.
3. Hall, KD et al. "Ultra-Processed Diets Cause Excess Calorie Intake and Weight Gain: An Inpatient Randomized Controlled Trial of Ad Libitum Food Intake." *Cell Metab.* 2019 Jul 2;30(1):67-77.e3. Epub 2019 May 16. Erratum in: Cell Metab. 2019 Jul 2;30(1):226.
4. Lane MM, Gamage E, Travica N, Dissanayaka T, Ashtree DN, Gauci S, Lotfaliany M, O'Neil A, Jacka FN, Marx W. "Ultra-Processed Food Consumption and Mental Health: A Systematic Review and Meta-Analysis of Observational Studies." *Nutrients.* 2022 Jun 21;14(13):2568.
5. Bahadoran Z, Mirmiran P, Azizi F. "Fast Food Pattern and Cardiometabolic Disorders: A Review of Current Studies." *Health Promot Perspect.* 2016 Jan 30;5(4):231-40.
6. "Fast Food Consumption Among Adults in the United States, 2013–2016." *Centers for Disease Control.* cdc.gov/nchs/products/databriefs/db322.htm. Accessed 1 October 2024.
7. "Access to foods that support healthy dietary patterns." *U.S. Dept of Health and Human Services.* health.gov/healthy-people/priority-areas/social-determinants-health/literature-summaries/access-foods-support-healthy-dietary-patterns. Accessed 15 October 2024.
8. "Coca-cola®." www.mcdonalds.com/us/en-us/product/coca-cola-large.html Accessed 3 November 2024.
9. "How many ml are in your small, medium and large fizzy soft drinks?" mcdonalds.com/gb/en-gb/help/faq/how-many-ml-are-in-your-small–medium-and-large-fizzy-soft-drinks.html. Accessed 3 November 2024.
10. Xiong K, Li MM, Chen YQ, Hu YM, Jin W. "Formation and Reduction of Toxic Compounds Derived from the Maillard Reaction During the Thermal Processing of Different Food Matrices." *J Food Prot.* 2024 Sep;87(9):100338.

11. "Big Mac®." mcdonalds.com/us/en-us/product/big-mac. Accessed 3 November 2024.
12. "Nutrition and Allergens." chick-fil-a.com/nutrition-allergens. Accessed 3 November 2024.
13. Gearhardt AN, Bueno NB, DiFeliceantonio AG, Roberto CA, Jiménez-Murcia S, Fernandez-Aranda F. "Social, clinical, and policy implications of ultra-processed food addiction." *BMJ*. 2023 Oct 9;383:e075354.
14. Bahadoran Z, Mirmiran P, Azizi F. "Fast Food Pattern and Cardiometabolic Disorders: A Review of Current Studies." *Health Promot Perspect*. 2016 Jan 30;5(4):231-40.

Chapter 13: Nutritious Lunches and Snacks

1. Haines, Jess et al. "Nurturing Children's Healthy Eating: Position statement." *Appetite* vol. 137 (2019): 124-133.
2. Loth, K et al. "Food-related parenting practices and child and adolescent weight and weight-related behaviors." *Clinical practice (London, England)* vol. 11,2 (2014): 207-220.
3. Hammons, Amber J, and Barbara H Fiese. "Is frequency of shared family meals related to the nutritional health of children and adolescents?." *Pediatrics* vol. 127,6 (2011): e1565-74.
4. Abdoli, Marzieh et al. "Affect, Body, and Eating Habits in Children: A Systematic Review." *Nutrients* vol. 15,15 3343. 27 Jul. 2023.

Chapter 14: Shopping Guide and Everyday Superfoods

1. Ravndi, Babak et al. "Prevalence of processed foods in major US grocery stores". *Nature food*. 13 Jan 2025.
2. "Allergic to the fine print: food allergies to additives, rare but real." *American Academy of Allergy, Asthma, and Immunology*. aaaai.org/tools/for-the-public/conditions-library/allergies/allergic-to-the-fine-print-food-allergy-to-additiv Accessed 9 November 2024.
3. Valley H. Misso NL. "Adverse reactions to the sulphite additives." *Gastroenterol Hepatol Bed Bench*. 2012 Winter; 5 (1): 16-23.
4. "Broccoli and cruciferous vegetables: Reduce overall cancer risk." *American Institute for Cancer Research*. aicr.org/cancer-prevention/food-facts/broccoli-cruciferous-vegetables Accessed 9 November 2024.
5. Wu QJ, Yang Y, Vogtmann E, Wang J, Han LH, Li HL, Xiang YB. "Cruciferous vegetables intake and the risk of colorectal cancer: a meta-analysis of observational studies." *Ann Oncol*. 2013 Apr;24(4):1079-87.
6. Liu X, Lv K. "Cruciferous vegetable intake is inversely associated with risk of breast cancer: a meta-analysis." *Breast*. 2013 Jun;22(3):309-13.
7. Xiong XJ, Wang PQ, Li SJ, Li XK, Zhang YQ, Wang J. "Garlic for hypertension: A systematic review and meta-analysis of randomized controlled trials." *Phytomedicine*. 2015 Mar 15;22(3):352-61.
8. Arreola R, Quintero-Fabián S, López-Roa RI, Flores-Gutiérrez EO, Reyes-Grajeda JP, Carrera-Quintanar L, Ortuño-Sahagún D. "Immuno- modulation and anti-inflammatory effects of garlic compounds." *J Immunol Res*. 2015;2015:401630.
9. Valverde ME, Hernández-Pérez T, Paredes-López O. "Edible mushrooms: improving human health and promoting quality life." *Int J Microbiol*. 2015;2015:376387.
10. Starck C, Cassettari T, Wright J, Petocz P, Beckett E, Fayet-Moore F. "Mushrooms: a food-based solution to vitamin D deficiency to include in dietary guidelines." *Front Nutr*. 2024 Apr 10;11:1384273.
11. Ravn-Haren G, Dragsted LO, Buch-Andersen T, Jensen EN, Jensen RI, Németh-Balogh M, Paulovicsová B, Bergström A, Wilcks A, Licht TR, Markowski J, Bügel S. "Intake of whole apples or clear apple juice has contrasting effects on plasma lipids in healthy volunteers." *Eur J Nutr*. 2013 Dec;52(8):1875-89.
12. Guasch-Ferre M, Hu FB et al. "Olive oil intake and risk of cardiovascular disease and mortality in the PREDIMED Study." *BMC Med*. 2014 May 13;12:78.

13. Martinez-Gonzalez MA et al. "Effect of olive oil consumption on cardiovascular disease, cancer, type 2 diabetes, and all-cause mortality: A systematic review and meta-analysis." *Clin Nutr.* 2022 Dec;41(12):2659-2682.
14. Mackonochie, Marion et al. "A Scoping Review of the Clinical Evidence for the Health Benefits of Culinary Doses of Herbs and Spices for the Prevention and Treatment of Metabolic Syndrome." *Nutrients* vol. 15,23 4867. 22 Nov. 2023.
15. "Trans Fat." *U.S. Food and Drug Administration.* fda.gov/food/food-additives-petitions/trans-fat. Accessed 31 January 2025.Recipes

Recipes

1. Doma KM, Dolinar KF, Dan Ramdath D, Wolever TMS, Duncan AM. "Canned Beans Decrease Serum Total and LDL Cholesterol in Adults with Elevated LDL Cholesterol in a 4-wk Multicenter, Randomized, Crossover Study." *J Nutr.* 2021 Dec 3;151(12):3701-3709.
2. Paudel D, Dhungana B, Caffe M, Krishnan P. "A Review of Health-Beneficial Properties of Oats." *Foods.* 2021 Oct 26;10(11):2591.
3. Keegan RJ, Lu Z, Bogusz JM, Williams JE, Holick MF. "Photobiology of vitamin D in mushrooms and its bioavailability in humans."*Dermatoendocrinol.* 2013 Jan 1; 5(1):165-76.
4. Gunawardena D, Bennett L, Shanmugam K, King K, Williams R, Zabaras D, Head R, Ooi L, Gyengesi E, Münch G. "Anti-inflammatory effects of five commercially available mushroom species determined in lipopolysaccharide and interferon-γ activated murine macrophages." *Food Chem.* 2014 Apr 1; 148: 92-6.
5. van Poppel G, Verhoeven DT, Verhagen H, Goldbohm RA. "Brassica vegetables and cancer prevention. Epidemiology and mechanisms." *Adv Exp Med Biol.* 1999; 472: 159-68.
6. Glenn, Andrea J et al. "Nuts and Cardiovascular Disease Outcomes: A Review of the Evidence and Future Directions." *Nutrients* vol. 15,4 911. 11 Feb. 2023.

Index

Acesulfame potassium, 73, 133
Acorn squash. *See also* Squash.
   recipes with, 259
Added sugar/s, 30, 40, 109, 114, 117, 118, 142, 153, 158-160, 173. *See also* Added sweetener/s and sugar.
   American Heart Association upper limit, 124
   in beverages, 125-127
   on food label/s, 69-71, 76, 77-78, 80
   natural verses added, 128-129
   teenager consumption of, 125
Added Sweetener/s, 117, 126, 173. *See also* Added sugar/s.
Adrenal glands, 113
Adrenaline, 54
Advanced glycation end products (AGEs), 63, 153
Agave, 45t, 124, 130
Agricultural revolution, 24
Alanine, 54
Alcohol, 23, 40, 106, 112, 114, 117-118, 119t, 120, 145
   alcoholism, 118
Allergies, 72, 106. *See also* Food allergies.
All Natural, 67, 83
Allium, 168
Allulose, 132
Almond/s, 54, 66t, 108, 138, 159, 170, 175
   butter, 58t, 138, 139
   calcium in, 93t
   fiber in, 51t
   protein in, 58t
   smoke point of oil, 185t
   recipes with, 193, 195, 203, 207, 208, 214, 216, 219, 221, 224, 231, 249
Alzheimer's disease, 106

Amaranth, 49, 54, 96
   cooking guidelines for, 179t
   fiber in, 51t
   protein in, 58t
   recipes with, 256
American Heart Association, 124
Amino acid/s, 53-55, 60, 130, 228
Anaphylaxis, 31
Animal agriculture, 26, 30, 60
Animal by-products, 80, 82
Antibiotic,
   use in animals, 17, 80, 92
   use in humans, 106,
   resistance, 60
Antibody/antibodies, 31, 53
Anti-inflammatory, 17, 21, 29, 30, 62, 82, 107, 169, 171, 216, 260
   diet, 12, 36, 225
   omega-3 fatty acids, 121t
Antioxidant/s, 26-29. 37-38, 43, 48, 63-64, 65t, 80, 82, 107, 118, 121t, 126, 129, 132, 153, 167-172, 204, 240, 242, 254, 255
   glutathione, 55
Apple cider vinegar, 71, 104, 108, 120, 128, 177, 179
   recipes with, 197, 198, 210, 228, 236, 240, 242, 243, 249
Applesauce as egg substitution, 252, 255
Aquaculture, 62, 63
Arginine, 54
Artificial colors, 69, 71, 73, 80, 83, 174
Artificial sweeteners, 70, 73, 132-134, 173
   acesulfame potassium, 73, 133
   aspartame (NutraSweet®, Equal®), 73, 133
   saccharin (Sweet N Low®), 73, 133
   sucralose (Splenda®), 71, 73, 133
Arugula, 105, 168

cooking guidelines, 183t
recipes with, 198, 249
Ascorbic acid. See Vitamin C.
Asparagine, 54
Aspartame (NutraSweet®/Equal®), 73, 133
Aspartic acid, 54
Asthma, 72, 106, 167
Atherosclerosis, 39, 114. See also Cardiovascular disease.
Attention deficit hyperactivity disorder (ADHD), 72
Autoimmune disease, 30, 31, 114
Autolyzed yeast, 69
Avocado, 33, 35t, 49, 66t, 81, 90, 139, 152, 161
fiber in, 50t, 170
potassium in, 155
recipes with, 191, 196, 204, 217, 223, 226, 240, 243, 244, 250, 261
Avocado oil, 19, 34, 38, 96, 138, 159, 182
smoke point of, 185t
Ayurvedic cooking, 171, 184t
Azodicarbonamide, 73, 74, 154

B

Bad cholesterol. See Low-density lipoprotein (LDL).
Baked Acorn Squash, 259
Baked Kale Chips, 199
Baked Root Fries, 212
Banana/s, 47, 66t, 81, 107, 159
fiber in, 50t
potassium in, 226
protein in, 58t
recipes with, 193, 195, 207, 216
Barley, 48
calcium in, 93t
cooking guidelines for, 179t
recipes with, 20
Basic Bone Broth, 228
Basic Green Salad with Protein, 244
Basic Vinaigrette Dressing, 235
Bean/s, 45t, 66t, 160, 166-167, 171
calcium in, 93-94t
cooking guidelines for, 179-180, 181t
fiber in, 51t
protein in, 57t
Bean and Veggie Chili, 250
Beef, 26-27, 39, 54, 61, 65t, 82-83, 154, 160. See also Tallow and grass-fed beef.
protein in, 57t
recipes with, 196, 205, 225, 247, 250
Beets, 90, 96, 169
fiber in, 52t
recipes with, 63, 201, 249
Beet sugar, 130, 131. See also Sugar beets
Beet greens, 169
cooking guidelines, 183t
fiber in, 52t
Bell pepper/s, 64, 90, 121t, 129, 158, 161
recipes with, 198, 201, 215, 223, 225, 227, 240, 247, 250
Beta-carotene. See Vitamin A.
Beta-glucan, 107
Bile, 39, 105
Bioengineered foods (BE). See Genetically modified organism (GMO).
Bisphenol-A (BPA), 85, 142, 250, 261
Black beans, 43, 171
cooking guidelines for, 181t
fiber in, 51t
recipes with, 225, 240, 261
Black Bean Pumpkin Soup, 261
Black-eyed peas cooking guidelines, 181t
recipes with, 254
Black-eyed Peas and Collard Greens Soup, 154
Blanching, 161, 183t, 215, 217

Bloating, 30, 103, 105, 151

Blood glucose, 47, 114-115, 120. *See also* Blood sugar and type II diabetes mellitus.

Blood pressure, xvii, 23, 40, 46, 66t, 75, 118, 145, 146, 154, 155, 168. *See also* Hypertension.

Blood sugar, 23, 44, 54, 105, 111-121, 121t, 126, 130, 131, 133, 136, 143, 144, 149, 158, 168, 170, 171, 173. *See also* Blood glucose and type II diabetes mellitus.
   fasting, 115

Bok choy, 89, 93, 168
   calcium in, 94t
   cooking guidelines for, 183t
   fiber in, 52t
   recipes with, 253

Bone broth, 138, 228
   protein in, 57t

Bone health, 64, 65t, 121t
   effect of calcium on, 92-93
   and osteoporosis, 93, 127

Bowel movement/s, 106, 141

BPA. *See* Bisphenol-A.

Bran, 25, 48, 65t, 84, 121t, 173

Breakfast Smoothie, 207

Breastfeeding, 55, 62, 142

Breast milk, 30

Breathing, 119, 145-146, 149
   diaphragmatic breathing, 132

Broccoli, 64, 65t, 66t, 89, 93, 105, 121t, 162, 168, 254
   calcium in, 94t
   fiber in, 52t
   protein in, 59t
   recipes with, 201, 223, 253, 258

Brown rice, 43, 48, 72, 90, 99, 152
   cooking guidelines for, 178t
   fiber in, 51t
   protein in, 58t
   recipes with, 201, 204, 237, 260
   recipes with flour, 193, 209, 252, 255

Brown rice syrup, 70

Brown sugar, 124, 130, 132. *See also* Sugar.

Brussels sprouts, 90, 168
   calcium in, 94t
   fiber in, 52t
   recipes with, 201, 223, 262

Buckwheat, 48, 54, 96
   cooking guidelines for, 179t
   protein in, 58t

Bulk section, 159, 166-167

Butter, xix, 27, 28, 34, 35t, 36-38, 75, 83, 90, 96, 162, 170-171, 182
   smoke point of, 184t

Butternut squash. *See also* Squash.
   calcium in, 94t

B-vitamin/s. *See* Vitamin B.

C

Cage-free, 83, 86

Calcium, 25, 26, 48, 49, 60, 66t, 76, 93t-94t, 127, 130, 142, 151, 191, 214, 216, 225, 233, 242, 254
   and dairy, 91-93

Calorie/s, 34, 41, 47, 49, 55, 88, 99t, 118-119t, 124, 136, 151, 153
   on food label/s, 74

Cancer, 23, 47, 59, 61, 63, 72, 73, 85, 106, 118, 127, 133, 146, 168, 169, 254, 262

Cane sugar. *See* Sugar.

Cannellini bean/s, cooking guidelines, 181t

Canola oil, xix, 28, 36, 38-39, 71, 84, 89, 174, 182
   smoke point of, 185t

Cantaloupe/s, 66t, 169
   fiber in, 50t

Carbohydrate/s, 43-52, 95-97, 99t, 117. *See also* Fiber, starch

in alcohol, 119t
complex, 44-45, 45t, 48, 76, 90
on food label, 76-77
refined, 40, 41, 54, 76, 98, 112, 117, 138, 153, 157
simple, 44, 45t, 112, 116, 173
Carcinogen, 63, 173
Cardamom, recipes with, 260
Cardiovascular disease, 36, 40, 75, 92, 137, 153, 170, 225, 226
Carotenoids, 254
Carrot Zucchini Muffins. 193
Cayenne pepper, 104, 172
recipes with, 199, 204, 212, 220, 225, 250, 254, 261, 262
Casein, 31
Cashew/s, 159, 170, 254
fiber in, 51t
protein in, 58t
recipes with, 195, 207, 215, 216, 253
Cattle, 61, 65t, 82, 61
CDC. *See* Centers for Disease Control.
Celiac disease, 31, 105
Cell membrane/s, 34, 36, 39, 121t
Centers for Disease Control (CDC), xvii, 114
Chard, 89, 168
cooking guidelines for, 183t
fiber in, 52t
recipes with, 207, 223, 242
Cheese, xix, 35t, 36, 54, 91-92, 96, 97, 99-100, 108, 109
protein in, 57t
recipes with, 198, 225, 247, 249
Chemical additive/s, 69-73, 78, 107, 122, 132-133, 142, 158, 176
Chia Pudding 4 Ways, 202
Chia seed/s, 35, 39, 49, 54, 96, 107, 121t, 138, 139
fiber in, 51t

protein in 58t
recipes with, 202, 208
Chick peas. *See* Garbanzo beans.
Chicken, 27, 35, 36, 39, 60-61, 66t, 100. *See also* Eggs.
cage-free, 83
free-range, 82
pasture-raised, 83
protein in, 57t
recipes with, 201, 209, 228, 244, 247
Chicory root, 107
Chloride, 75, 142, 154
Chlorine, 133, 142
Cholecalciferol (D3). *See* Vitamin D.
Cholesterol. *See also* Low-density lipoprotein and high-density lipoprotein.
blood levels, 23, 34, 37, 39-40, 43, 45t, 47, 113, 204
in food, 39-41, 67, 75
Cilantro, 172
recipes with, 191, 204, 210, 225, 226, 240, 250, 260, 261
Cinnamon, 104, 120, 129, 171
recipes with, 193, 195, 202, 208, 212, 216, 221, 224, 238, 250, 256, 261, 262
Citrus, 63, 65t, 90, 105, 121t, 169
CLA. *See* Conjugated linoleic acid.
Clean Fifteen, 81
Cocoa Loco Bars, 219
Coconut, 35t, 36, 90, 97
milk, 92, 97
oil, xix, 27, 34, 38, 170-171, 182, 184t
recipes with, 195, 221, 256
recipes with milk, 238, 256, 261
sugar, 124, 131
smoke point of oil, 184t
water, 127, 142

Coconut Berry Bliss, 238
Coconut sugar, 124, 131
Cod liver oil, 28, 65t, 121t
Collagen, 65t, 121t, 228
  peptides, 59t
Collard greens, 26, 168
  calcium in, 94t
  fiber in, 52t
  recipes with, 215, 254
Colon, 46, 143
  cancer, 47, 61, 118
Colorful Cole Slaw, 210
Complete protein. See Protein.
Complex carbohydrates. See Carbohydrates.
Conjugated linoleic acid (CLA), 27, 82, 92
Copper, 216
Corn, 25, 48, 72, 81, 82, 84, 90, 127, 131. See also High fructose corn syrup.
  cooking guidelines for cornmeal, 179t
  syrup, 70, 71, 124
  fiber in, 51t
  protein in, 58t
  recipes with, 191-192, 209, 214, 225, 240, 250, 252, 255
Corn oil, xix, 28, 36, 38, 71, 153, 174, 182
  smoke point of, 185t
Cortisol, 113-114, 115, 116, 144
Cottonseed oil, smoke point of, 185t
Cruciferous vegetables, 64, 105, 168, 254, 262
Cucumber, 90, 95, 127, 141, 158, 161
  recipes with, 198, 210, 217, 233, 243, 244
Cumin, 172
Curcumin. See Turmeric.
Cysteine, 55

D

Dairy, 26-27, 30, 31, 33, 34, 35t, 36, 37, 39, 46, 54, 59, 60, 66t, 75, 90, 91-92, 121t. See also Lactose intolerance.
  and bone health, 92-93
  calcium in, 94t
  probiotics in, 108-109
  protein in, 57t
  sensitivity, 31
Dandelion greens, 105, 107, 108 182
  cooking guidelines for, 183t
  recipes with, 242
Dark green leafy vegetables, 26, 46, 65t, 66t, 168
  cooking guidelines for, 183t
Date sugar, 124, 131
Dehydration, 98, 149. See also Hydration.
Delicata Squash Over Broccoli and Quinoa, 258
Depression, 40, 106, 136, 148
Detoxification, 65t, 168
Dextrose, 124, 131
DHEA, 39
Diaphragmatic breathing. See Breathing.
Diarrhea, 30
Diabetes. See Type II diabetes mellitus.
Diet soda, 111, 132-134, 153
Dietary fiber. See Fiber.
Digestion, 46, 98, 101-110, 146, 149, 151, 153, 172, 173
  nervous system effect on, 102-103
Digestive enzymes, 102, 103
Digestive tract, 43, 46, 47, 105-106
Dirty Dozen, 81
Disaccharide/s, 44. See also Carbohydrates.
Docosahexaenoic acid (DHA), 35, 62
Dried fruit, 159, 160
  fiber in, 50t
  sulfites in, 167

E

Easy Cornbread, 252
ECO Project, xv, xx, xxi
Eczema, 106
Eggs, xix, 26-27, 30, 54, 59-61, 66t, 90, 95, 121t, 138, 139, 161
   cage-free, 83
   cholesterol in, 34, 39-41, 75
   egg substitution, 255
   food intolerance, 31
   pasture-raised, 83
   protein in, 57t
   recipes with, 193, 215, 223, 244, 252
Egg and Veggie Scramble, 223
Eicosapentaenoic acid (EPA), 35, 62
Electrolytes, 142, 154
Emotional eating, 164
Endocrine disruptor, 85, 142
Endorphins, 55
Endosperm, 25, 48-49, 84
Energy drink, xix, 43, 45t, 117, 124, 125, 126, 129, 132, 145, 173
Enterocytes, 54
Environmental Working Group, 81
Equal. *See* Aspartame (Nutrasweet®).
Ergocalciferol (D2). *See* Vitamin D.
Erucic acid, 38
Erythritol, 131, 132
Essential fatty acids, 34, 48, 233
Estrogen, 39, 59, 85, 93, 114
Evaporated cane juice. *See* Sugar.
Extra virgin olive oil, 28, 38, 71, 75, 90, 120, 170, 182, 185t
   recipes with, 197, 199, 210, 220, 235, 236, 240, 243, 249, 258

F

Factory Farm/s, 26, 27
FAME. *See* Food as Medicine Everyday.
FAME Plate, 87-100, 201, 210, 253
FAME Plate Sheet Pan Meal, 201
FAMI. *See* Food as Medicine Institute
Fast food, 36, 37, 60, 75, 76, 151-155
Fasting. *See* Intermittent fasting.
Fasting blood sugar, 115. *See also* Blood sugar and blood glucose.
Fat/s, 27-28, 33-42, 90, 96-97. *See also* Monounsaturated, omega-3 fatty acids, omega-6 fatty acids, polyunsaturated, saturated, trans fat.
   on food labels, 70-72, 75
   food sources of, 35t
Fat-soluble vitamins, 26, 34, 41, 60, 65t
Fatty liver disease, 114, 118, 127
Fava beans, 24, 109, 117
   cooking guidelines for, 181t
Fennel, 104, 227
   recipes with, 231
Fermentation, xix, 24, 25, 48, 59, 117, 131
Fermentable
   carbohydrate, 31
   fiber, 46, 47
Fermented foods, 59, 92-93, 105, 107-110
Fiber, 26, 29, 37, 39, 44-50, 45t, 90, 91, 99t, 107, 115, 136, 138, 152, 168, 170, 202, 204, 216, 226, 254, 256, 262. *See also* Carbohydrates.
   daily intake, 49-50
   on food label, 76-78,
   food sources of, 50t-52t
   insoluble, 46, 76,
   soluble, 46, 47, 76, 107, 170, 208
Fight or flight, 102. *See also* Sympathetic nervous system.

Fish, xix, 30, 31, 35, 35t, 39, 54, 62-63, 65t, 66t, 75, 96, 121t, 160, 170
   farmed, 62, 63
   oil, 28
   protein in, 57t
   recipes with, 191, 214, 233, 244
   wild-caught, 62, 63
Fish Tacos, 191
Flaxseed/s 35, 38, 46, 47, 49, 107, 108, 121t, 138, 139, 159, 160, 161
   as egg substitution, 252, 255
   fiber in, 51t
   protein in, 58t
   recipes with, 195, 203, 207, 208, 219, 238
Fluoride, 142
Folate. *See* Vitamin B.
Food allergies, 30-31, 91
Food as Medicine Everyday series, ix, xii, xv, xvi, xx, xxi
Food as Medicine Institute, ix, xv, xvii, xx
Food label/s. *See* Ingredient list and nutrition facts.
Food intolerance/sensitivity, 30-31, 98, 105
Free radicals, 26, 35
Free-range, 82, 86
Frozen Yogurt Bars, 195
Fructan, 107
Fructose, 44, 70, 124, 126, 127, 129, 130. *See also* High-fructose corn syrup and carbohydrates.

G

Galactose, 44. *See also* Carbohydrates.
Garbanzo beans (chick peas)
   cooking guidelines for, 181t
   fiber in, 51t
   recipes with, 197, 220, 236
Garden-fresh Summer Squash Salad, 236
Garlic, 107, 168

Gastrin, 53
Generally Recognized as Safe (GRAS), 37, 71, 72
Genetically engineered (GE). *See* Genetically modified organisms.
Genetically modified organisms (GMOs), 38, 84, 185t
Germ (grain), 25, 48-49, 65t, 84, 173
Ghee, 27, 34, 36, 37, 38, 90, 170, 182, 184t
Ghrelin, 144
Ginger, 104, 171, 172
   recipes with, 207, 215, 253, 256
Ginger Tempeh Stir Fry with Quinoa, 253
Glucagon, 113, 115
Glucose, 44, 124, 126, 127, 129, 130, 131, 134. *See also* Carbohydrates.
Glutamine, 54
Glutathione, 55, 82
Gluten, 31, 109
   -free, 231, 253, 255
Glycine, 55
Glycogen, 43, 113
Glycoside, 131
Glycosuria, 114
GMO. *See* Genetically Modified Organisms.
Goitrogens, 59
Golden Delicious Granola, 221
Good Cholesterol. *See* High-density lipoprotein.
Grains, xix, 24-25, 76-77, 166, 167
   cooking guidelines for, 177-178, 179t
   enriched, 77, 173
   fiber in, 51t
   protein in, 58t
   refined, 45t, 72, 117, 153, 173
   whole, 45, 46, 48-49, 65t, 66t, 84, 90, 95-96, 121t, 152
Granola, 159
Grapefruit, 105, 169
   fiber in, 50t

Grapeseed oil, 36, 38
    smoke point of, 185t
Grass-fed beef, 27, 39, 82. *See also* Beef.
Grass-finished beef, 82
Great northern beans,
    calcium in, 84t
    cooking guidelines for, 181t
Growth hormones, 27, 80, 82
Guacamole, 226
Gut flora, 105, 107

H

HDL. *See* High-density lipoprotein.
Healthy Chicken Bites, 209
Heart disease. *See* Cardiovascular disease.
Heartburn, 105
Hearty Salmon Salad, 233
Hemoglobin A1c (HbA1c), 115
Hemp seed, 35, 39, 54, 58t, 96, 121t, 138, 170, 203, 208, 248
    milk, 207
    recipes with, 208, 248
Herbal tea, 127, 132, 172
Heterocyclic amines (HCAs), 63
High-fructose corn syrup (HFCS), 126, 127, 128, 129, 130, 173. *See also* Corn syrup.
High-density lipoprotein (HDL), 39, 40, 113. *See also* Cholesterol.
Histidine, 53
Hives, 31, 167
Homemade Almond Milk, 224
Homemade Hummus, 220
Honey, xix, 44, 45t, 70, 71, 117, 124, 129-130, 138
    recipes with, 195, 208, 210, 235, 244, 249, 253
Hormones, 27, 39, 53, 54, 72, 80, 92, 106, 112, 114, 115, 120
    BPA and, 85, 142

Hummus, 49, 98, 158, 159, 160, 161
    recipes with, 217, 220
Hydration, 47, 127, 141, 142. *See also* Dehydration.
Hyperglycemia, 112, 114, 115. *See also* Type II diabetes mellitus.
Hyperpalatable, xviii, 88, 151
Hypertension, 40, 113. *See also* Blood pressure.
Hypoglycemia, 112

I

IgE antibody, 31
Immune system, 31, 53, 105, 110, 143, 168, 173, 216, 225, 259, 262. *See also* Autoimmune disease.
Industrialized food, 24, 26, 92
Inflammation, ix, xx, 29, 30, 34-37, 43, 63, 105, 106, 113, 153, 168, 170, 174, 233, 254. *See also* Anti-inflammatory.
    effects of cruciferous vegetables on, 64, 168, 254
    effects of conventional beef on, 27, 82
    effects of omega-3 fatty acids on, 27, 35-36, 38, 62, 82, 121, 170, 233
    effects of trans fat on, 37
Inflammatory bowel disease, 105, 106
Ingredient list, xviii, 68-75, 77, 83, 85, 109, 123, 153, 160, 173
Insoluble fiber, 46, 76. *See* Fiber.
Insomnia, 144
Insulin, 43, 53, 88, 112-115, 119, 126, 131, 132, 144
    Resistance, 43, 88, 112-114, 121t, 144
Intermittent fasting, 136-137,
Inulin, 107
Iron, 25, 26, 30, 48, 60, 61, 66t, 93, 130, 216
Isoleucine, 54, 55

J

Jerusalem artichokes, 107
Jicama, 107
Junk food, 162

K

Kale, 43, 49, 52t, 64, 65t, 66t, 81, 89, 93, 94t, 100, 105, 168, 182, 183t
  calcium in, 66t, 93, 94t
  cooking guidelines for, 182, 183t
  fiber in, 52t
  recipes with, 199, 225, 242, 250
Kefir, 92, 108, 109, 173
Ketchup, 153, 173
Kidney disease, 56, 75, 114, 120, 155
Kimchi, 108, 109, 173
Kombucha, 108, 109, 128, 173

L

Lactase, 31
Lacto-fermented, 108
Lactobacillus, 108
Lactose, 31, 44, 91, 124, 128, 184t
  intolerance, 31, 91
Lard, xix, 27, 34, 35, 37, 90, 182, 184t, 242
  smoke point of, 184t
LDL. See Low-Density Lipoprotein and cholesterol.
Lean muscle, 120, 149
Legumes, 29, 45t, 46, 49, 54, 56, 57t, 59, 68, 96, 121t, 152, 160, 166, 168, 171,
Lemon/s, 101, 104, 105, 127, 169, 177, 179
  recipes with, 196, 197, 198, 201, 220, 230, 233, 237
Lemon Rice, 237
Lentils, 46, 47, 51t, 57t, 90, 94t, 107, 171, 180
  calcium in, 94t
  cooking guidelines for, 180, 181t
  fiber in, 51t
  protein in, 57t
  recipes with, 230, 260
Leucine, 54, 55

Live active cultures, 108, 109
Liver, 34, 39, 106, 113, 114, 118, 126, 127, 130, 143, 169, 173
  disease, 106, 114, 118, 127
  food sources from animal or fish, 28, 65, 121
Low-density lipoprotein (LDL), 39, 40, 47, 204. See also Cholesterol.
Low-fat, 33, 41, 67, 91, 100, 138
Lycopene, 225, 240
Lysine, 53

M

Macronutrient/s, 31, 32, 33, 43, 64, 90, 95, 98, 99, 100
Magnesium, 25, 48, 66t, 76, 93, 130, 142, 216, 262
Manganese, 130, 205, 216
Mango, 81, 159, 191
Mannitol, 131
Maple syrup, xix, 45t, 117, 129, 130, 132
  recipes with, 193, 195, 197, 202, 203, 221, 235, 238, 252, 253, 255, 256, 258, 259
Margarine, xix, 28
Marinated Steak Bites, 196
Mayonnaise, 153, 161
Mediterranean Diet, xii, 26, 35, 118, 170, 172,
Meat, xix, 26-27, 30, 33, 34, 35t, 36, 37, 39, 46, 49, 56, 60-61, 63-64, 65t, 66t, 68, 75, 80, 82, 83, 90, 96, 105, 121t, 152, 160, 166, 172. See also Grass-fed beef.
  conventionally raised, 30, 36, 92
  industrial, 26-27
  labeling of, 80, 82, 83
  organic, 80
  pasture-raised, 35, 61, 65t, 80, 83, 92, 121t, 152, 160, 170, 184t
  processed, 27, 36
  recipes with, 196, 244, 247
Medium-chain fatty acids, 171

Melatonin, 54, 144
Melon/s, 65t, 66t, 81, 90, 132, 142, 169
Menaquinone (K2). 65t See also Vitamin K.
Menopause, 40, 93, 114
Metabolic, xviii, 23, 24, 30, 39, 41, 47, 54, 55, 88, 95, 96, 98, 112, 113, 116, 123
  disorders, xvii, 123, 173
Metabolic syndrome, 88, 112, 113-114, 120, 152, 155
Metabolism, 35, 41, 42, 64, 116, 126, 141, 144, 149, 169, 171
Methionine, 53
Micronutrient/s, 64, 65t, 91, 92, 99, 116, 137
Microbiome, 46, 47, 72, 105-108, 110, 133, 173, 208
Milk, xix, 30, 31, 35t, 36, 44, 54, 57t, 58t, 65t, 66t, 91-93, 94t, 96, 97, 108, 109, 128, 139, 159, 173, 184t. See also Dairy.
Millet, 48, 179t
  cooking guidelines for, 179t
Mindful, 104, 141, 145-146.
Mineral/s, 25, 41, 45, 48, 60, 62, 64, 66t, 74, 75, 76, 77-78, 80, 93, 126, 129, 130, 137, 142, 154, 168, 169, 171, 205
  on food labels, 77
Miso, 59, 109, 171, 173
  recipes with, 249
Molasses, 66t, 70, 124, 130
Monk fruit, 128, 129, 132, 203
Monosaccharides, 44. See also Carbohydrates.
Monosodium glutamate (MSG), 69, 71, 73
Monounsaturated, 35, 61, 75, 170, 182, 185t, 186t, 254. See also Fat/s.
MSG. See Monosodium glutamate.
Muscle, 30, 53, 54, 55, 60, 61, 66t, 75, 103, 119, 120, 141, 147, 149
Mushroom/s, 65t, 81, 90, 121t, 158, 169, 216
  recipes with, 201, 215, 223, 247

Mustard, 84, 153, 161
  recipes with, 235, 236, 244, 258
Mustard greens, 81, 94t, 105, 168
  calcium in, 94t
  cooking guidelines for, 183t
  recipes with, 242
Myoglobin, 61
MyPlate (USDA), 88

N

National University of Natural Medicine (NUNM), ix, xii, xv, xx
National Health and Nutrition Examination Survey (NHANES), 124
Natto, 59, 109
Natural,
  on food label, 83
Naturopathic doctor (ND), xi, xii, xx, 49, 56
Navy beans,
  calcium in, 94t
NCDs. See Non-communicable disease.
Nervous system, 48, 62, 85, 102-103, 104, 149, 172
Neurological, 30, 41, 62, 65t, 106, 171
Neuropathy, 114
Neurotransmitter/s, 53
NHANES. See National Health and Nutrition Examination Survey.
Nitrates/Nitrites. See Sodium nitrates/nitrites.
Nitrosamines, 63
Non-GMO Project, 84
Non-communicable diseases (NCDs), 23
Non-starchy vegetables, 89-90, 95, 98
Not Just Oatmeal (Rolled Oats), 208
NOVA classification, xix
NUNM. See National University of Natural Medicine.
Nut Butter Banana Jam Sandwiches, 216
Nut butters, 49, 58t, 78, 90, 96, 97, 155, 159

recipes with, 195, 207, 208, 216, 219
Nutrasweet®. *See* Aspartame.
Nutrient inhibitors, *See also* Phytic acid.
Nutrient-dense, 24, 26, 27, 29, 30, 98, 168, 170, 173, 182, 228
Nutrition Facts, 67, 68, 70, 74-79, 88, 123
Nut/s, xix, 28, 29, 31, 33, 35, 36, 39, 45t, 46, 49, 51t, 54, 59, 65t, 68, 80, 90, 95, 96, 97, 98, 107, 108, 120, 121t, 129, 138, 139, 155, 159, 160, 166, 167, 170
    allergy, 31
    fiber in, 51t
    protein in, 58t, 96

O

Oats, 46, 47, 48, 49, 50, 58t, 72, 77, 90, 96, 107, 138, 152
    fiber in, 51t
    cooking guidelines for, 179t
    recipes with, 139, 208, 221
Obesity, ix, 40, 41, 72, 88, 106, 113, 118, 123, 127, 132, 136, 137, 144, 146, 173, 174
    metabolic syndrome and, 113-114
Oligosaccharides, 107
Olive/s, 33, 35, 90, 97, 170
    oil, xix, 26, 28, 34, 35, 37, 38, 71, 75, 90, 95, 96, 120, 138, 139, 161, 162, 169, 170, 182. *See also* Extra-virgin olive oil.
    smoke point of oil, 185t
Omega-3 fatty acids, 27, 35-36, 38, 39, 48, 61, 62, 63, 82, 92, 121t, 170, 192, 202, 214, 233. *See also* Fat/s.
Omega-6 fatty acids, 35, 36, 38, 48, 61, 63, 82, 185t. *See also* Fat/s.
    conjugated linoleic acid, 27, 82, 92
Oregano, 63, 172
    recipes with, 209, 236
Organic, 59, 86, 92, 126, 130, 160, 171
    labeling, 80-81, 84

Organochlorine, 133
Osteoporosis. *See* Bone Health.
Oxalic acid, 93
Oxidation, 33, 35, 37, 38, 48, 153, 182
Oxidative stress, 168

P

Palm oil, 27, 36
    smoke point of, 184t
Palm sugar, 124, 131
Pancreas, 112, 113, 114
Parasympathetic nervous system. *See also* Digestion.
Parsley, recipes with, 196, 198, 214, 230, 233, 235, 236, 243
Parsnips, 162
    recipes with, 201, 212
Partially hydrogenated oil, 37, 71, 75, 182, 185t. *See also* Trans fat.
Pasteurized/pasteurization, xix, 109
    honey, 129
    milk, 109
Pasture-raised animals/meat, 35, 39, 41, 61, 65t, 83, 92, 121t, 152, 160, 170, 184t, 209, 223. *See also* Beef, chicken, eggs.
    omega-3 fatty acids in, 35, 39, 61, 92, 121t, 170
Peas, 46, 47, 81, 107, 129, 158, 159, 171, 180, 181t
    fiber in, 51t
    protein in, 57t
    calcium in, 94t
    recipes with, 197, 201, 253, 254
Peanut/s, 31, 35, 54, 78
    butter, 58t, 78, 83, 124
    fiber in, 51t
    protein in, 57t
    smoke point of oil, 185t
    recipes with, 195, 207, 208, 216, 219
Pectin, 107

Percent Daily Value (%DV), 74-75
Pesticides, 80, 81, 133, 142
Phenylalanine, 53, 54
Phenylketonuria, 133
Phosphoric acid, 127
Phosphorous, 25, 60, 91
Phylloquinones (K1) 65t. *See* Vitamin K.
Phytic acid, 25, 48, 177, 179
Phytoestrogen/s, 59
Phytonutrients, 43, 107, 118, 130, 168, 171
Pinto beans, 99, 100
   calcium in, 94t
   cooking guidelines for, 181t
   protein in, 57t
   recipes with, 204, 250
Plantains, 47, 107, 159
Polycyclic aromatic hydrocarbons (PAHs), 63
Polydipsia, 115. *See also* Type II diabetes mellitus.
Polysaccharides, 44. *See also* Carbohydrates.
Polyunsaturated fat 33, 35-36, 37, 61, 75, 153, 171, 182, 185t. *See also* Fat/s.
Polyuria, 115. *See also* Type II diabetes mellitus.
Polyphenols, 28, 107-108, 118, 170
Pork, 26, 36, 54, 61, 83, 160
   protein in, 57t
Portion size, 62, 88, 95, 96, 98, 99, 126
Portion Size Guide, 95, 96
Postbiotic, 107
Potassium, 26, 49, 66t, 76, 91, 130, 142, 155, 170, 226
Potato/s, 43, 45, 47, 50, 81, 90, 94t, 96, 107, 129, 162
   chips, 76, 199
   fiber in, 52t
Power Bowls, 197
Prebiotic, 46, 47, 107, 109, 208
Prediabetes, xvii, xx, 41, 112, 113, 120, 126. *See also* Type II diabetes mellitus.
Preservatives, xviii, 27, 63, 64, 69, 73, 80, 83, 127, 153, 159, 160, 167, 174
Probiotics, 105, 107, 108-109, 173
Progesterone, 39, 114
Protein, 41, 48, 53-63, 96, 115
   amino acids in, 53, 54, 60
   complete, 53, 54, 60, 90, 170
   dietary intake of, 55-56
   food sources of, 57t-59t, 96
   on food labels, 77
   plant based, 54, 60, 57t-59t
   powder, 59t
   Recommended dietary allowance, 55
Protein powder, 59t, 139
Psyllium husk, 46
Pumpkin, 54, 262
   recipes with, 202, 256, 261
Pumpkin Pie Amaranth Porridge, 256
Pumpkin seeds, 66t, 121t, 138, 170, 262
   fiber in, 51t
   protein in, 59t
   recipes with, 195, 219, 221, 261

Q

Quinoa, 48, 49, 54, 90, 95, 99, 139, 216, 240, 256
   cooking guidelines for, 179t
   fiber in, 51t
   protein in, 58t, 96
   recipes with, 197-198, 201, 215, 240, 253, 258
Quinoa Veggie Stir-Fry in Collard Wraps, 215

R

Rainbow Nachos, 225
Rainbow Quinoa Salad, 240
Rapadura, 130
Rapeseed. *See* Canola oil.

Red pepper. *See also* Bell pepper.
   recipes with, 197-198, 201, 215, 223, 225, 227, 240, 247, 250
Refined carbohydrates. *See* Carbohydrates.
Refined grains. *See* Grains.
Refried Pinto Beans and Rice, 204
Reproductive system, 85
Resistant starch, 47, 49, 107, 208
Rest and digest. *See* Parasympathetic nervous system.
Resveratrol, 118
Rice. *See* Brown, white, and wild rice.
Rice syrup, 70, 131
Rice vinegar,
   recipes with, 215, 253
Roasted Beet Salad with White Miso Vinaigrette, 249
Roasted Brussels Sprouts, 262
Root vegetables, 45, 81, 131, 162, 169
Rosemary, 63, 127, 172
   recipes with, 209, 212, 227, 231, 258

S

Saccharin (Sweet N Low®), 73, 133
SAD. *See* Standard American Diet.
Safflower oil, 28, 36, 38, 71, 174, 182
   smoke point of, 185
Salmon, 35, 62, 160, 161, 170
   calcium in, 94t
   recipes with, 214, 233
Saturated fat/s 27, 33-34, 36-37, 40 41, 61, 75, 80, 151, 171, 182. *See also* Fat/s.
   smoke points of, 184t
Sauté/ing, 38, 95, 97, 139, 168, 169, 170, 183t
Sautéed Seasonal Greens, 242
Savory Salmon Cakes, 214
Sea salt, xix, 76
Sedentary lifestyle, 112, 146, 147
Selenium, 60

Serotonin, 54, 55, 106
Serving size, 56, 88, 118
   on food label, 74
Sesame oil, 38
   smoke point of, 185t
   recipes with, 215, 253
Sesame seeds, 35, 66
   calcium in, 94t
   recipes with, 220
Shortening, 185t
Simple carbohydrates. *See* Carbohydrates.
Sitting disease, 146
Sleep, 40, 54, 55, 106, 111, 114, 115, 118, 120, 141, 143-145, 146, 147, 148, 149, 172
Small intestine, 31, 54
Smoke point, 37, 38, 170, 182, 184t-186t
Snap peas, 129, 158
Snacks, xix, 49, 76, 97, 98, 116, 117, 155, 157-160, 162, 193, 195, 197, 202, 220, 259
Soaking,
   beans, 179
   whole grains, 177-178
Social determinants of health, xvii, 152
Sodium, 66t, 67, 80, 142, 151, 154-155, 160, 174
   on food label, 75-76
Sodium nitrites/nitrates, 27, 73, 160
Soluble fiber, 46, 47, 107, 170, 208. *See also* Fiber.
Sorbitol, 131
Sorghum cooking guidelines, 179t
Soybeans, 160, 171, 249, 253-254
   fermented, 109, 173
Soybean oil, 36, 77, 84, 89, 153, 174
   partially hydrogenated, 182
   smoke point of, 185t
Spaghetti squash, 247-248
Spaghetti Squash Pasta with Hearty Marinara Sauce, 247

Spices, 69, 129, 162, 166, 167, 168
   medicinal benefits of, 104, 171-172
Spiced Red Lentils (Dal) with Spinach, 260
Spring Herb Crackers, 231
Spring Lentil Soup, 230
Splenda®, 73, 133. *See also* Sucralose.
Split peas, 180
   cooking guidelines for, 181t
Sprouting, 24, 25, 48
Squash, 65t, 90, 96, 129, 168
   calcium in, 94t
   fiber in, 52t
   recipes with, 201, 236, 247, 258, 259
Standard American Diet, xviii, 24, 26, 28, 36, 105, 107, 112
Starch/es, xviii, xix, 44-45, 47, 48, 49, 76, 89, 90, 95-96, 107. *See also* Carbohydrate/s.
Starchy vegetables, 89-90, 95-96
Stevia, 128, 129, 131, 132
Stone milling, 25
Stress, 40, 54, 66t, 104, 106, 112, 113, 114, 115, 116, 119, 135, 136, 143. *See also* Cortisol.
   and diabetes, 115
   effects on digestion, 102-103
   and hormones, 112-113
Sucanat, 130
Sucralose (Spenda®), 73, 133
Sucrose, 44, 126, 130, 131, 133. *See also* Sugar and carbohydrates.
Sugar, 44-45, 45t, 70, 76-77, 117, 123-134, 173. *See also* Added sugar.
   brown, 124, 130, 132
   cane, 77, 124, 128, 129, 130-131
   on food label, 70, 124, 128-129
   table, 126, 132, 133
   turbinado, 130
Sugar alcohols, 131-132
Sugar beets, 131

Sugar-sweetened beverages, 125, 126-127, 129, 134, 152
Sulfites, 73, 167
Summer Squash, 90. *See also* Squash.
   recipes with, 236
Summer Tomato Avocado Salad, 243
Sunflower oil, 28, 36, 71, 174, 182
   smoke point of, 185t
Sunflower seeds, 36,
   fiber in, 51t
   protein in, 59t
   recipes with, 219, 221, 244, 258
Superfood/s, 167-173, 182
Superoxide dismutase, 82
Sweet leaf. *See* Stevia.
Sweet N Low®. *See* Saccharin.
Sweet Potato, 43, 90, 129, 162
   calcium in, 94t
   fiber in, 52t
   recipes with, 201, 212, 214, 255
Sweet Potato Cornbread, 255
Swiss chard. *See* Chard.
Sympathetic nervous system, 102-103, 105. *See also* Digestion.

T

Table syrup, 130
Tahini, 220. *See also* Sesame.
Tallow, 27, 37, 90, 182
   recipes with, 242
   smoke point of, 184t
Tamari, 59, 109. *See also* Soybean.
   recipes with, 215, 253
Tarragon, recipes with, 233, 235
Teff, 48, 179t
Tempeh, 54, 56, 59, 90, 96, 109, 161, 171, 173, 254. *See also* Soybeans.

calcium in, 94t
protein in, 58t
recipes with, 244, 253
Tequila, 130
Testosterone, 39, 114
Thermic effect, 54
Thyme, 63, 172
recipes with, 196, 209, 227, 231, 258
Thyroid, 39, 54, 59, 72, 85
Time-restricted eating, 136
Tobacco, 23, 40
Tocopherols. *See* Vitamin E.
Tomato, 64, 69, 85, 90, 121t, 138, 141, 152, 159, 161, 225, 240
fiber in, 52t
recipes with, 197, 201, 204, 223, 225, 226, 233, 236, 240, 243, 244, 247, 250, 261
Trace minerals, 48
Traditional diets, 23-28, 37
Trans fat, 37, 71-72, 75, 174, 185t. *See also* Partially hydrogenated oil.
Triglycerides, xx, 113, 126, 130
Tryptophan, 53, 54
Turbinado sugar, 130. *See also* Sugar.
Turkey, 36, 57t, 60, 82, 83, 138, 139, 160, 161
recipes with, 217, 228, 244, 247, 250
Turkey Avocado Roll-ups, 217
Turmeric, 63, 104. *See also* Curry.
medicinal benefits of, 171
recipes with, 260
Type 2 diabetes mellitus/diabetes, xvii, 23, 29, 36, 37, 39, 40, 41, 43, 44, 47, 60, 63, 106, 112, 113, 114-115, 116, 117, 123, 127, 129, 131, 132, 136, 137, 144, 146, 147, 152, 155, 170, 173, 174
artificial sweeteners and, 132
effects of fiber on, 45t, 47
insulin and, 112-114
metabolic syndrome and, 113-114

Tyrosine, 54

U

Ultra-processed, xviii, xix, 23, 26-30, 36, 37, 41, 60, 62, 68-73, 76, 78, 87, 88, 107, 127, 129, 132, 133, 151, 165, 173, 174, 182, 185t
United States Department of Agriculture (USDA), 49, 60, 75, 80, 81, 82, 83, 84, 88, 91
Unsaturated fat/s, 33-37, 41, 61, 75, 182. *See also* Fat/s.
smoke point of, 185t-186t
USDA. *See* United States Department of Agriculture.

V

Valine, 54, 55
Vanilla, 129
recipes with, 193, 195, 202-203, 221, 224, 238, 256
Vegan, 59
Vegetable Broth, 227
Vegetarian, 59, 96, 99
Vitamin/s, 25, 26, 41, 45, 60, 62, 65t, 74, 80, 93, 107, 126, 129, 137, 168, 169, 171
fat-soluble, 34, 41, 65t
on food label, 77-78
Vitamin A, 26, 65t, 168, 225, 242, 259
beta-carotene, 26, 27, 65t, 82, 92, 93, 168, 169, 170, 225, 242, 255, 259
Vitamin B (B-vitamins), 30, 41, 60, 65t, 91, 92, 107, 225
folate, 65t, 225, 254
Vitamin C/ascorbic acid, 65t, 121t, 169, 225, 240, 254
Vitamin D, 39, 49, 62, 65t, 91, 92, 93, 121t, 169, 216
Vitamin E, 27, 28, 48, 65t, 82, 92, 170
Vitamin K, 26, 65t, 93, 107, 225

W

Walnut/s, 35, 36, 39, 54, 121t, 159, 170
    fiber in, 51t
    smoke point of oil, 186t
    recipes with, 193, 203, 219, 221

Water. *See* Hydration.

Water-soluble vitamin, 65t

Weight-bearing exercise, 93, 147

Wheat Gluten. *See* Gluten.

Whey, 31, 59t

White rice, 49, 97, 99, 117, 152, 173

Whole food/s, xii, xvii, xviii, xix, xx, xxi, 24, 28-29, 31, 32, 33, 41, 43, 45, 46, 49, 64, 68, 76, 78, 86, 89, 91, 98, 107, 118, 123, 142, 158, 160, 168

Whole foods diet, xi, 36, 64, 70, 91, 92, 152

Whole grain, 25, 26, 29, 45, 45t, 46, 48-49, 50, 54, 65t, 66t, 68, 72, 76-77, 80, 84-85, 90, 95-96, 98, 107, 108, 109, 121t, 138, 139, 152, 160, 161, 166, 167, 173
    cooking guidelines for, 177-179
    on food label/s, 72, 76, 84-85
    parts of, 48-49

Whole Grains Council, 84

Whole grains stamp, 84

Wild game, 54, 90, 96, 121t

Wild rice, 48

Wine, 38, 111, 117, 118, 119, 145, 185

World Health Organization, 23, 133

X

Xylitol, 131

Y

Yacon syrup, 131

Yams, 45, 90, 162, 255

Yoga, 119, 146

Yogurt, xix, 35, 36, 54, 56, 57t, 91, 92, 96, 97, 108-109, 124, 128-129, 159, 173, 177, 179, 203
    Greek, 57t, 100, 138, 139, 208, 221
    recipes with, 191, 195, 207, 261

Z

Zinc, 25, 30, 48, 60, 66t, 121t, 130, 262

About The Authors

Julie Briley, ND

DR. JULIE BRILEY received her naturopathic doctorate degree at the National University of Natural Medicine and her Bachelors of Science in Biology and Certificate in Environmental Studies from the University of Wisconsin-Madison.

Dr. Briley is a co-founder of the Food As Medicine Institute at NUNM in Portland, Oregon. She helped develop and facilitate the FAME series and the FAME Educator training program. She has been a consultant for developing nutrition and naturopathic content and curriculum development.

At her private clinical practice in Portland, Dr. Briley focuses on the prevention and treatment of chronic diseases, addressing hormone imbalances, and optimizing digestive health. Dr. Briley's longstanding interest in community health and education was sparked through her research and teaching experience in the U.S and Latin America, including her service as a Peace Corps volunteer in Paraguay.

DR. COURTNEY JACKSON earned her Doctorate in Naturopathic Medicine from the National University of Natural Medicine (NUNM) and holds a Bachelor of Science in Resource Ecology Management from the University of Michigan.

She is a co-founding physician of the Food as Medicine Institute at NUNM in Portland, Oregon, where she developed the Food as Medicine Everyday program. She is an experienced writer who has worked with academic and healthcare organizations to develop evidence-based nutrition content. Dr. Jackson currently practices at a women's health clinic in Portland, where her clinical focus includes cardiometabolic health, perimenopause, and menopause management. Dr. Jackson also volunteers with organizations dedicated to strengthening local food networks.

Courtney Jackson, ND

About NUNM Press

NUNM PRESS is the publishing arm of the National University of Natural Medicine (NUNM) in Portland, Oregon where we produce high-quality, mission-aligned publications that reflect the principles and evolving practice of natural medicine.

Our flagship title, Food as Medicine Everyday, exemplifies our commitment to advancing integrative health education and honoring the historical and contemporary roots of natural healing systems. Through select works, NUNM Press aims to contribute meaningfully to scholarly and clinical conversations in naturopathic and integrative medicine, public health, and sustainability.

Founded in 1956, NUNM is home to North America's longest-standing accredited naturopathic doctoral program, as well as graduate and undergraduate degrees in nutrition, global health, and Chinese Medicine.